The Stitches of Creative Embroidery

Jacqueline Enthoven 1962

Jacqueline Enthoven

The Stitches of Creative Embroidery

Revised and Enlarged Edition

West Chester, Pennsylvania 19380

Acknowledgments

My notes and drawings on embroidery stitches were compiled over a period of years as an aid to teaching. I am grateful to the many pupils who urged me to convert the material into a book, and to my friend Marion Gartler, author of childrens' textbooks, who kindly but firmly started me on the project.

I owe a great deal to Sister Joanne Mary SNJM, head of the Art Department of Holy Names High School in Seattle, Washington, who generously drew the letters which harmonize so well with my drawings; to Karin Williams for her technical help; and to Marcelle Péfourque in France for her devoted and painstaking research on a number of stitches.

I would also like to thank Virginia Harvey, Curator of the Costume and Textile Museum of the University of Washington, Seattle, and the learned staff of the Textile Museum, Washington, D.C., for their help, interest, and encouragement. I am very grateful to Dorothy Willis for her skillful and perceptive editing.

Most of all I want to express my gratitude to my family, especially to my husband whose command of English was invaluable to me, and who never objected—well, almost never—to my writing when I should have been cooking.

Drawings by the author.
Photographs by Don Normark unless otherwise credited.

Cover:
Sampler of some of the new stitches in this Revised Edition, worked by the author. (Photograph by Robert McClellan.)

Frontispiece:
Sampler, 28" x 18", by the author.

Title page:
LION by Lois Packer. The inspiration for this decorative stitchery was a photograph of a painting by a folk artist of Tonala, Mexico (see page 233). This was Lois' first attempt at designing with a needle. The whole effect is lively and delightful.

Copyright © 1987 by Jacqueline Enthoven.
Library of Congress Catalog Number: 87-61433.

Printed in the United States of America.
ISBN: 0-88740-111-2
Published by Schiffer Publishing Ltd.
1469 Morstein Road, West Chester, Pennsylvania 19380

This book may be purchased from the publisher.
Please include $2.00 postage.
Try your bookstore first.

Contents

Introduction 9
I Starting to Stitch
  Begin Now—Choosing the Material 19
  Size of the Sampler—Doodling Cloth 20
  Threads 21
  Choosing Colors 22
  Needles—Other Things You Need 23
  Transfering Designs 24
  Your Embroidery Notebook: Sources of Ideas 25
  Starting the Sampler 26
  Notebooks of Stitch Samplers 28

II The Stitches
  Flat Stitches 31
  Looped Stitches 101
  Chained Stitches 121
  Knotted Stitches 149
  Couching and Laid Work 165

III Creating with Stitches
  Finishing and Using the Sampler 181
  Creating Borders with Straight
    and Curved Lines 184
  Building Borders Spontaneously 187
  Working with Geometric Designs 189
  From Geometric Designs to Various Shapes 193
  Working on Printed and Plain Materials 196
  How to Create Spontaneously with Stitches 200
  Wall Hangings and Space Dividers 201
  More Ideas for Your Home 203
  Clothes 208
  Embroidering Flower Shapes 213
  Detached and Semidetached Petals 219
  Joinings 223
  Edgings 227

Conclusion 231
Index of Stitches 234

Left, *Scroll of Stitches*, 57" x 10", which has most of the stitches shown in this book, made by the author.

Right, *Chromatechnics* by Wilcke Smith. Wilcke is an artist in complete control of her medium. This piece was inspired by her collection of kaleidoscopes, which she worked into a study of color using six controlled hues and values on a black wool background. Her use of stitches is superb. I particularly enjoy her random multilayered areas, which create exciting color gradations. It is not only the work of a true artist but of a superb craftswoman.

Below, *Summer Meadow* This fresh and gay mural, worked on paper-backed burlap, was a summer project designed and embroidered by a group of children under the direction of two mothers, Elizabeth Moses and Joan Carbary. Martha and Christine Moses, aged 8 and 6; and Wendy and Susie Carbary, aged 7 and 5, did the major portion. Other contributors were David and Scott Carbary, aged 10 and 9; Lisa Samson, aged 5; Lisa Ayrault, aged 4; and Sarah Moses, aged 2½. Sarah embroidered most of the slightly wild dandelion and the tiny butterfly near it. Each child embroidered his or her own butterfly and flower. All worked on the rest of the meadow and the tree. The two mothers coached and coaxed. By the end of the summer the young embroiderers had become very adept in a number of stitches.

The Laced and Whipped Running Stitches were the favorites, but the Chain Stitch was almost as popular. Couching, Chevron, Satin, Open Chain, Buttenhole, Fly Stitch, French Knots, and Fern Stitch were mastered. The children showed an amazing amount of enthusiasm during the whole project and had great pride and a sense of accomplishment in the completed mural.

Caption for page 7, see page 8.

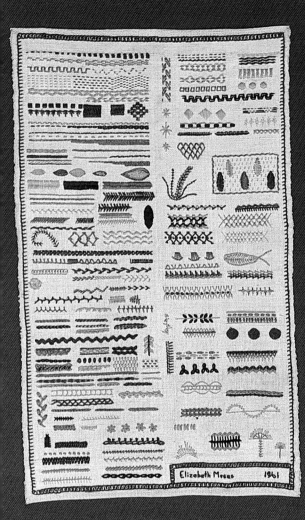

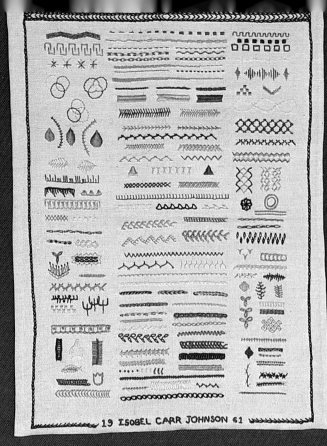

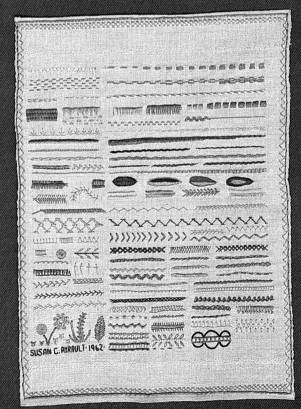

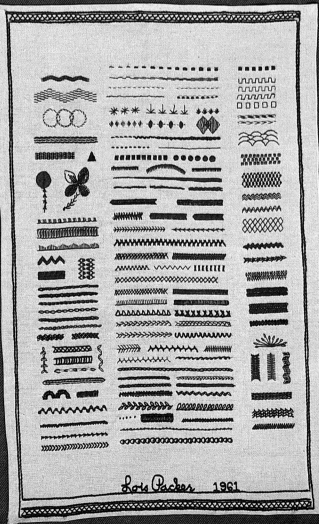

Samplers by Elizabeth Moses, Isobel Carr Johnson, Susan Ayrault, and Lois Packer (page 7). The four young women who made these samplers shared the conviction that they could not design. They had never done any kind of needlework before but were eager to learn. As they learned stitches, each one experienced the thrill of producing a beautiful sampler which was her own creation. Although they worked at the same time, each sampler is completely different and expresses the personality of its creator. Even before these young women had completed their samplers, they were applying their knowledge and producing beautiful things. Above all, they experienced the joy that comes from creating with a needle, sharing this experience with women of all ages and cultures.

Susan C. Ayrault and Elizabeth Moses whose samplers are shown on page 7. Their blouses were designed and worked by the author. The design on Susan's Blouse was inspired by an eighth century Viking scroll on a Swedish memorial stone. The Morone painting shown on page 18 was the source of the design on Elizabeth's blouse.

Isobel Carr Johnson and Lois Packer whose samplers are shown on page 7. Isobel's blouse was designed and worked by the author in the Viking scroll pattern.

Introduction

There is today a real need for a book in which people will find the inspiration and the guidance to explore the possibilites of contemporary embroidery, a book in which stitches are so clearly and completely described that anyone can master them with little effort. The purpose of this book is to fill this need—to teach many stitches, some of which have not been recorded before.

A tremendous resurgence is taking place in the area of individual expression in the arts and crafts. Women, and men too, are rediscovering the joys of hand work; they are tired of the monotony of assembly line products. Interest in embroidery was lost mainly because it was not exciting; it was old fashioned, and the tempo of modern living seemed to leave no time for it. Today, more and more people are experiencing a strong desire to create with their hands. They are rediscovering the possibilities of an old medium expressed in contemporary terms, using modern techniques, not those of 100 or even 50 years ago. It is my hope that this book will provide the inspiration and the knowledge they seek. It is written for people of all ages—for teachers and students; for career girls, mothers, and grandmothers; for men and boys.

Many people assume that they cannot design embroidery for their own use. They are indoctrinated with the idea that the planning can be done only by experts. We can all design if we overcome the notion that we cannot draw. We can all design if we keep our eyes open to new ideas and to the beauty around us—if we just give ourselves a chance. If a woman in a remote corner of Lapland or a small island in the Mediterranean can produce something beautiful and pleasing with a needle, why can't you? This book will show you how.

Most of what is termed "peasant" embroidery of Europe is made with simple stitches used effectively. For instance, the embroidery of Brittany which has so much charm consists almost entirely of a few simple designs made with Chain, Stem, and Buttonhole Stitches, along with the native Breton Stitch. If the women of Brittany can do this today, so can you. Don't be afraid of expressing yourself and you will find, as I did, that a new world of creativity can be yours. We have so many sources of designs that our ancestors did not have. It is simply a question of knowing how to go about it. My aim is to teach you how.

Before books were printed, women—and men—embroidered. They learned by word of mouth. Knowledge was passed on from one generation to the next. New stitches, or imaginative combinations of stitches, were tried out on a piece of linen on which the embroiderer recorded examples, or "sampled" what she wished to remember. Hence the word sampler. A sampler was a personal encyclopedia of stitches.

Left-handed stitchers: Turn the stitch diagrams upside down and follow the letters.

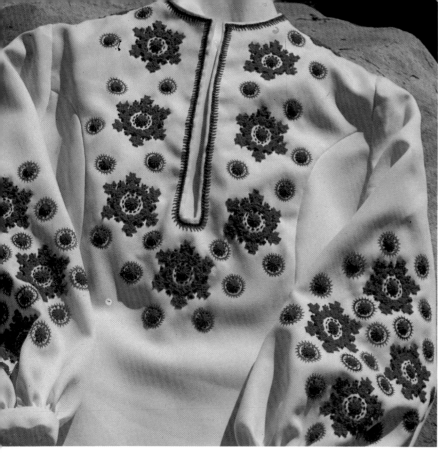

Above, caftan with Indian interlacing stitches made by the author.

Christmas necktie, snowflakes on blue background. Designed and worked by the author.

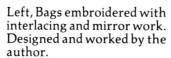

Left, Bags embroidered with interlacing and mirror work. Designed and worked by the author.

Right, Bottom of pants legs embroidered in anticipation of a cruise with snorkeling. Designed and worked by the author.

Right, Evening bag by Edith Hansen. (Courtesy of Danish Handcradft Guild.)

Embroidered Patchwork Quilt [detail] by Mary Ann Spawn. Mary Ann is a painter turned stitcher who enjoys playing with colors and textures. Working spontaneously, she is fond of breaking space into small areas, creating a mosaic of sparkling jewels. The cribsize quilt is composed of puffy little patches of many colored, antique satin swatches from a decorator's sample book. These are heavily enriched with stitches and joined together into an exciting, colorful whole.

Embroidered sleeves on blouse—one from shoulder to elbow, the other from elbow to wrist. Designed and worked by the author.

Cotton dress with multicolored Orlon yarn embroidery, designed and worked by the author.

In the Middle Ages European women were inspired by the embroidery brought back from other countries by their warrior husbands. There was a time when historical scenes were in vogue, such as the famous Bayeux Tapestry made in the eleventh century. After the Crusades women experimented with the brilliant colors described by the men, the colors that inspired the intense colors of stained glass in the cathedrals. Later on, embroidered and printed cloths from the Near East and the Far East provided a new and exciting inspiration from which English crewel embroidery emerged.

In the sixteenth century a few books of embroidery patterns were printed in Italy and Germany. These were expensive and were passed on from one group to another, each woman recording samples of the stitches or of the designs. At first, only the ladies of the court had access to designs for embroidery. Gradually the country people who waited on the court ladies copied the stitches on samplers of their own. Only the better designs were transmitted, which may explain in part the excellence of some of the peasant embroideries of Europe. Each woman added something of her own personality; her combination of stitches was influenced by the materials available, the threads, the very feel of the age. She adorned her home and enriched her festive clothes. Samplers became valued possessions handed down in the family from mother to daughter. Each one in turn added the combinations of stitches that she created.

Later on, samplers lost their true meaning. They became an exhibition of patience and proficiency. Many a little girl was made to spend long hours of patient (or was it impatient?) labor, working on Cross Stitch alphabets and verses with a moral which it was hoped would sink in. I smypathize with the little girls of past centuries. To this day I have a slight aversion to Cross Stitch because, when I was in grade school in Paris, I had to work over and over again on Cross Stitch alphabets. The idea was to learn to mark clothing. Today we use printed name tapes. What thrilling things we could have embroidered; what fun it could have been; what a missed opportunity! With a little direction, children can produce exciting work with needle and thread.

The past has become interesting again. We marvel at the intricate stitchery used by our great-grandmothers, and would love to produce something as effective. But we think we have neither the time, nor the patience, nor the skill. Today's embroidery can be quick, easy, and fun; it can be beautiful.

It is my feeling that women should go back to the original idea of our ancestors and make "samplers" of the stitches they learn; rather than copying someone else's sampler, each woman should create one all her own, expressing her own creative bent in color and texture variations of her choosing. Such a sampler is a useful reference whenever new work is planned—a reference to the stitch, the size, and the combination of stitches that she finds most pleasing. That is how early samplers were used.

A sampler should not be an end in itself, but a means to an end. However, by good use of color and careful placement, a sampler of real beauty can be achieved. The samplers on page 7 were planned and stitched at my suggestion by four young women who had never sewn or designed before. Each sampler is lovely, completely different, and each one expresses the personality of the individual who made it.

Today, there is a new vitality in the art of embroidery. Museums exhibit works made by artists for home decoration such as wall hangings, panels, screens, table linens, as well as church vestments and articles of clothing. Don't try to do something elaborate at first. Learn and work for the fun of it, for relaxation, for the pleasure it will bring to you and those around you. There is something stable and basically reassuring about a woman embroidering, and you don't need to look like Whistler's Mother either!

Men and boys are rediscovering what they can do with a needle. In past centuries professional embroidery was done by men. It still is today in many parts of the world. Men and boys bring a fresh, imaginative, free flowing approach to the craft. Some of the most exciting contemporary work I have seen was done by men and school-age boys.

FERNINAND. An original stitchery designed and worked by 13-year-old Tom Glenn in an art class taught by Margaret Seil, John Marshall Junior High School, Seattle, Washington.

They have also been quicker to discover the therapeutic value of creative stitcheries, and how they help to relieve tensions. It is my hope that the use of stitcheries in therapy will be more thoroughly explored, and that this book will provide a needed impetus in this direction.

While not an exhaustive treatise on the subject, this book does explain clearly the great majority of stitches, especially how a basic stitch can be varied, and what can be done with it. It groups stitches in their natural sequence. There is a logical development in stitches. Flat stitches form the first group. Flat stitches with a curve or loop

Embroidery threads from Kutch, India. (Photograph by Robert McClellan.)

Designs from Hindu Toran, late 19th century, Kutch, India; sampler made by the author.

Embroidered yoke for dinner dress. Three values of turquoise, with gold; inserted turquoise stone. Designed and worked by the author.

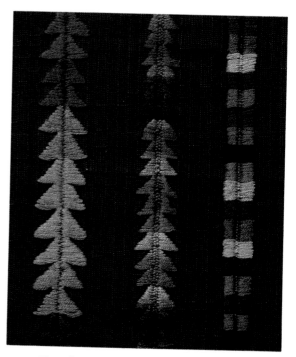

Notebook page sampler of Guatemala seam joining by the author.

Sampler of Brittany hearts embroidered for Mme Le Minor, Pont l'Abbé.

Modern Sampler by Mariska Karasz. Mariska Karasz was one of the first artists to work with what she called "liberated stitches." This joyful sampler emerged as she played with basic stitches and spontaneous variations. The Outline Stitch meanders and widens into the Satin Stitch followed by the Chain Stitch and her favorite Open Chain, then the Buttonhole and finally the Vandyke Stitch. Using a variety of colorful yarns, she created the textures and shapes that make this sampler one of my most treasured possessions.

Notebook of samplers worked by the author. (Photograph by Robert McClellan.)

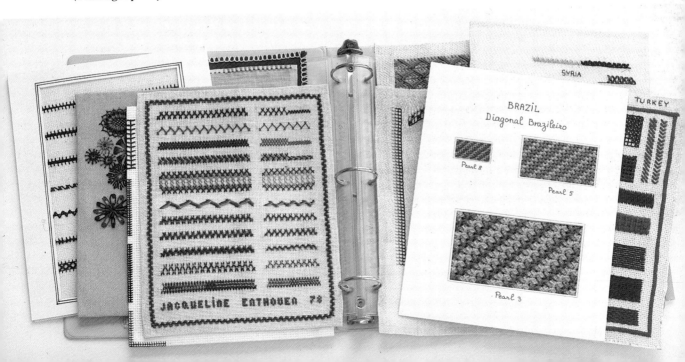

become looped stitches. Closing the loop makes chained stitches. Twisting and tightening the loop makes knotted stitches.

It is best to start with simple stitches. As each stitch is learned, practice it on a separate cloth until a rhythm is established. Then embroider it on the sampler in the color and weight of thread that you find most effective. There is no substitute for practice. Fortunately, with bold, modern stitches, facility is rapidly acquired. But it is only after you have mastered a technique that you can use it to express exactly what you want to say.

The spontaneity which marks so much of contemporary art doesn't just happen; it is born of painstaking practice from which freedom emerges. A ballerina's perfect leaps and twirls appear relaxed because she has so mastered the technique that mechanics are forgotten. It is much the same with embroidery. But unlike ballet, freedom can be obtained rapidly with less than half an hour of practice for each new stitch. From the mastering of technique, creation will flow and bring its own reward. Learn one step at a time, building on a solid foundation.

You can be spontaneously creative with forms issuing from your needle. This will happen only after stitches flow freely from your fingertips, so that when a shape wants to be born, the stitch that will best express your feeling will spring forth unconsciously. Spontaneity emerges after you have freed yourself from the mechanics of the medium.

Gradually, from simple stitches, effective groupings appear. When you come up with a combination you like, make a record of it on your sampler. Stitches can gain vitality when used together with other stitches or when emphasized through repetition. Take, for instance, the simple Running Stitch. By lacing or whipping it, repeating or alternating rows, you can create a smart, interesting border. The best effects are often obtained with the simplest stitches.

Learn to doodle with a needle. After you have learned or become reacquainted with a few stitches, play with them and see how you can vary them. Lengthen them, shorten them, bring them closer together or farther apart, try thinner or heavier threads, and experiment with texture. Once you have mastered a number of stitches, you will find that ideas for using them will come to you. Before long, expression will blossom forth and you will know just what you want to do. It will bring satisfying reward and even exhilaration.

As you learn stitches and record them on your sampler, anchor your newly acquired knowledge by applying it. There are many pieces of clothing you can embroider. You can make articles to decorate your home such as tablecloths, table mats, cushions, curtains, bedspreads, and the wall hangings so popular today. You can create original presents. This is a craft that can be mastered at home with a minimum outlay of materials and time. Always keep a work basket or bag handy—near your favorite chair—with a few threads and needles of matched sizes and a piece of coarse linen or cotton homespun. A few minutes of practicing and doodling will help you to relax and unwind. You may even come up with an unexpected combination that will thrill your. If you have children, you will find that while you are quietly embroidering, they will be more apt to come to you, share their experiences, and talk over their problems. You will be in a mood to listen because, with your hands occupied, you will feel that you can spare the time. So few mothers today feel they can spare the time to listen. Your work should always be easily available and your doodling cloth handy. There is always a stitch that can be practiced. It will pay dividends in more ways than you think.

Some of the happiest recollections of my childhood are centered around my grandmother while she embroidered and listened to me. What I said was no doubt utterly trivial, but it was important to me. My mother was an author whose work required concentration. She rarely had time to listen. What recollections do you have? What recollections will your children have? You can do so much for your children and for others if you listen. Busy hands make for easy listening.

It is my hope that this book will open a new world of spontaneous creativity for you and that, in addition to practicing new stitches and inventing original combinations, you will make a record of what you learn on a sampler of your own. I hope you will sign and date it, and that it will become not only your pride and joy, but also something to be treasured by those who will inherit it.

I hope that you will fall in love with stitches, waking up in the morning eager to see what you created the day before, eager with new ideas to put down. There are few joys in life comparable to that of creating something original and beautiful. If you try, you can experience the joy of creating with stitches.

MADONNA AND CHILD by Domenico Morone. Late fifteenth century. Have you
thought of going through an art gallery seeking embroidery possibilities? I went through
the Italian rooms of the National Gallery of Art in Washington, D.C., with just that
thought in mind. (Courtesy of National Gallery of Art, Washington, D.C., Widener
Collection.)

I Starting to Stitch

BEGIN NOW

Your sampler is going to be a permanent record of the stitches you already know and also of those you are about to learn. However, it may take you a little time to assemble the materials and the threads you need. Don't wait until you have found the ideal material and the ideal threads. Start practicing stitches now on any piece of material you have around, perferably one with a coarse weave, even a dish cloth. Use any thread, yarn, or twine you have, even the soft string from that package you just brought home. Heavy threads are best. If it will make your learning easier, pull out a thread or two from the cloth for a definite stitching line, or draw a line with a blue pencil. A black pencil is apt to smear.

Practicing will teach you the mechanics of the stitches that are unfamiliar to you. By the time you have assembled all the things you want for your sampler, you will know several stitches and start with confidence.

CHOOSING THE MATERIAL

It is important to choose the right kind of material for your sampler. You will need two pieces of material: one for your sampler, and one for your "doodling" or practice cloth. Traditionally, in western countries, samplers were made on handwoven, unbleached linen with a slightly loose weave. Linen is still ideally suited for samplers because of its beauty, durability, and ease of working. It need not be handwoven. Beautiful linens are manufactured today. A good linen weight for samplers has approximately 26 threads to the inch with fairly even warp and weft, so that the threads can be counted when necessary. Anywhere from 24 to 30 threads to the inch is good.

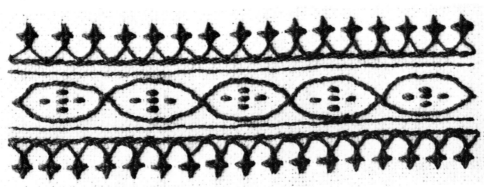

Sampler by the author interpreting the lowest border of the Morone painting. It was worked in red cotton on white material to be used vertically on the sleeve of a blouse. The stitches used were Cross Stitch Flower, Fly, Outline, Whipped Back, and Seed.

Other textiles, less expensive, also lend themselves to stitching. Cotton homespun comes in an off-white and in striking colors, with threads coarse enough so that lines can easily be followed, between 24 and 28 threads to the inch. It has a pleasing texture and makes a beautiful sampler. There are also many blends with synthetic fibers. Coarse weaves are often found in drapery materials. Look for remnants with an even weave. Children enjoy making samplers on striped materials, using the stripes as a guide. Have a needle in your purse for testing cloth to see if it is easy to pierce. Besides off-white cloth, colored cloth can be used to make attractive samplers. The advantage is that the embroidery can be worked with white thread, resolving the problem of what color to use. I made a much-admired sampler on a royal blue napkin, stitched in white.

SIZE OF THE SAMPLER

There is no ideal or perfect size for samplers. In your planning, allow an extra inch on all four sides for a hem. You may eventually want to make a very small hem, but if you leave enough in the beginning, you don't have to make up your mind until later on.

Because materials frequently come in widths of 35 or 36 inches, half a width—around 18 inches before hemming—is a convenient size. (This means 16 inches, allowing for a 1-inch hem on each side.) This is a good basic width for a sampler, with enough room for a pleasing margin.

Some linens come in 14- or 16-inch widths. The selvedge can remain as the edge of your sampler, with hem at the top and the bottom. If you want to make a wall hanging of your sampler, for your sewing corner for instance, allow for a larger hem at the top and the bottom into which a rod or wood slat can be slipped. The length of your sampler should be left flexible because you may need more or less space. If you buy ¾ yard, or better still, 1 yard of material, you will be safe.

A good length for your finished sampler would be between 20 and 26 inches. Twenty inches might prove to be too short for you because there might still be stitches to record, or you might have been a little generous in the spacing of your rows. If your sampler runs to 26 inches, ¾ yard would just allow for this. Cut the edges straight by drawing a thread for guidance and overcast the raw edges to avoid fraying.

DOODLING CLOTH

Along with the material for your sampler, you should have another piece of material on which to practice unfamiliar stitches, or experiment with different weights of threads, textures, colors, proper tension, and so forth. If you start directly on your sampler and have to undo some stitches, your threads will develop a tired look.

I call this second piece of material my doodling cloth, because just as some people doodle with pen or pencil, I like to doodle with a needle, inventing new combinations of stitches, and trying mixtures of color. On a doodling cloth you can experiment and decide how you will record a stitch on your sampler. Think of it as a sketching pad. Mine is always handy with thread and needle, ready to be picked up as I listen to people or to music. The results of my doodlings often suggest new designs.

The doodling cloth is a place to practice and a place to make mistakes, presuming you ever make mistakes! By the time you have worked 2 or 3 inches of a stitch, you will know just how you want to record it on your sampler. On my doodling cloth, I don't even both to end the threads. It is the place where you will discover whether the lacing thread looks better when it is darker than the base stitch, or the other way around. There you develop the color combinations that please you. Try a stitch in pearl cotton, size 5 or 8, and in stranded cotton, and see which appeals to you most. Record it that way on your sampler, or if two or three ways look interesting, do small samples of it each way.

If the sampler material you bought is 36 inches wide, use half the width for your sampler and the other half for your doodling cloth. Since it has the same thread count and the same background shade as your sampler, it would be an ideal cloth for trying out ideas.

THREADS

There should be a congenial relationship between the materials and the threads you use, between the textures, the colors, and the stitches. Different threads will produce varied effects, and are manufactured under different trade names. Experiment with cotton, linen, silk, and wool. To learn and practice stitches, twisted threads such as embroidery pearl cottons are useful for a crisp definition.

Pearl cotton is a twisted thread which comes in skeins or balls. The common sizes are 3, 5 and 8. The lower the number, the heavier the thread. Size 3 is useful; it is the heaviest pearl which covers ground quickly. Size 5 is the most popular, and size 8 is used for finer work. Needlecraft stores, some department stores and weavers' suppliers carry assortments by a variety of manufacturers in the United States and abroad. Weavers are good people to know; they often have interesting, unused thread ends.

Crochet and knitting cottons have varied textures. If you are dyeing your own threads, they are good ones to use.

A different effect is obtained with stranded cotton, the most available thread in the United States. It comes in an unlimited range of colors, which differ according to brands. It can be split in order to vary the weight. A thick, soft, untwisted cotton without sheen is available in many colors in the Scandinavian countries, France, England, Japan, and elsewhere. These create effects particularly wellsuited to contemporary design and interior decoration. The same type of thread is found in the United States in white or ecru unmercerized crochet cotton and in candlewick cotton.

An exciting substitute is plain, uncolored, soft string which can be found inexpensively in various weights. It is exciting because you can dye your own string or white crochet and knitting cotton to create the effect you want. This is precisely what our great-great-grandmothers used to do, and to this day American Indian women dye their own straws and barks to weave baskets that truly express their personalities. Think of what an exciting sampler you could make with crochet cotton dyed in several values of the same color, from very dark to very light. Start with the darkest, dyeing 5 yards of thread. Then dilute the solution a little for the next 5 yards, and so on until you reach off-white. That sampler would really be your creation! My grandmother used to boil white embroidery cotton in very strong tea that had been strained through muslin, also in linden blossom tea; the color was like a tea with a blush to it.

A number of beautiful linen embroidery threads are manufactured. There is something very permanent about linen. I hope, too, that you will discover the thrill of embroidery with silk; nothing can match its beauty. Wool in a wide range of colors is easily available. Man-made fibers are now used extensively.

Start collecting threads. You will find many countries manufacture their own typical brands. Do you have friends traveling to Scandinavian countries, to Japan, to India? Ask them to bring back a few skeins of local embroidery threads in your favorite colors.

When you start a new skein, attach the color number and brand-name label to the end of the skein so that it will always be there as a reference. Keep a page of threads to refer to in your notebook. Tape or sew through the paper to fasten a small piece of thread in each color and weight. It will save you time and make buying duplicates easy. Make a note of which theads were used for a specific piece— the type, the size, and the color of each.

CHOOSING COLORS

Think in terms of colors that appeal to you. Begin with the shade that expresses your feelings best. The other shades will fall into place around it. When the background material is neutral, there is no limit to the choice of thread colors. When the material is colored, the threads can be neutral; they can also accentuate the background color or contrast with it.

If you need a source of inspiration, look at paintings you like by famous artists. They may start you on a new and exciting combination of colors. The golds and greens of a Van Gogh might make a lovely color scheme for a sampler. See how the artist used his colors, whether bright colors are dominant or muted ones. Watch for variations in value from light to dark. Look for accents and note their proportions. Good magazine pictures can be helpful.

Many books are available illustrating the art of various countries such as India, Persia, China, and Egypt. There are also color reproductions of tapestries and of stained glass windows. Two Persian fourteenth century miniatures at the Freer Gallery of Art in Washington, D.C., were a source of inspiration for me. Another was an advertisement for an oil company, showing a color photograph of a country landscape in beautiful shades of green with gold, reddish brown, and a touch of blue-green. Good photographs of outdoor scenes will provide an endless source of color combinations. The colors of early spring or fall are another source. Are there trees around you? Look at the variations in greens and browns. Are there flower borders? Delphiniums provide endless and exciting variations in shades of blue.

You can make a beautiful sampler by using threads in several values of one color. For example, you might make an all blue sampler, with threads ranging from brilliant royal blue to the palest sky blue, or an all red sampler, from the darkest Burgundy red to light pink or coral. Think also of color progression, for example, from yellow to orange to red. Gather together your threads in groups, blending, complementing or contrasting, just as an artist arranges the colors he wants to use on his palette.

For variety in texture as well as color, you will find that a few balls of pearl cotton—three in size 5, three in size 8, and three skeins in size 3—also three or four skeins of stranded cotton will give you a good range with which to start. Variegated cottons in pearl and in stranded cotton are fun to use and give motion to a pattern.

If you are not in the mood to experiment with color, use different weights and textures of white on colored material. Once you start on your sampler, you will find yourself on the lookout for new shades and new weights of thread. Collect all the threads you can. Even a small length may be all you need for accent on a future mural or cushion.

NEEDLES

The thread should be able to pass through the eye of the needle smoothly and easily. If you have to tug, you lose the rhythm and the fun is gone. Plan to have needles in assorted sizes on hand so that threading is never a problem; the smaller the size number, the heavier the needle.

An assorted package of each of three types of needles should take care of most of your needs.

Crewel needles are long-eyed with a pointed end. A package of assorted sizes from No. 3 to No. 9 is convenient.

Tapestry needles are long-eyed with rounded ends. They are useful for many stitches, for heavy threads and loose material. They are particularly suited to whipped or threaded stitches, and for weaving in and out. They are available in packages of assorted sizes from No. 18 to No. 24.

Round-eyed milliner's needles with sharp ends are useful for knotted stitches, especially Bullion Stitches, as the loops slip off easily. They come in assorted sizes, No. 3 to No. 9. You will soon discover which needle works best for you for each type of thread and material. For instance, for pearl cotton in size 5, you might use a No. 5 crewel needle, but if the material is loose a No. 22 tapestry needle might work better. If the needle is difficult to thread, use a larger size.

OTHER THINGS YOU NEED

In addition to material, threads, and needles, you will need sharp scissors, a thimble, and a hoop. A thimble is a must if you really want to embroider well; it takes only a short time to get used to it. I don't always use a hoop when I am doodling, but I usually do if I am really embroidering. Working with a hoop makes your work easier and quicker; the stitches are regular, and take on a neat, crisp look; the material stays taut and does not pucker.

Embroidery hoops, sometimes called tambour frames (*tambour* is the French word for drum), are made of two rings which fit over each other. Choose a hoop with a screw on the outer ring. A screw is essential, enabling you to keep the material really taut. Hoops are made of wood, plastic, or metal; wood ones are particularly pleasant to use. A convenient working size is 6 inches in diameter. The 8-inch size is useful for larger areas. There are also lap hoops, table hoops that clamp onto tables, and standing floor hoops.

To stretch your work, put the inner ring on a table. Place the material over it. Loosen the screw on the outer ring until it fits over the material without forcing. Then tighten the screw. For a tight surface, stretch your material both lengthwise and crosswise, true to the grain, before the final turn of the screw. If your material is very fine, first warp a piece of open bias tape around the inner ring to prevent slipping. You will enjoy working with a hoop, once you acquire the habit.

If you are working very fine stitches such as the lettering on the baptismal robe shown on page 50, or if eyesight is a problem, a full-field magnifying glass is a great help. Some come with an adjustable cord that goes around the neck, leaving both hands free for embroidering; others come on stands.

As you design for embroidery, experimenting with placement or reproduction of designs, you will find a pad of good quality layout paper invaluable. These come in various sizes. Also useful are a few sheets of dressmaker's tracing carbon paper in two or three colors. Do not use typewriter carbon paper; it smudges.

TRANSFERRING DESIGNS

There are several ways of transferring designs on to cloth. The technique used varies with the nature of the design and the cloth. Professionals use a pricking and pouncing method, a technique that would be confusing to beginners.

The most popular and easiest method is to use dressmaker's or other nonsmear transfer paper. Lay the material on a smooth, hard surface. Place a piece of transfer paper of suitable color over the material, and place the design—outlined on a sheet of layout paper—over the transfer paper. The design can be traced with a hard, sharp pencil.

When the material is light in weight and color, my favorite way of transferring a design is to use a piece of glass raised over a strong light. First outline the design in black ink on layout paper. Tape the paper, with the material over it, on top of the lighted glass. You can trace the design directly on the material either with a pencil of suitable color, or with a fine paint brush dipped in watercolor. The result is a freer design.

For large designs a warm-iron transfer pencil or transfer ink is useful. Trace the design over again on the back of the layout paper so that the imprint will come out right side up. It takes a little experimenting, but once you known how sharp your pencil should be and how hot your iron, using a transfer pencil becomes a quick and easy way to transfer a design. However, the lines are not always evenly sharp. This makes it unsuitable for fine detail.

For an occasional line or shape, a useful trick is to draw a stitching guide on the *back* of the material with a blue pencil. I find this very helpful. It gives me a precise point, when precision is needed, to insert the needle from back to front. For the spider web shown on page 176 circles were drawn on the back around coins.

When designs are made of repeated shapes, templates can be cut out of light cardboard and used as a tracing guide. You can also use a French curve or the shapes around you—cups, saucers, dishes—as pioneer women did.

YOUR EMBROIDERY NOTEBOOK: Sources of ideas

As you learn stitches and look for ideas in applying them, you will begin to see with new eyes, keyed to embroidery possibilities. Start collecting ideas for designs, pictures, anything related to your embroidery. Keep them in a special loose-leaf notebook (8½-11-inch sheet size), so that the collected material can be divided into sections. In my notebook I paste or staple magazine articles; scraps of paper with designs I might use, such as a beautiful Christmas wrapping paper with stylized snow flakes; advertisements for articles of clothing or home furnishings with lines or designs that could be adapted to stitches; travel pictures of foreign countries, showing native art and embroidered or woven native costumes.

You will develop a new approach to the art forms of today and of the past. Keep a written record of your ideas. Make simple sketches of combinations of stitches and of borders you might want to try. I still have an embroidery design I drew when I was ten years old. A photograph of a detail on a medieval cathedral can inspire a border which you can recreate in your own textures and colors.

One of my ancestors designed the stalls of the cathedral at Rouen in France in the fifteenth century. It is one of my great desires to go back there and bring home my forefather's designs, interpreting them five centuries later in my own stitchery. What fun it would be to design a bonnet for a grandchild and know that I had collaborated with a long-ago grandfather.

Did your own grandmother make a quilt? If so, you might like to adapt her design to something contemporary. It could start you on a new and exciting combination of colors. A bowl from Iran might give you an idea for a stylized bird on a cushion. A Greek urn might have a symmetrical border that you can interpret in simple Running Stitch on a table cloth. One border I developed came from an Angkor Wat Cambodian sculptured headdress in a magazine.

Look around you for sources of designs. For round designs exciting sources are manhole covers in the streets. There is quite a variety and some are beautiful. Think in bold, imaginative terms; develop your own designs. It will give you far more satisfaction than embroidering a piece of material with a design already stamped on it. All artists look around them for ideas to inspire designs. An idea is not necessarily something which suddenly strikes you from the blue. There are so many available sources to inspire us. We have excellent reproductions of designs through the ages, from primitive cave paintings, so contemporary in their stylized motion, to the work of artists now living.

Many cities have traveling exhibits of art from other countries. For those who do not live near museums, magazines faithfully reproduce the treasures of other lands. Look up the jewelry from Tutankhamen's tomb, Cretan pottery, Byzantine mosaics, African and Polynesian art, or that of our own American Indians. I used stylized bisons from prehistoric cave paintings as a source for the mural "Indians and Buffalos" (pages 230-231).

Arrange and recreate designs until they feel "like you." Interpret them in colors that mean something to you. Each stitch has qualities of its own, used singly or in combinations with others. Think in terms of form and texture, not in terms of imitating the technique of the paint brush. Think rather of what stiches can do, turning the limitations of material and threads to beauty. When you have an idea, record it on your sampler. Ideas have a frustrating way of vanishing, make a record of them to keep.

STARTING THE SAMPLER

No sampler should be completely designed in advance. It should grow as new stitches are learned. Basically the sampler should not be an end in itself. It should be a record of the stitches one has learned, done in the form, the color, and the weight of thread most pleasing to you. For this reason no two samplers should be exactly alike. I have yet to see a sampler that is not beautiful. A four-year-old's sampler of Running Stitches irregularly worked in vivid colors of the child's choosing was a joy to look at.

Some stitches you will love and enjoy. Others may not appeal to you at first, but keep a record of them because stitches have a way of growing on one. A particular stitch may be just what you need later on for a special effect. Several stitches which I did not like as a child are now among my favorites. Each new stitch opens a new door to a path you may not travel for some time, but do record it on your sampler. Try it twice, first in the original size and then half size. If you have made rows of Running Stitches ¼ inch long, make additional rows ⅛ inch long.

Let stitches become your vocabulary. Each new stitch is like a new word added to your repertoire; the richer your vocabulary, the better you can express yourself.

When a stitch particularly appeals to you, practice it on your doodling cloth in different colors. A change of color can add interest. Use different types of threads, coarse or thin, shining or dull, twisted or flat. If you have used pearl cotton in size 5, try using stranded cotton. You will be surprised at how different the same stitch can look. Repetition of the simplest stitches creates interesting designs, try several rows close together or rows at different intervals.

On a sampler it is best to start with a knot on the "wrong" side, since the sampler is a record of *how* stitches were worked out. Then

Sampler by Maria Clementina Carneiro de Moura. It is a record of the colors and stitches used on peasant girls' vests in the province of Minho. The cloth is red wool, embroidered in multicolored wools and metallic thread, with added spangles; also used are glass beads in interesting groups of eight. (Photograph by Robert McClellan.)

when you are trying to decide what stitch will meet the purpose you have in mind, the knot itself will be a guide as to where to start. Keep the back of your sampler as neat as possible with no dangling pieces of thread.

Work, other than samplers, should not be started with a knot. Instead use a few small Running Stitches towards the starting point and work over them.

Although the stitches are listed in this book according to traditional classification, some are much easier than others. You may want to start with all the stitches you already know, which is one way to go about it. However, a sampler is more useful for reference later on if some general classification is adhered to.

There are many ways in which the stitches can be recorded. My favorite way is to work each basic stitch and some variations in a center panel, 6 inches wide. On each side of the center panel, and ½ inch away, there is a panel 3 inches wide in which ideas and combinations of stitches and color are noted. This is the way I worked the sampler shown on the frontispiece.

If your fancy runs to leaf forms, illustrate a stitch recorded in the center panel as a leaf. Try a flower such as those made in Jacobean crewel embroidery, stylized birds, insects, fish, animals, or any shape or design. You might illustrate the Running Stitch in a zigzag or wave pattern, the Darning Stitch as a leaf filling. In the center of your sampler, record the stitch learned; on the side, see what you can do with it.

Some stitches look quite different when massed together rather than put in a single line. This is illustrated with the Running Stitch, the Surface Darning Stitch, the Back Stitch, and the Outline Stitch.

Another way to plan your sampler is to have your basic stitches on one side in a panel 6 inches wide, and use a 6-inch panel on the other side for examples, with 1 inch between the two panels.

Try to express your own ideas. The more individual your work, the more it will express you, and the happier you will be. You are not trying to impress anyone; you are making a useful record in a way that is pleasing to you.

If your material is 18 inches wide and you allow 1 inch on each side for a hem, there will be a margin of about 1½ inches on each side. If your hem is smaller, you might have a 2-inch margin. At the top, leave 1 inch for a hem, and 2½ to 3 inches for a margin before starting the first row. This will give you space in which to embroider a frame of favorite stitches.

All the stitches need not be worked on the 6-inch length. Some stitches, such as the Single Threaded Backstitch and the Double Threaded Backstitch, can be worked halfway or a third of the way, or vertically instead of horizontally.

Don't try to decide ahead of time what color the next illustration will be. Just lay skeins of different colors next to the last row. By a process of elimination, you will quickly decide which shade will look best. If you are not sure where to place the next design, lay a piece of tracing paper on your work. Draw on it what you have in mind; move it up and down, toward the sides and toward the center. When you have found the right position, mark the place by piercing the design on the paper with a few needles; then slip the paper off the needles. The needles should show the general outline of the design.

NOTEBOOKS OF STITCH SAMPLERS

A satisfying way to keep a record of what you are learning is by working individual samplers to fit 8½-by-11 inch three-ring notebooks. The finished size of each one can vary. Mine are usually 7½ by 9½ inches. Samplers of this size worked by eighth and nineth grade pupils are shown on pages 32, 80, 100, 120.

Whenever you come across suitable sampler cloth in a variety of textures and colors, cut pieces about 8½ by 10½ inches to allow for a ½-inch turnback; hem it with a fine thread of matching color using a simple Herringbone Stitch (this will not show on the front). I keep one or two in my purse in a little plastic bag, with a needle already threaded, ready to do the hemming. Then if I am waiting for someone or something, in no time I have another page ready. You can of course hem them on a machine but it is nice to make your stitch records attractive and pleasing to the eye.

Each page is protected by a three-hole clear plastic cover, which allows the back as well as the front to be seen. If plastic covers are not available, the page can be tacked at the top of a piece of heavy three-hole paper.

A page of explanations is useful opposite each sampler, with a stitch diagram if necessary or the history of the stitch or design.

Classify them as to type of stitch (flat, looped, and so on), by design, or by continent and country. I have separate notebooks for these. They give me a real sense of accomplishment, satisfy my sense of order, make me feel that I am growing in learning and retaining a reassuring record of that growth. Because they often serve to record a newly learned technique, something you saw or originated, you do not have to fill the whole page right away. A sampler is something you add to as the occasion arises. It provides ideas for the use of stitches. You are building a continually growing record for ready reference.

I also have a whole notebook of little samplers worked by friends, special variations of theirs or an interesting grouping of colors. One of my treasures is a small sampler worked for me in 1980 by Clementina de Moura Manta of Lisbon, Portugal's most distinguished artist/embroiderer. I have another by Barbara Snook, and best of all I own Mariska Karasz's famous "Modern Sampler" (not notebook size!).

Notebook samplers can illustrate a family of stitches or the many variations of one stitch, in a basic way or in free interpretation. They can represent the stitches of different countries or ethnic groups and how they are used, in colors used in that country. It is particulary satisfying whenever possible to start these on indigenous cloth. I worked a Guatemala sampler on hand woven cloth from that country, one from Japan on Kogin cloth, one from India on handwoven cotton and pineapple fiber, and many others. Some samplers can record edges and joinings. I have made samplers using traditional Moslem joinings and some from the Balkans, the Ukraine, and other cultures, so that now, when I want to join the seams of a garment, I have the pleasure of looking at these pages and selecting the seam joining that is most effective.

Samplers can record ways of filling shapes, such as the Chinese using knots, the Balkans using a variety of close Double Running or Darning Stitches, and the French using Seed Stitches. Another subject would be how different ethnic groups fill spaces between shapes: the Moslems in several countries use a number of small attractive motifs; the Hindu have their own motifs, the Mexicans make a filling of small, complete circles of Bullion Stitches.

Samplers can show different ways of expressing leaves and flowers. They can focus on one shape—the heart shape for example—showing how different cultures such as those of Poland, Portugal and Brittany interpret it with stitches in a variety of ways. Note your sources and be sure of them. This is not only good scholarship, the work becomes much more interesting.

I enjoy medallion and border samplers. Often, as I doodle with a pencil, I work out stitches in a circle. If I like the result, I am apt to work it out on a blouse or around a skirt.

Some of my favorite samplers are those picturing typical designs of a country, worked with its special stitches, like those of India or Hungary. Different countries use different techniques. I find it particularly rewarding to research and work samplers of countries whose needlework is mostly a thing of the past. It becomes an important historical document. The Tuareg nomads don't work hand-embroidery anymore, yet their gorgeous interlacing should live forever. Carl Schuster, the great collector of Cross Stitch embroideries of rural western China wrote in *Asia* magazine in January 1937: "The art is dead, it is a thing of the past . . . held in varying degrees of contempt by the women of the younger generation . . ." There are countless unique works of embroidery begging to be studied and condensed into records for future reference. Such organized records are much more likely to survive and be valued than a pretty embroidery hung on a wall. Be sure you name and date them. What an heirloom for future generations!

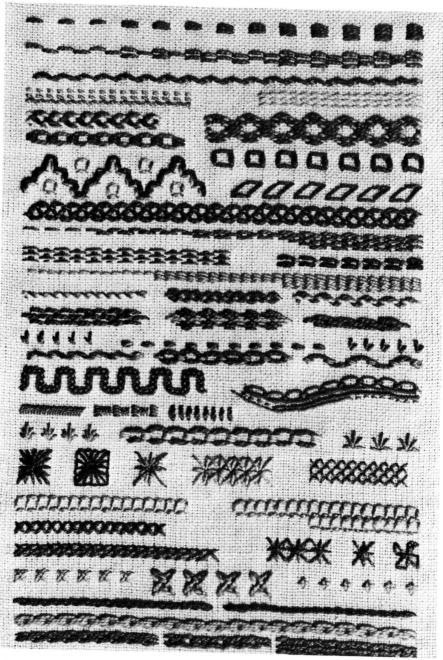

Flat Stitch sampler worked by the author on cream handwoven linen 10 inches   wide.

II The Stitches

FLAT STITCHES

Introduction

Flat Stitches form the largest family of stitches. They are on the whole the easiest stitches. They are used to follow lines or to fill shapes. With a little imagination, exciting effects can be produced simply by varying the size of the stitches, the distance between them, or the distance between rows. They lie flat on the surface of the material, either close together or spaced.

The simplest Flat Stitches are worked as straight or curved lines. Some Flat Stitches are worked detached and at random; many others cross each other. There are also a few which are worked in an angular pattern.

Running Stitch

The Running Stitch is the simplest and quickest of all stitches. It is the basis of countless variations. As its name implies, the needle runs in and out of the material at regular intervals. It is used as an outline or as a filling with rows of parallel or staggered stitches to create textures.

Work from right to left, using a heavy cotton to practice, such as pearl in sizes 3 or 5, or six strands of stranded cotton, or any thread you may have. Start with a knot on the wrong side; remember that your sampler is a record of your stitches, and you will want to see where you started.

The size of the stitches depends on the texture of your material and the threads at your disposal. On a coarse linen or cotton homespun, you can count the threads easily if you wish to be accurate, or you can draw lines on the back of the material to guide you.

Starting on the right, make a row of straight stitches of equal length with equal spaces between them (about ¼ inch or slightly less); work from A to B, covering 6 inches in the center of your sampler (Figure 1). Start again just below A at C and make a similar row of stitches to D. Continue working rows from E to F, G to H, and I to J. You are recording what different blocks of Running Stitches look like. The varying depths will suggest decorative uses.

1

Flat Stitch sampler worked by Linda Richie, eighth grade, Holy Names Academy, Seattle, Washington. Linda used white cotton of varying weights on red cotton homespun.

1 Eskimo Laced Edge 2 Running Stitch 3 Checkerboard Running Stitch 4 Threaded Running Stitch 5 Whipped Running Stitch 6 Border in Threaded Running Stitch 7 3 Rows, Bottom Whipped 8 3 Rows, All Whipped 9 Double Threaded Running Stitch 10 Double Running Straight Stitch 11 Double Running Zigzag Stitch 12 Double Running (Holbein) Stitch 13 Surface Darning 14 Back Stitch 15 Whipped Back Stitch 16 Seed Stitch 17 Threaded Back Stitch 18 Seed Stitch (angled) 19 Double Threaded Back Stitch 20 Whipped Seed Stitch 21 Pekinese Stitch and Two Rows Whipped Together 22 Satin Stitch 23 Guilloche Stitch 24 Straight Stitch 25 Cross Stitch 26 Slav Cross Stitch 27 Double Cross Stitch 28 Cross Stitch Flowers 29 Outline Stitch 30 Stem Stitch 31 Alternating Stem Stitch 32 Alternating Stem Stitch 33 Long Stem Stitch 34 Long Stem Stitch Filling 35 French Filling

Three rows of close Running Stitches with heavy threads make an attractive border for a table mat (Figure 2). If you are lengthening a little girl's dress, this is a quick and attractive way of making a border to hide the creased line of a previous hem.

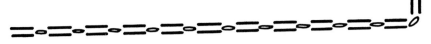

2

Checkerboard Running Stitch

Start a second group of Running Stitches about ¼ inch below the first group, using the same weight of thread but perhaps a different shade. The choice of weight of thread and color is what will make the sampler your own. This time, work in checkerboard fashion, with the second row just under the spaces of the first row (Figure 3).

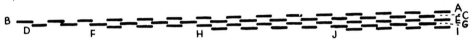

3

On the side panels of your sampler, work examples to show what these stitches will look like when you use pearl cotton in size 8, or three strands of stranded cotton. Try different shades, stitches one-half or one-third of the size they were before, in straight lines, wavy lines, or zigzag lines.

Whipped Running Stitch

This stitch is a quick and effective way to outline a shape. It gives texture to the line, producing a twisted cord effect. It is economical of thread. The whipping thread can be the same color or a contrasting one. A rich effect is obtained when the whipping thread is gold or silver. This makes it a useful filling stitch for ecclesiastical embroidery. The metallic thread stays on the surface, whipped through a silk or mercerized cotton of the same shade. Children love to work the Whipped Running Stitch, especially in red, whipping it in white for a candycane effect.

Work from right to left. Start with a row of even Running Stitches from A to B (Figure 4). Whip with a tapestry needle (it has a rounded point), from right to left.

4

Bring the needle and whipping thread out just under the first Running Stitch at C, over and under the second stitch, and so on. Do not catch the material; pass the thread between the stitch and the material as from D to E. Watch the tension so the whipping thread is neither too tight nor too loose. End behind the middle of the last stitch. The whipping thread goes through the material only at the beginning and at the end.

Small Running Stitch sampler showing variations 1, 2, and 3.

Whipped Running Stitch Variations

Rows of Whipped Running Stitches *parallel to each other* make a stunning border. They are a quick, effective way of filling a shape. In the stitchery "Michael, The Archangel," shown on page 35 rows of Whipped Running Stitches are used on the wings. Try the following variations, using approximately five Running Stitches to the inch and three strands of six-stranded cotton for the first four. Work either in color on white cloth or in white cotton on colored cloth. Some of these variations are illustrated in the two small samplers shown above and below.

    1. Three rows of close Running Stitches with the bottom row whipped, the other two rows not whipped.

    2. Five rows of close Running Stitches, the first and fifth whipped, the three center rows not whipped.

    3. Three parallel, close rows of Whipped Running Stitches.

    4. Two parallel rows of Running Stitches whipped together (not illustrated).

    5. Three parallel rows of Whipped Running Stitches with large stitches, ⅜ to ¼ inch, in pearl cotton, size 3.

    6. The above variations in different values of the same color, such as light, medium, and dark blue (not illustrated).

When you are working several rows of Running Stitches, if you wish to continue with the same thread at the end of a row, rather than start again at the beginning point, turn your work so that the next row will still be worked from right to left, both for the running and for the whipping. Make sure that all rows are whipped in the same direction, over and under.

Variation 5.

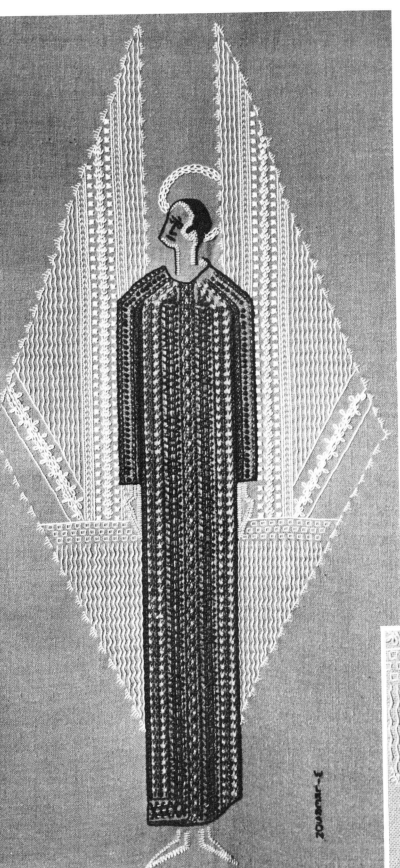

MICHAEL, THE ARCHANGEL.
An original stitchery designed
and worked by 17-year-old
Terry Lee Wilkerson. She was
one of a group of 16 girls at Holy
Names High School, Seattle,
who were taught stitches during
a four-week period as an experiment in the use of stitches as an
art form. The girls made original
samplers, like Kay McWalter's,
recording some 50 stitch variations. In the next four weeks,
each girl produced a stitchery of
her own design. Terry's use of
simple stitches is particularly
imaginative. The wings are gold,
the robe is in shades of blue,
turquoise, and green. The size
of the actual embroidery is 30 by
15 inches.

Detail of MICHAEL, THE ARCH-
ANGEL, showing use of
Whipped Running Stitch in the
wings.

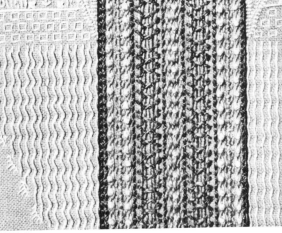

PASTORAL. Small wall hanging by Mrs. G. Baumann-Wartmann, Switzerland. Note the original treatment of the background and the use of parallel Running Stitches with vertical connecting stitches. (Photograph by courtesy of Swiss Craft House, Zurich, Switzerland.

Threaded Running Stitch

Make a Running Stitch from right to left, using pearl cotton in size 5. Start with stitches and spaces approximately ⅛ inch long.

For the lacing, use thread of the same weight or if possible, heavier, such as size 3 (Figure 5). A darker shade is more effective. Use a tapestry needle to work in and out so that no material will be picked up. Keep the tension of the lacing thread neither too tight nor too loose.

For a rich-looking, quick and easy border, make four parallel rows of Threaded Running Stitches, with the two middle rows close enough so that the lacing threads will lay side by side in the center.

On my sampler shown as the Frontispiece, I used a light green pearl cotton in size 5, with stitches and spaces ⅛ inch long. Rows 1 and 3 are 3/16 inch apart, and so are rows 3 and 4. Rows 2 and 3 are ⅛ inch apart. The first two rows are threaded with a dark green pearl cotton in size 3 in the same direction, up and down; the third and fourth rows in the opposite direction, down and up.

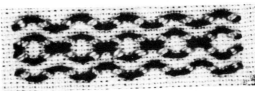

Detail of sampler with Threaded Running Stitch made by the author.

Such a border is very effective around the top of a table cloth, or on the sides of place mats. I have worked it around a little girl's skirt to hide the marks left by lengthening the hem, and also have used it on the edge of a bonnet. Worked in heavy soft cotton with no sheen, the effect is quite handsome on cushions, bedspreads, bags, and so forth.

Double Threaded Running Stitch

This stitch is worked over one or two rows of parallel Running Stitches, threaded from right to left, from outside in (Figure 6). At the end of the row, turn your work around and thread back. The yarns can be of different weights or textures, and they may be in the same or in different values of the same color, or in contrasting colors. Vary the size of the stitches—large, small or delicate—using two fine threads (Figure 7). These look well on colored cloth embroidered in white.

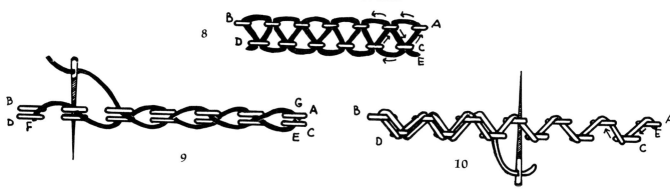

There are many possible variations. One is between a base of alternating Running Stitches (Figure 8). Another is over two rows of parallel Running Stitches, threaded from inside out for a braid effect (Figure 9). One of my favorite unintentional discoveries started with two rows of alternating Running Stitches, with a space between them equal to the length of one stitch (Figure 10). Starting at E, thread upward from right to left, from inside out; then thread the first bottom stitch from inside out. On the return journey, repeat the steps always threading from inside out. The result is a beautiful, unusual border.

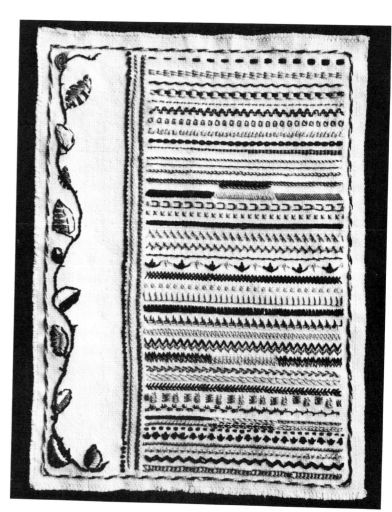

Sampler by Kay McWalter, Holy Names High School, Seattle. Kay used light, medium, and dark blue thread to work 50 stitch variations.

Tuareg nomad blouse from Niger. (From the author's collection; photograph by the author.)

Tuareg Double Laced Band

From the moment I saw pictures of Tuareg nomad women in Niger wearing white blouses with striking red embroidered designs, I wanted to document the designs and the unusual stitch which was new to me. As in most ethnic embroidery, I knew that the stitch must be economical in its use of thread, wasting little in the back. It must be basically easy to work, with a definite rhythm. After many trials, I came up with diagrams that looked similar to the pictures and produced a very handsome band (see Quadruple Laced Woven Band on page 42.) But I had not held a blouse in my hands. Not able to verify the technique, I was not satisfied because I could not attribute it to the remarkable Tuareg women.

My years of persistant search for one of these vanishing blouses was finally crowned with success. An unbelievable set of circumstances sent a friend of mine on a safari in the Sahel where these particular nomads live. When Cynthia mentioned her trip to Africa to me, I remarked, "Of course you will be going to the area around Agades, and I have a mission for you." Cynthia was astounded because she had not mentioned to anyone where in Africa she was going and she *was* going to Agades! I showed her pictures and gave her sketches of the blouse and stitch, explaining that this was the stitch I had to actually see and analyze so that a true, permanent record could be made and shared, honoring these unknown, talented women.

When Cynthia reached Agades, she showed my pictures, but nobody recalled ever seeing such blouses, not even a collector of ethnic clothing who had lived seven years in Agades and knew most of the nomadic tribes. At long last, a few hours before Cynthia was to leave by the weekly plane, a young nomad at the market volunteered that he had seen such a blouse in a small oasis 50 kilometers from Agades and was sure he could get it for her in time if a Land Rover and driver could be provided for the drive over the desert. There was no road! After a wild ride, the blouse was found. I now own it and it is even more beautiful than the ones in the pictures I had. My friend was told that they were traditionally worn by Tuareg nomad women on festive occasions and are hard to find. Nomads have little storage space to keep things.

They are all similar: the cotton background cloth varies in weight but it always consists of a long rectangle folded over, with a small seam on the outer edges to mark the underarm and a long narrow rectangle cut in the center for the neck. The Laced Woven Band I had devised was made in four journeys. The Tuareg work it in two. Although the effect is almost identical, they used a fine sewing thread for the Running Stitches while I used the same thread for both Running and lacing creating a slight difference in the edge. The four journeys produce a regular over and under; the two journeys do not and the lacing must therefore be tacked down for stability. None of the braided yarn appears on the back; only the irregular tacking stitches show. There are a few square medallions made up of groups of green and yellow Eyelet Stitches embroidered through the cloth. On the various pictures I have, each blouse shows slight differences, but the basic stitch is always the same. The only way I have been able to duplicate it is by the procedure I describe.

For the Running Stitches and the reinforcing, the Tuareg used a cotton sewing thread of the same color as the lacing thread. For the lacing, they used a mercerised, colorfast, four-stranded braided yarn. I find that DMC pearl cotton red 321 in size 3 gives almost the same effect. (Before using it, rinse it until all bleeding stops.) I have used pearl 5 on fine cloth.

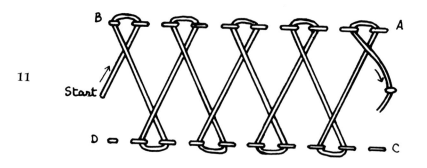

Work two rows of Running Stitches, AB, CD, five to the inch exactly opposite each other, the two rows ⅞ inch apart (Figure 11). For your first try, you might use 10-to-the-inch canvas or aïda-type cloth. On smooth cloth such as the Tuareg use, mark the stitch placement, either with chalk or with an erasable pencil. I prefer to use 10-to-the-inch graph paper, cutting a strip 8/10 inch wide and basting it to the cloth (you can use dots on plain paper). The little 1/10-inch squares make it easy to work even relaxed stitches of the right size just outside the paper, using cotton thread. Once the Running Stitches are worked, remove basting and paper. Stretch the cloth in a hoop, as the lacing tends to draw the sides together.

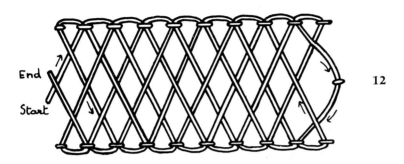

12

Using pearl cotton size 3 (or similar yarn) and a tapestry needle, follow the diagrams for the lacing, working from left to right (Figure 12). The Tuareg work the lacing so that no beginning or end shows. The heavy yarn does not pierce the cloth anywhere. New lengths of yarn are neatly overcast on top of each other, almost invisibly. Since economy of yarn is not a problem for us, it is simpler to leave a small end on the back for a beginning and end, catching them under when the final tacking is worked. The Tuareg reinforce the lacing with sewing thread, tacking each of the intersections with a small Back Stitch. It then becomes very stable, and the result is well worth the effect. Figure 13 shows an ending. Once you have mastered the technique, try varying the width of the band and the size of the yarn.

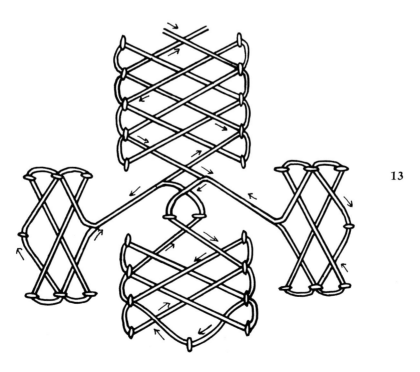

13

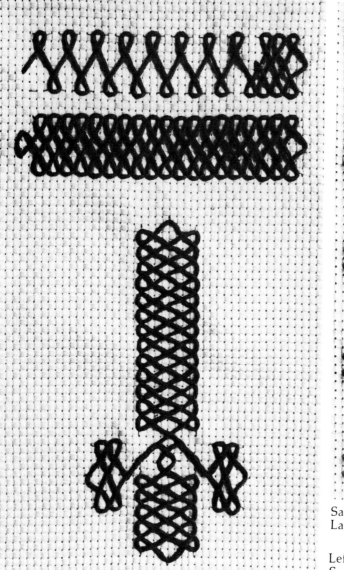

Sampler by the author illustrating the Quadruple Laced Woven Band. (Photograph by the author.)

Left:
Sampler by the author illustrating the Tuareg Double Laced Band. (Photograph by the author.)

Quadruple Laced Woven Band

I made up this beautiful band from photographs of embroidered blouses worn by Tuareg nomads before I actually held the embroidery in my hands (see Tuareg Double Laced Band page 39). It is similar yet quite different illustrating the importance of obtaining definite proofs in research before publishing material. Each of the two bands has a beauty and uses of its own. The completely woven feature of my approach makes tacking down unnecessary; this also makes it suitable for a handsome joining, with the Running Stitches on both edges.

On my sampler, I used DMC Retors mat cotton size 4. Pearl cotton size 3 would also be suitable as would any yarn of similar weight. To bring out clearly each successive row, I used a slightly darker value for each new one. The directions for the two rows of Running Stitches are the same as those shown in Figure 11 for the Tuareg Double Laced Band except that the lacing yarn is also used for the Running Stitches, instead of fine thread (Figures 14-17).

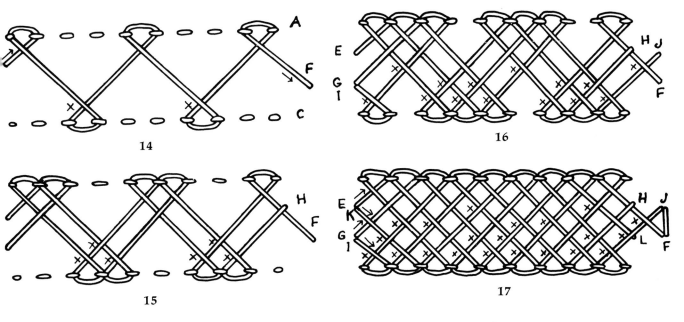

14 16 15 17

The lacing is different, made in four journeys instead of two. Using a tapestry needle, follow the diagrams, remembering to go over and under the yarn when indicated to achieve perfect weaving. A small x marks the places where the yarn weaves under. As each row is worked note that the upper loops go *OVER* on the way down. At the lower edge, all the loops go *UNDER* on the way up, sliding the needle under. Before you fasten the thread at the end of each row, check to see that both top and bottom are correct.

Running Stitch—Variations in Connecting Stitches

A variety of effects can be achieved by using different connecting stitches between rows of Running Stitches. Connecting stitches can be vertical or slanting, and Running Stitches can be worked in parallel or alternating rows (Figures 18-21). Three or four rows of parallel Running Stitches can be joined in numerous ways (Figures 22-24).

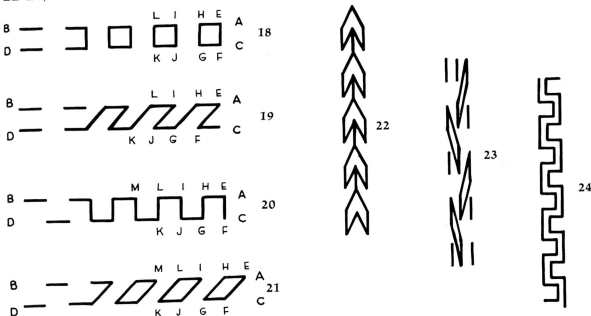

Anna Meyer. Detail of MADONNA OF MERCY AND THE MAYOR MEYER FAMILY
by Hans Holbein the Younger. Painted around 1528. (Courtesy of Schlossmuseum,
Darmstadt, Germany. Property of Prinz von Hessen und bei Rhein. Photograph by
Kunstmuseum, Basel, Switzerland.)

Double Running or Holbein Stitch

The Double Running Stitch is often referred to as the Holbein Stitch because designs worked in this stitch occur in some of Holbein's paintings. It is strikingly illustrated in his famous "Madonna of Mercy and the Mayor Meyer Family's altarpiece, in Darmstadt, Germany.

The white dress of Anna Meyer, the mayor's daughter, is embroidered in black, with bands of Double Running Stitch at right angles in a geometric design, reminiscent of Assisi embroidery. This is interesting because when Holbein made this portrait, he had just returned from a trip to Italy where no doubt he came across Assisi embroidery. Holbein was such a precise draftsman that he could not fail to be attracted to it. It would be interesting to know if the embroidery was actually on the dress or if Holbein chose to adorn it with this decorative stitchery.

The Double Running Stitch is usually used to outline designs on material of clearly defined weave with even warp and weft. It is quick and easy.

A row of Running Stitches of equal length with equal spaces is worked from right to left. The gaps are filled in a return journey by inserting the needle in exactly the same holes as the first row (Figures 25, 26). The material can be turned around so that you are still working from right to left.

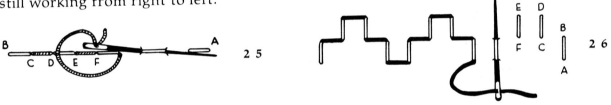

The stitch is used a great deal in Italian work. It is especially effective when worked with a heavy, no-sheen cotton. The return journey can be worked in a lighter or darker shade, or in a contrasting color. Greek type borders can be worked quickly this way (Figures 27, 28).

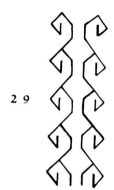

In central Europe, close rows of Double Running Stitches are worked to fill shapes by staggering the rows in laid brick fashion. Color variations can be worked to produce a checkered effect. The Holbein Stitch can also be worked diagonally (Figure 29).

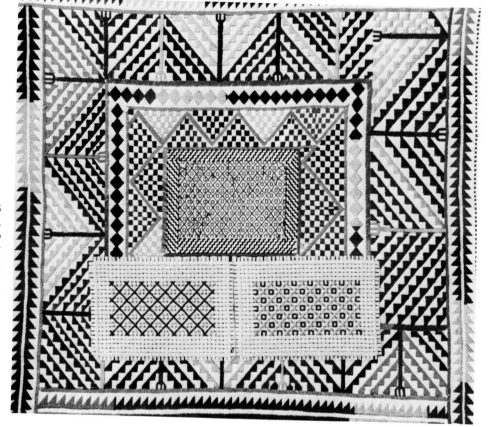

Embroidered square, 15 inches, from Afghanistan, partially covered by two identical small samplers by the author reproducing the front and back of the center rectangle of the original square. The center rectangle, worked in Double Running Reversible Stitch, is 3¼ by 2¼ inches. The two little samplers by the author were worked twice the size of the original. (From the author's collection; photograph by the author.)

Afghanistan Reversible Stitches

This Afghan piece is from the Kandahar area. Such pieces were often used as a dress front or for the top of a table to show off a lady's skill. The center was probably worked by a beginner trying to master the traditional intricate pattern of counted thread on cotton muslin 56 threads to the inch, and NO magnifier! The surrounding embroidery, in reversible Satin Stitch, is the work of a skilled craftswoman, perhaps of a mother framing her child's work. The designs are typical of the area, inspired by very old patterns from pottery in Majenjadaro. The multiple colors are also typical.

The center pattern is the most exciting reversible stitch I have come across. It also proved to be one of the hardest stitchery puzzles for me to solve. Yet I felt that if a woman in Afghanistan could do this work, I should be able to. They would have been amused at my efforts. Finally I found the clue, marveling at the ingenuity and skill involved. Once you know how, the procedure is quite easy.

The front and back of the center pattern are identical, with colors reversed. One side has a diamond grid of red thread with small green squares in each center; the reverse side has a green diamond grid with red square centers. The squares are worked over four threads of muslin (56 threads to the inch muslin!). I worked out the design with pearl cotton size 5, on eight to the inch aïda cloth, two diamonds to the inch instead of four. It simplified the task.

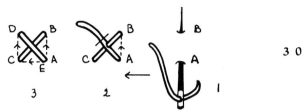

Work from right to left. Since front and back are reversible, there should be no knots and almost invisible starts and ends. Use a thread as long as you can manage and when you have to end and start, do so invisibly on the edges. Aïda cloth made it possible to slide the needle throught the cloth so that the starting thread is not visible on the back. A smooth muslin as in the Afghan piece does not leave this alternative. In this case leave a tail end diagonally on the side you are working on, go down at A (Figure 30, 1-2-3) and up at B. Before going down at C, use the point of the needle to split the thread in two. Go down at C, up at D, down at E (splitting the thread at A to anchor it), and up at F (Figure 31). Cut off the end of the tail extending beyond the cross, tucking the end under AD. When you need more thread, repeat the beginning procedure.

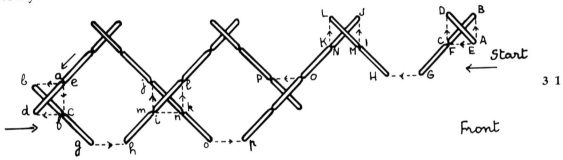

Continue, going down at G, up at H, down at I, up at J, down at K, up at L, and so on to the end of the row; then work from left to right, reversing the first row. Continue back and forth until the area is covered. From time to time, check the back; it should show evenly spaced squares (Figure 32). The last row is worked with a cross between the diagonal stitches to complete the pattern. When you have completed one side, turn the piece around and repeat with a different color between the squares. It is exciting to see the whole design take shape.

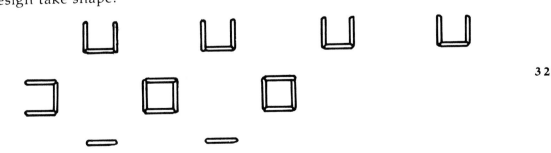

Eskimo Laced Edge

This simple and effective edging is based on the Running Stitch. It was devised by the Eskimos and the Aleuts to bind together the many seams of their seal gut parkas, making them waterproof. There is a real thrill in adapting this utilitarian stitch originally worked with caribou or walrus sinew to new beautiful edges with a contemporary feeling. It can look very different according to the texture of the material and the weight of the thread used. Until recently I had seen the stitch only once, many years ago, around the edge of a child's cap. Miss Blanche Payne, Professor of Home Economics at the University of Washington, has seen it used ornamentally around the hood of an Eskimo child's parka.

On linen or cotton homespun, I like to use pearl cotton in size 5 for the Running Stitch and in size 3 for the lacing, with a hem between ¼ to ⅜ inch deep. On organdy, for example, around the edge of a collar, with a ⅛-inch hem, I like to use three strands of six-stranded cotton.

It is a good idea to try samples of colors on the edge of your doodling cloth. Different effects can be achieved according to the way colors are used. I wanted to use pearl cotton in size 3 in vivid red and royal blue on a table mat of oyster white, cotton homespun. I first tried blue Running Stitches with red lacing. The effect was not at all pleasing to me, so I tried the Running Stitches in red and the lacing in blue, and loved the result. Other pleasing combinations are white on a colored material, and two shades of the same color, such as a light green and a deep forest green on a white material.

Start by basting a hem all around the edge you want to decorate. The Running Stitches should be worked quite near the inner edge of the hem. With pearl cotton in size 5, work from right to left on the back side (Figure 33). Place the beginning knot at A, inside the hem, so that it does not show. Come out on the *right* side for the first stitch. This is important; if you come out on the back side, the pattern will not work out. If your hem is between ¼ and ⅜ inch deep, make your stitches and the spaces between them about 3/16 inch long. They should be worked one at a time, inserting the needle straight in, all the same size *without pulling*. In fact, they should be a little relaxed to make the lacing easy. Always end and start a new length of thread from inside the hem so that it won't show.

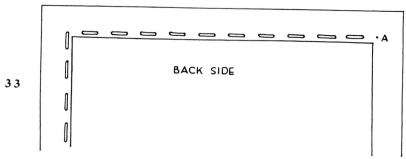

33

BACK SIDE

• A

When the Running Stitches are completed, take a size 3 thread of a different color. With a tapestry needle, lace it over and under,

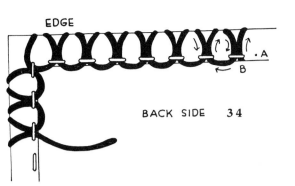

EDGE

BACK SIDE 34

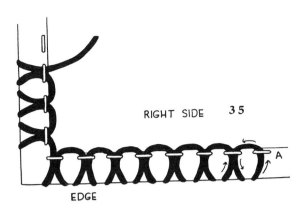

RIGHT SIDE 35

EDGE

working from the back side to the front or right side, and from right to left (Figures 34, 35). To do this, hold the material with the back side up and the outside edge away from you.

1. Start the beginning knot *inside* the hem at B and come out just below the first Running Stitch.
2. Lace under the first Running Stitch without picking up the material.
3. Turn the edge over so that the right side edge is toward you, and again lace under the first stitch (which should be a little to the right), this time lacing from the edge in.
4. Then lace through the second stitch toward the edge.
5. Lace over the edge to the back again under the first stitch from the edge inward.
6. Continue along the base of the hem under the second stitch toward the edge.
7. Continue over the edge of the hem to the second stitch on the right side of the material, and so on.

Surface Darning

Some of the most sophisticated French embroidery is done with Surface Darning. It is used for making outlines and borders, and for filling shapes. It is beautiful on handkerchief linen or on organdy-like material, worked in white or color. Six-stranded cotton is good for this, using the number of strands that gives the texture you want. Buttonhole silk twist gives a rich look.

On your sampler, using six strands, work stitches ¼ inch long or less from right to left, picking up a thread or two of material at regular intervals (Figure 36). The beauty lies in regularity.

```
B                                    A
D  =================================  C    36
F                                    E
```

Work the first row from A to B. In the second row, CD, the threads picked up are just below the middle of each stitch of the first row. The third row is a repetition of the first, and so on. The rows should lie close together, with no material showing between.

On the sampler, work five rows decreasing in length (Figure 37).

```
B ___ ___ ___ ___ =====================  A
          D _____ ================== C  E
                F ___ ============== G
                       H ========== I
```
37

Make the first row from A to B. The second row, CD, should be three-quarters as long as AB; the third row, one-half; and the fourth and fifth rows, one-quarter. This will give you a record of the different effects produced by varying the number of rows.

Baptismal robe designed by the author. Of fine handkerchief linen, 18 inches long, it is embroidered with white linen thread. The straight bands are worked with five close rows of Surface Darning. The waving lines, symbolizing the waters of baptism, consist of three close rows of Surface Darning. The body of the Holy Spirit is worked in Long Stem Filling, the feathers in French Filling Stitch. The lettering is worked in fine Chain Stitch. The name of the child, the place of baptism, and the date are stitched in fine Chain Stitch at the bottom of the back.

Opposite:
Sampler and handbag worked in Kogin embroidery. The sampler shows three interpretations of one motif, a typical Kogin pattern. It is worked in unbleached cotton thread on indigo cotton. "The white-blue contrast," says Mrs. Misao Kimura, "lends itself readily to the formation of various patterns and designs and often extremely interesting decorative results." (Courtesy of Misao Kimura Technical School of Embroidery, Sendai, Japan.)

Pattern Darning

This easy form of embroidery has been used for centuries in many countries, either as a background for design or as a filling. It is made up of rows of stitches of varying lengths worked into definite patterns (Figures 38-41).

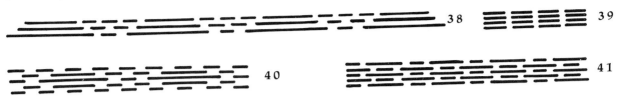

It is essential that the stitches be worked in accurate lengths. Use a material of easily counted threads or baste a canvas or curtain cable net material as a guide on the material to be embroidered. In the latter case the stitches are worked carefully in the canvas or cable net holes without piercing the threads of the canvas or cable net. When the design is finished, the canvas or cable net is gently shredded and pulled away. This method is used also in Europe for Cross Stitch on fine material.

The Japanese worked this type of embroidery many centuries ago; the poor farmers of the island of Honshu used it to reinforce and prolong the life of their garments. Known as "Kogin" embroidery, it was often worked in white cotton thread on rough indigo linen. Today, students of Mrs. Misao Kimura at the Technical School of Embroidery in Sendai, Japan, are adapting these old utilitarian embroideries to contemporary designs with great success. Examples of work done by students at this school are shown above.

Try to invent your own design of Pattern Darning.

Sashiko

Sashiko is a form of Japanese embroidery that uses small, even Running Stitches to create designs. Like the Darning Stitches of Kogin, it was also used originally to reinforce garments, holding two layers of cotton cloth together to add warmth and strength to worn clothes and at the same time embellishing them. Sashiko is worked with a soft white cotton thread on cotton cloth dyed a dark indigo. There are many traditional designs, each with its own name.

This Sashiko sampler was worked for the author by Kimi Ota, one of Japan's specialists in Sashiko quilting and embroidery. The cloth used is very old indigo cotton. The three designs are traditional: Higaki (cypress fence), Asanoha (hemp leaf), and Shippo Tsunagi (seven treasures of Buddha). (Photograph by the author.)

Back Stitch

The Back Stitch can be a highly decorative stitch, used either by itself as an outline or in conjunction with other stitches. Its beauty depends on perfect regularity. It is easiest to work on even, coarse textures where threads can be counted without strain. If the material is fine, baste canvas or curtain cable net material as described in Pattern Darning.

Work from right to left. Use pearl cotton in size 5 to practice, also size 8. Try six-stranded cotton. Heavy threads give effective results.

Bring the needle and thread out at A and take a small Back Stitch to B, coming out at C (Figure 42). Go back in at A, the previous hole. AB should equal CA.

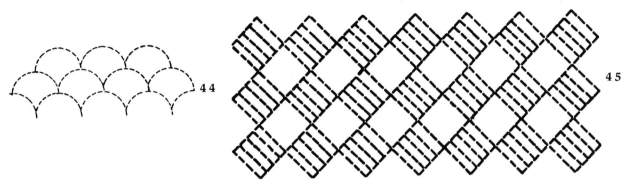

43

On your sampler, work a 6-inch row of Back Stitches, from A to B, making each stitch about ⅛ inch long (Figure 43). Make the next two rows, CD and EF, two-thirds as long as AB, and the last two rows, GH and IJ, one-third as long. You are recording what various depths of close rows of Back Stitches look like.

Linear patterns may be suggested by quilting designs (Figure 44) or American Indian basket designs (Figure 45).

44

45

Back and Running

Back and Running is a Back Stitch followed by a Running Stitch. Usually the Running Stitch is a little longer than the Back Stitch. The Back Stitches stand out and form a slightly raised rib texture alternating with flat areas. Work a Back Stitch A to B and back to A (Figure 46). Pull through. Go down at C. AC is about one and a half times the length of AB. Come up at D (Figure 47) work a Back Stitch D to C and back to D, and so on.

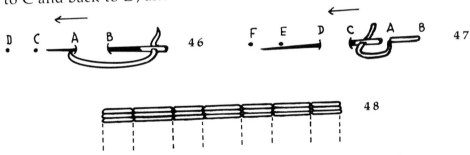

46

47

48

The stitch combination shown in Figure 48 was found on a sash woven by American Zuni Indians. Although it is a weaving technique in which the yarns are worked in as the weaving progresses, the result looks as though it were embroidered. Some pieces are worked with a needle. An even weave makes the work easier to learn, but the stitch can be used on curved lines too. (Figure 49).

49

You might try varying lengths or working two Back Stitches over each other (Figures 50, 51).

50

51

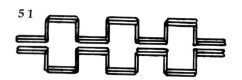

Ceremonial dance sash, southwestern United States. Both front and back show the effect obtained by the Back and Running Stitch, whether worked on an upright loom or with a needle. (Courtesy of the Smithsonian Institution.)

Whipped Back Stitch

For the outline of a curved shape, the Whipped Back Stitch is more accurate than an outline stitch (Figure 52). It also produces an effective raised surface. For a thin line, use fine thread and small Back Stitches, but do not pull the stitches too tightly. Try two or three strands of stranded cotton with small Whipped Back Stitches. This is useful for fine lettering. With pearl cotton in size 3 and Back Stitches ⅛ inch long, the effect is a strong cord.

Threaded Back Stitch

53

This is a quick and effective way to outline a shape (Figure 53).

Double Threaded Back Stitch

54

This stitch makes a rich looking, textured outline, using either the same color or a darker color for the lacing (Figure 54).

Triple Back or Hungarian Stitch

This attractive line stitch is particularly effective when it is worked in heavy threads of pearl cotton in size 3 or in six strands of stranded cotton, with stitches approximately ¼ inch long. It can be worked spaced or closed. Exact regularity is essential. For ease in counting threads, use coarse materials.

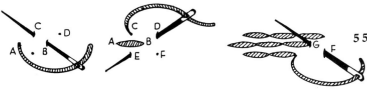

55

Start with the middle row, from A to B (Figure 55), coming out at C in the top row, halfway between A and B. Go in at D, coming out at E in the third row, halfway between A and B. Go in at F and back to B in the middle row. A border of spaced stitches is shown in Figure 56.

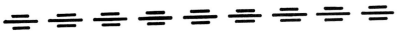

56

Closed Triple Back Stitch

This stitch makes a rich looking line, worked with no material showing between the three lines (Figure 57). The back looks like Cross Stitch. It can also be worked as a solid pattern using one or two colors (Figure 58).

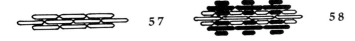

57   58

Seed or Dot Stitch

To fill areas where you need a light airy effect, use small even Back Stitches placed either at random or in patterns over the surface to be textured. You can use single or double stitches of any size, placed at an angle, or even overlapping.

For a double Seed Stitch, make two Back Stitches in the same holes, neatly relaxed side by side (Figure 59). Try two Back Stitches meeting at an acute angle, making the upright stitch longer (Figure 60).

Whipped Seed Stitch

Like the Running Stitch and Back Stitch, the Seed Stitch may be whipped (Figure 61). The Whipped, Threaded, and Double Threaded Seed Stitches look most effective when a double Seed Stitch is used for the foundation.

Threaded Seed Stitch

The Seed Stitch can be threaded as shown in Figure 62. It is particularly effective when threaded with gold or silver cord.

Double Threaded Seed Stitch

A row of Seed Stitches can be double threaded for a richer effect (Figure 63). Try adding a French Knot in the space between the Double Seed Stitches, using a heavier thread and a variation in color value.

Seed Stitch Filling

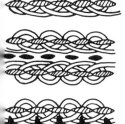

The Seed Stitch is effectively used to fill monograms outlined in close Stem Stitch or a fine Chain Stitch (Figure 64). Other shapes or backgrounds can be filled by working the stitches in one direction or at random (Figures 65, 66).

65

66

Pekinese Stitch

The Pekinese Stitch was used with great skill and artistry in the embroideries of China, both as an outline and a filling stitch. It was worked in silk, frequently in different values of one shade. The stitches are so fine that one needs a magnifying glass to understand their structure.

The Pekinese Stitch has a distinctive texture. It is an interlaced stitch which follows any linear design with great ease. Interesting borders can be made with two parallel rows worked in opposite directions with a small open space between them, or close together laced (Figure 67).

First work a row of relaxed Back Stitches from right to left. If the Back Stitches are worked with pearl cotton in size 5, the stitches would be about ⅛ inch; with size 8, they would be a little shorter.

As I use the Interlaced Stitch, I think with admiration and concern of the Chinese women who worked 30 to 44 stitches to the inch without magnification, and of the young girls whose task it was to interlace them!

The interlacing is worked from left to right. For this a rounded-point tapestry needle makes the work easier. The lacing thread can be in the same weight and color or in a contrasting color. A pleasing effect is obtained when the lacing thread is heavier and darker than the Back Stitch base. If size 8 is used for the Back Stitch, lacing with size 5 is effective. Also try using metallic threads for the lacing. The result is a rich looking braid. It is useful in ecclesiastical embroidery.

Bring the needle and lacing thread out at A, just below the beginning of the first Back Stitch (Figure 68). Hold the thread down with your left thumb. Without picking up any material, lace the thread up through the second Back Stitch BC, leaving a loop. Go back down through the first Back Stitch AB. Pass the needle *over* the loop coming from A. Before pulling the needle through, gently pull the thread above BC so as to close the loop. Then pull the needle through and gently close the loop above B. Hold the thread down with your left thumb. Go up through the third Back Stitch CD, leaving a loop. Go down through the second Back Stitch BC on top of the previous loop and complete the stitch as before. The loops should lie snugly side by side. Although the diagram shows them slightly loose, they should lie gently relaxed against the Back Stitches, slightly curved, neither flat nor loose.

The Laced Cretan Stitch (see Figure 279) is sometimes referred to as the Double Pekinese Stitch. Try interlacing over two close rows of Back Stitches. The effect is quite different.

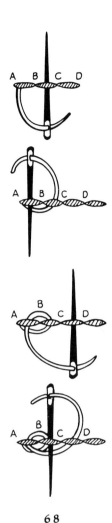

68

Spaced Pekinese Stitch

The Spaced Pekinese Stitch is a free-moving stitch which lends itself to imaginative variations. It is especially suited to freehand stitcheries and allows for experimentation with threads of various textures and weights.

To practice, use pearl cotton in size 5, working Back Stitches ⅛ inch long and ⅛ inch apart. Interlace the Back Stitches with two thinner threads threaded together in the needle (Figure. 69). The two threads might be in different colors or in contrasting textures—one dull and the other metallic. Some of the lower threads could be anchored down with small perpendicular stitches. I have interlaced a deep turquoise pearl cotton in size 5 with two fine, no-sheen threads of dull gold and light turquoise, anchoring some of the lower loops with the dull gold thread.

69

Chinese embroidered piece from a nineteenth century Mandarin coat. It is worked entirely in Pekinese Stitch as an outline and as a filling, 35 stitches to the inch. Notice the contemporary feeling of the stitch and how the straighter edge is used on the outside. Detail is shown on the following page. (Gift to the author from Colonel and Mrs. McAllister, Arlington, Virginia; photograph by Colonel McAllister.)

It is stimulating to take a stitch and see how you can change or expand it by adding other stitches—overlapping and doubling. Invent your own combination. Try working free-flowing loops or floral shapes. Practicing imaginative uses of a stitch is one of the steps that will lead you to freedom with a needle and creative embroidery.

Detail of Chinese embroidered piece shown on page 58. (Photography by Colonel M. D. McAllister.)

Satin Stitch

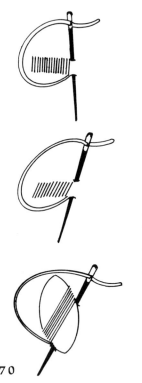

The Satin Stitch consists of Back Stitches worked close together, side by side, to cover a shape (Figures 70, 71). If the area to be covered is large, the space should be broken up into units, making this part of the design. When stitches are too long, they tend to pull out of place and do not wear well. (When long stitches are essential to your work, it is better to use the Roumanian Stitch because each stitch is anchored down in the middle.) For designs worked in straight lines, evenly meshed materials make the Satin Stitch easier to work. For a raised effect, it can be padded with Running or Chain Stitches before starting. Watch for a neat line along the edges. To obtain this, start by working a close outline stitch on the edge around the shape. Work the Satin Stitches to the outside edges, covering the outline stitches. If the edge is not perfect, cover it over with a second outline of Back Stitches, Threaded Back Stitches, Pekinese Stitches, or other outline stitches. Work Satin Stitches straight or on the slant. (See Chain Outlined Satin Stitch, page 125).

70

71

Twisted Satin Stitch

Individual Satin Stitches can be twisted for a textured effect. They can be worked close together in groups, or as individual stitches with spaces between. Figure 72 shows a design worked with Twisted Satin Stitch.

Bring the needle and thread out at A and in at B (Figure 73). Go back to A and pull through. Slide the needle under AB without picking up any material, and pull through gently. Insert the needle at B (not in the same hole but a little above) and come out at C for the beginning of the next stitch.

72

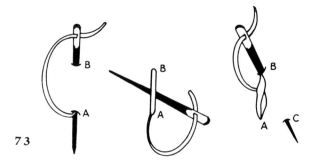

73

Satin Stitch Filling and Groupings

Suggested variations in spacing and repeated groups in different sizes are shown in Figures 74-77.

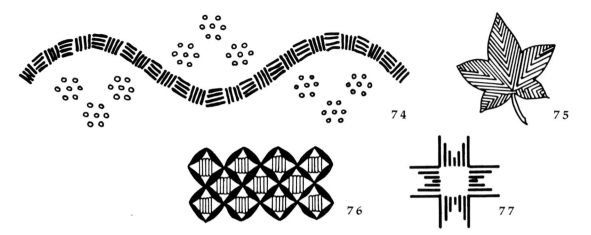

74

75

76

77

Basket Filling Stitch

The Basket Filling Stitch is used in Jacobean embroidery for a close flat filling with a basket weave pattern. It is worked in alternate groups of three or four horizontal and vertical Satin Stitches (Figure 78). It should not be confused with the Basket Stitch (see page 97).

78

Guilloche Stitch

The Guilloche Stitch is a double threaded Satin Stitch. Work groups of three or more Satin Stitches at regular intervals. With a rounded tapestry needle, thread in and out under the Satin Stitches without picking up material. At the end of the row, turn the work around and thread back to the beginning (Figure 79).

79

The Guilloche Stitch can be worked on curved lines. With a blue pencil (not a black lead pencil which smears), mark the line you wish to follow, such as a semicircle, on the *wrong* side of the material. Place your beginning knot on the line and use the penciled line as a guide for placing the bottom stitch of each group of three Satin Stitches. By adding a row of a linear stitch on each side, you can create an interesting border.

Long and Short Stitch

The name describes the stitch; the first row is made up of alternately long and short stitches (Figure 80). Particularly useful on a curve, this stitch is much used in crewel embroidery. It makes attractive shadings, either in several colors or in various values of one color. Stranded cotton works well for shading.

80

61

Bring the needle and thread out at A inside the shape; go in at B on the outside edge, coming out at C (about two-thirds of the length of AB). Go in at D, and continue to EF, and so on.

After the first row of Long and Short, subsequent rows are worked with equal sized Satin Stitches in the intervals.

If you want a crisp laid-brick effect, the stitches should meet in the same holes. If you want a smooth blended effect, the needle should split the tip of the stitch above.

Straight Stitch

Straight Stitches of equal or varying lengths can radiate out from a given point. They can be worked in rows or in geometric patterns to fill a large shape quickly, or they can be scattered at random to achieve various effects (Figures 81, 82).

81

82

On an eighteenth century Czechoslovakian curtain, striking flowers were embroidered with petals made of two vertical Straight Sttiches tied down in the middle with a small Back Stitch (Figure 83). Straight Stitches radiating from given points can be spaced decoratively around a shape (Figure 84).

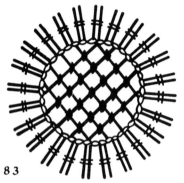

83

84

Eye Stitch

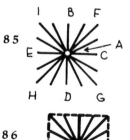

85

86

87

The Eye Stitch consists of 16 stitches radiating from the same center, with their outside edges forming a square (Figure 85). On their inner edges, the 16 stitches all pass through the center hole. This stitch is easiest to work on coarse material with threads that can be counted. Instead of beginning with a knot which would get in the way at the center, leave a length of thread in the back and work it later over the back of the stitches. Come up at A, down at B, up at A, and so on. The squares can be finished with a row of Back Stitches, outlining the shape (Figure 86). A different effect can be obtained by working freehand and varying the lengths of the stitches or using different threads and color values (Figure 87).

Algerian Eye Stitch

88

Many early samplers had alphabets worked in Algerian Eye Stitch. They were worked on loosely woven cloth, using a thread without a tight twist. Come up at A (Figure 88), down at B through the center. Repeat a second time, pulling the thread taut. Come up at C and down at B twice, and so on all around, with the stitches neatly side by side around the center forming a hole. The stitch makes a good edging (Figure 89) and filling (Figure 90).

89

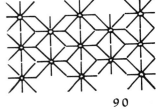

90

The Italians often work the same filling in a different way, overlapping the stars and working from left to right (Figure 91).

91

Star Filling

For Star Filling, start at the center of the star, coming out at A (Figure 92). Insert at B, come out at C, and go over and back to A. Go under and out at D, over and back in at A, under and out at E, and back in at A.

92

Come out at the center of a new star, either to the right or below the first star, and continue the same way, with arms meeting.

Italian Hemstitch and Four-Sided Stitch

These two stitches are similar though worked differently. For borders, I like to use the Italian Hemstitch because it is easy, effective, and quick to work. For crisp sharp squares and for a filling, I like the Four-Sided Stitch.

The easiest way to master these two stitches is to practice them on a piece of coarse linen with an even weave or on cotton homespun. Pull out two threads, leaving four threads between them and work each stitch over four threads.

For the Italian Hemstitch work from top down, coming out at A, on the left side (Figure 93). Go over and in at B (four threads over) and under and out at C (four threads under B). Go over and back in at B. From B go under diagonally across to D, back up over to A, and down under to D. You are then ready to start again. Go over and in at C, under and out at E, back to C, and so on.

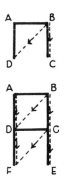

93

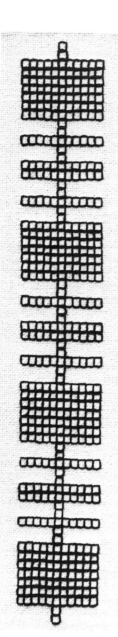

For the Four-Sided Stitch work from right to left, coming out at A on the right side (Figure 94). Go over and in at B (four threads up). From B go diagonally under and out at C, and over back to A. From A go under diagonally across to D, from D back to B, and then diagonally under and out at C. You are then ready to start again. From C go over to D, under diagonally and out at E, back to C, and so on. With the Four-Sided Stitch, the stitches on the right side are straight; those on the wrong side are all diagonal, forming a cross. Try using Four-Sided Stitches freely, with spaces between them, with sides uneven, or overlapping (Figure 95).

94

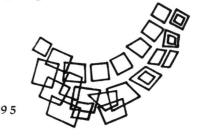

95

Four-Sided Stitch Filling

Work rows of Four-Sided Stitch under each other by turning your work around so as to work from right to left. The stitches of adjoining rows can be worked in the same holes. Any of the squares can be ornamented with stitches (Figures 96, 97).

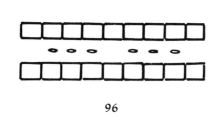

96

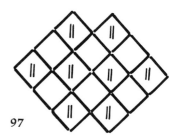

97

Detail of tray cloth designed and worked by the author. Royal blue cotton thread is embroidered on oyster white cotton homespun. The Four-Sided Stitch was the obvious choice to interpret this design from a slit-embroidery Koryak belt, as pictured in the papers of the Jesup North Pacific Expedition in Eastern Siberia, 1897-1903.

Cross Stitch

Cross Stitch embroidery has been used for centuries by the rural people of many countries to adorn their clothing, home furnishings, and church vestments.

On coarse material, it is worked by counting threads. On fine material, a canvas of appropriate mesh is basted on the material, and the Cross Stitch is worked through both, without piercing the threads of the canvas. Later, the canvas is gently pulled out. If canvas is not available, a suitable substitute is "cable net," a curtain material found in drapery departments. Variations of Cross Stitch worked on canvas form the basis of many tapestry stitches.

There are several ways of working Cross Stitch embroidery, but in all of them the stitches should be crossed in the same direction. Bring the needle and thread out at A (Figure 98). Go over to B, under to C, and over to D. From D go under back to C, over to E, under to F, and so on. Figure 99 shows an edging worked in Cross Stitch.

98

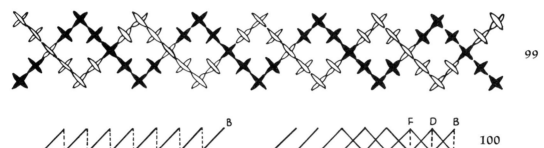

99

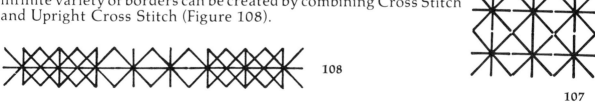

100

For rows of Cross Stitch, it is quicker to work in two movements—from left to right followed by from right to left, crossing on the return journey (Figure 100). In many cultures, the appearance of the back is as important as that of the front, with all stitches either vertical or horizontal. On page 136 you will find, the Chained Cross Stitch, which has a particularly good texture.

There are many Cross Stitch variations:

Upright Cross Stitch

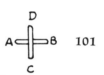 **101**

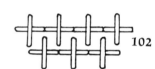 **102**

Upright Cross Stitch (Figure 101) can be worked into interesting grids and borders (Figures 102-104). It also combines well with Cross Stitch (Figure 105).

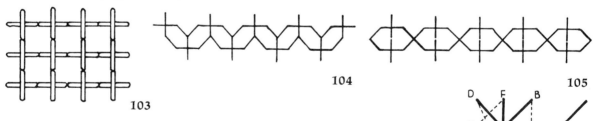

103

104

105

Double Cross Stitch

This is a Cross Stitch with an Upright Cross Stitch over it (Figures 106, 107). It is especially attractive when worked in blocks. An infinite variety of borders can be created by combining Cross Stitch and Upright Cross Stitch (Figure 108).

106

107

108

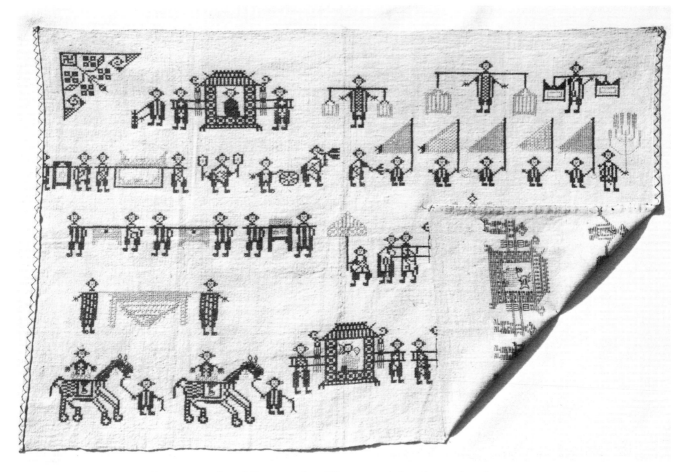

Chinese rural wedding sampler. (Photograph by the author.)

Oblong Cross Stitch

An elongated Cross Stitch can be worked vertically or horizontally (Figures 109, 110). By combining both and joining the ends, flower patterns are obtained (Figure 111). Figure 112 is a mixture of Oblong Cross Stitch and Cross Stitch.

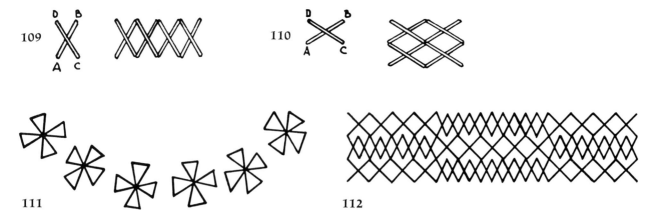

Sampler worked by Carol Thrailkill recording motifs from Chinese rural embroidery. The original pieces were collected in 1935-36 by Norman Hamwell during an expedition in Szechwan province with Carl Schuster.

This sampler was worked from two of the many original pieces loaned to the author by Dorothy Coryell, using for the stitches fine dark indigo cotton brought back from China. For the cloth, we could not find homespun cotton of the same thread count and had to substitute a fine evenweave linen that looked similar. The upper scene with sedan chair is a detail from a delightful wedding procession. The lady's clothing is a lightly grayed turquoise; the child's clothing is lavender. The stitches on the back are all horizontal. On some pieces, such as the willow from a bed valance, the stitches are all vertical. This attention to the placement of stitches on the back is traditional in many cultures. For most motifs, the key to success lies in starting at the right point—a piece of information that must have been passed from mother to daughter. On the front, the crosses are not all crossed in the same direction. With the help of a magnifier, I made a graph showing the direction of each cross. (If you want all the crosses to slant in the same direction, the needle has to be slipped under the first half of that particular cross.) The stitches are worked in two journeys with some crosses completed on the first journey.

After much experimenting, Carol was able to work out the procedure used for each design so as to make her sampler a valid record of a traditional folk art already dying out in 1935. It is accurate in every detail, a truly historical document not only of design but of method. (Photograph by the author.)

Star Stitch

This stitch consists of a Double Cross Stitch with a third small Cross Stitch worked on each side of the vertical stitch (Figure 113). The Star Stitch is particularly useful when the Double Cross Stitch is large and needs anchoring. It has color variation possibilities with darker centers. Star Stitch, regular Cross Stitch, Upright and Oblong Cross Stitches can be combined in many decorative ways (Figure 114).

 113

     114

Slav Cross Stitch

The Slav Cross Stitch is also known as the Long-Armed or Long-Legged Cross Stitch. It is a beautiful stitch which always reminds me of Julie, a spirited little girl from Yugoslavia who was a classmate of mine in Paris. Once a week we had a sewing class. Year after year, in the lower grades, it meant working interminable Cross Stitch alphabets. No room was left for personal interpretation, a hard restriction for imaginative children.

Toward Easter, we started working on the borders of our samplers, everyone doing the same border, a plain Cross Stitch in red marking cotton. Julie was a rebel with strong national leanings, and sping was in the air. She was working something different and I wondered with excitement what would happen when this obvious deviation from the established pattern would be noticed by the teacher. Julie worked fast, with determination. "What is this?" demanded the teacher. "In Serbia", answered Julie, "this is the way we work our Cross Stitch borders. French people do it one way, we do it another. I am a Serb and must work my border as my people do." This was not said rebelliously but with real conviction. Nevertheless, it was open defiance. Originality was not tolerated in sewing class. There was a long pause. To our amazement, the usually unbending teacher said, "It's all right, Julie. This is the Slav Cross Stitch and you may use it for the border."

I was filled with visions of new and exciting Cross Stitch patterns I could work; Julie had opened the floodgates. But in one glance, the teacher took in the sprouting rebellion and added, "Only Slav students may work the Slav Stitch." (Julie was the only one.) "French students will continue to use the classical Cross Stitch!" What a blow! To this day, I am not fully reconciled to the "classical Cross Stitch." We all learned Julie's stitch during recess, and I have never forgotten it.

I still like Julie's description: "You reach way out with your arm, then cross back, reach way out, cross back." The stitch goes very fast and is particularly attractive when worked with coarse threads.

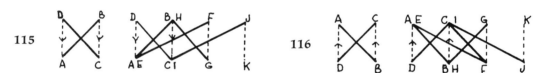

For the Long-Armed Cross Stitch, start with a regular Cross Stitch ABCD (Figure 115). From D come up at E (same hole as A), down at F, go two squares over, and up at G. Go back down at H (same hole as B), up at I, and so on. For the Long-Legged Cross Stitch (Figure 116), the process is reversed, with the long stitch AE to F going two squares over and down at F. The back shows parallel stitches, two together at even intervals.

A beautiful variation is the Diagonal Long-Armed Cross Stitch. It was taught to me by Sally Carter whose study of Brazilian Stitches has opened new doors to many people. These stitches originated in the traditional Portuguese use of the Long-Armed and Long-Legged Cross Stitch. From these roots, the Brazilians expanded the stitch and developed many variations of their own. They use wool yarn heavy enough to cover the background cloth. I use pearl cotton size 3 for four squares to the inch, pearl 5 for 7 squares to the inch. It is worked diagonally over a series of square units in pairs (Figure 117). Squares one and two are regular Long-Armed Cross Stitch. From I (Figure 118)—instead of continuing horizontally—go up vertically to J, and so on (Figure 119). The last stitch would be as shown from S to V. Start the next diagonal row at G, going up as you did before from A to B, and so on. An interesting effect is obtained by alternating colors or values.

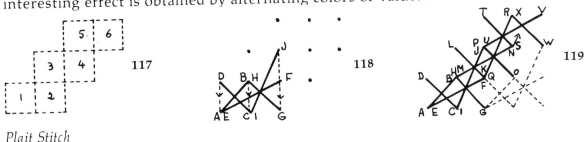

Plait Stitch

When the Slav Cross Stitch is worked close together with little or no material showing between the stitches, it becomes the Plait Stitch. How close the stitches are worked depends on the weight of the thread. For a thick border, try using pearl cotton in size 3 between parallel lines ⅜ inch apart, with about ⅛ inch distance between stitches (from D to B and from B to E in Figure 115). Try it also with six-stranded cotton with both your parallel lines and your stitches from 1/16 to ⅛ inch apart. The result is a beautiful braided line, useful for a raised outline.

Right:
SPRING DYNAMICS (11 x 18 inches) by Wilcke Smith. A magnificent illustration of an imaginative use of the Raised Cross Stitch, with variations in size and texture. (Photograph by Robert Smith.)

Below:
Bag designed and worked by the author on heavy linen four-squares-to-the-inch aïda-type cloth, using pearl cotton size 3. The stitch used is the Brazilian Diagonal Long-Armed Cross Stitch, worked in two alternating values of turquoise. (Photograph by the author.)

Raised Cross Stitch

The Raised Cross Stitch can be used in many ways. It is worked over the sides of an Upright Cross Stitch with Buttonhole Stitches worked detached, turning it into a raised square or circle.

For a square (Figure 120), practice with pearl cotton size 3 with a ½ inch diameter cross. At first keep the buttonholing snug; then relax it a little. The squares can be worked in different sizes—¼, 1/3, or ½ inch. A larger size would increase the size of the stitches too much and require anchoring down. Designs can be constructed, fitting units together. Wilcke Smith, the stitchery artist, calls it Jacqueline's tile and makes a magnificent use of it, changing values within each tile. Raised circles work best with ¼-inch-diameter crosses, working snugly around and coaxing the stitches into a circular shape (Figure 121). They can be used singly as the center of a flower, close together in clusters of different color values, or scattered.

120

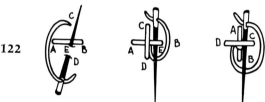

122

121

Work an Upright Cross Stitch ABCD (Figure 122). Come up at E in the center *under* AB. Pull through. Circle the thread from E counterclockwise and slide the needle under B without picking up any cloth. With the thread under the point of the needle, pull through, buttonholing snugly toward the center. Turn the cloth a quarter turn clockwise, and slide the needle under C. Repeat what you did under B, holding the buttonhole on the center (this one tends to slide on DC). Continue around, buttonholing snugly toward the center, until the arms are completely covered and make a textured raised square or circle.

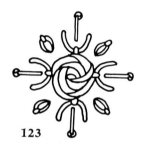

123

For a different effect, the arms can be partly covered. You can also thread under the four arms and add stitches (Figure 123). Instead of Detached Buttonhole Stitches, try Raised Coral Stitches over the arms of the small cross, with the thread over and then under the point of the needle, starting under A and turning counterclockwise (Figure 124). The result is a raised, nubby square or circle.

124

Cross Stitch Flower (Interwoven Cross Stitch)

The Cross Stitch Flower is a decorative Cross Stitch variation. When this book was first written, this stitch had not appeared in any of the standard works. I had learned it in France, where it is called Double Cross Stitch, a name that refers to something different in English. Since then, the stitch has become well-known and widely used, which gives me much satisfaction. It can be worked in single units, in rows, or in massed groups to indicate the individual florets of a composite flower such as bachelor's buttons. In the stitchery "Michael the Archangel," several rows of Cross

Stitch Flower are used on the wings (see page 35). Cross Stitch Flower makes an attractive filling when scattered over a surface. Heavy threads are particularly effective. Practice it with varied weights and types of thread.

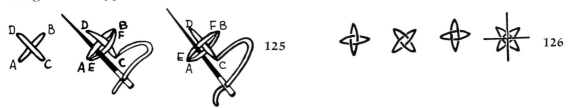

125

126

The Cross Stitch Flower is made of two Cross Stitches on top of each other, in the same holes, the second Cross interwoven with the first (Figures 125, 126). Start with a regular Cross Stitch ABCD. From D, return to A, in the same hole; go over to B, and then down to C. On your way back to D, with the point of the needle (without picking up material), go over the last stitch EF and under AB. Pull through and go down at D. If when you come up at C the AB stitch presents itself first, go under AB and over EF. Weaving can be continued over and under several times. The arms of the first Cross Stitch can be made uneven, creating interesting shapes (Figure 127).

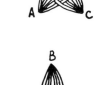

Stem, Crewel, or Outline Stitch

127

Stem Stitch is used for any line or outline of shapes. It is also used as filling by working rows closely side by side until the shape is filled. When Stem Stitch is used as a filling, it is advisable to start from the outside so as to preserve a sharp edge.

Winged man. Detail of a Peruvian Paracas mantle, dating from the first century A.D. It is solidly embroidered in Stem Stitch, with Chain Stitch snakes around the eyes (Courtesy of The Textile Museum, Washington, D.C.)

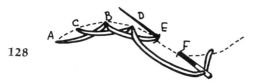

128

Work from left to right (Figure 128). Bring the needle and thread out at A. Holding the thread down with your left thumb, insert the needle at B. With the thread still down, come out at C, halfway between A and B. Pull the thread through. (The stitches appear curved on the diagram so that you may see how they are made.) Go over and in at D (with the thread down), coming out at B in the same hole; pull the thread through. Go over and in at E, coming out at D, and so on. Establish a rhythm, and regularity will come with it. Always bring the needle out in the hole of the previous stitch.

The stitch is called Stem or Crewel when the thread is kept down. The result is a textured line. It is called Outline when the thread is kept above the needle with a resulting straighter line.

Whether the stitch is called Stem, Crewel, or Outline, you must always keep the thread on the same side of the needle—either below the needle or above it. Do what comes easiest to you and try for the effect you like best. Work 1 or 2 inches each way to experience the difference. On sharp curves, keep the thread outside the curve. The back should look like a neat row of Back Stitches.

Alternating Stem Stitch

This stitch is worked like the Stem Stitch from left to right. But instead of holding the thread down for every stitch as in Figure 128, the thread is held alternately down for the first stitch, up for the second, down for the third, and so on (Figure 129).

129

An interesting effect is obtained by working two rows close to each other. Start the second row just below the first row at C, reversing the first row, holding the thread up for the first stitch, down for the second, up for the third, and so on. The two rows will look like four rows of stitches. It is a quick way of working a border, and is particularly effective when worked with heavy threads such as pearl cotton in size 3.

Long Stem Stitch

Instead of going back to the preceding hole as in the regular Stem Stitch, pick up a small amount of material (Figure 130). The length of the stitch is related to the weight of the thread. If three stands of six-stranded cotton are used, the stitches will be about ⅜ inch long with about ⅛ inch of material picked up.

130

The French use the Long Stem Stitch effectively to fill shapes, especially flowers and leaves. The rows are staggered close together with no material showing, and all move in the same direction, with the thread in the same position. When the end of the first line is reached (Figure 131), in order to start again next to A at C (if the line is not too long), the thread is run through the stitches at the back of the material; this is quicker than ending and starting the thread each time.

When the shape is filled, it is then outlined with a close Stem or Outline Stitch. On a fine material, one strand is used for a delicate filling, with two strands for the outline. This way of filling a shape is quicker and easier than working the often used Long and Short Stitch. The result is a beautiful textured surface.

If the floral shapes have stems, work one row of Outline Stitches from left to right, with the thread up, towards the outside of the shape (Figure 132). When B is reached, take small, even Running Stitches from C to D. Follow this with another row of Stem Stitches EF, with the thread held down, towards the outside.

Whole shapes can be filled in this quick, easy, satisfying way. Long Stem Stitch filling is much used in France because of its interesting texture. It is economical of thread, a feature dear to the thrifty Frenchwoman's heart.

French Filling

Work an Outline Stitch from A to B (Figure 133). When the end of the line is reached, take small even Running Stitches all the way back to the beginning, paralleling the first line. The third row, EF, is like AB, with the thread in the same position. The fourth row, GH, is like CD, and so on. This filling goes quickly and is effective.

As a chid, I used to call this "the little mouse" stitch because of a French nursery rhyme, "*La petite souris qui monte, qui monte, qui monte...*" ("the little mouse who climbs and climbs and climbs..."): this was for the Outline Stitch going up, followed by "*qui descend, qui descend, qui descend...*" ("down he goes, down he goes, down he goes...") for the Running Stitch going down.

When used as an outline for shapes such as figures, animals, plants, and abstract forms, the edge acquires more dimension and strength if one, two, or three rows of small Running Stitches are added (Figure 134).

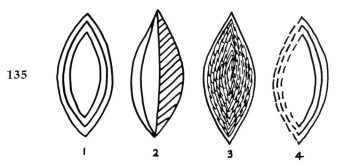

135

1   2   3   4

There are many ways of using the Stem Stitch to fill a shape (Figure 135). Several rows of regular Stem Stitch can be used to outline the shape (1). Straight rows can also be worked with even intervals between them (2). The Long Stem Stitch can be used as the French do, working rows close together (3). Try intervals of Stem Stitch and Running Stitches (4).

Work some of the Running Stitch variations. Use the Whipped Stem for a heavier line with dimension.

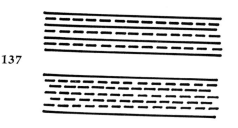

136

The stitches can be evenly slanted (Figure 136), picking up broader lines, which leads one back to the Satin Stitch. Stem Stitch can be combined with Running Stitch for rich borders (Figure 137).

Monograms can be worked with spaced Stem Stitch. The outline can be darker, the inside lighter (Figure 138).

137

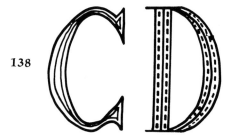

138

Line Shading

Line Shading is achieved by working rows in contrasting colors or in different values of one color. Values can be graduated from dark to light, for example, from a royal blue to medium to light blue. This is found in old embroideries of China and India, contributing much to their beauty.

Portuguese Stem Stitch

The Portuguese Stem Stitch has an interesting rugged texture with a knotted look. It creates unusual, sturdy lines, giving the effect of a couched cord, but it is much stronger. It is not difficult to work, and should be particularly useful to those who like to experiment with textures and extra dimension in working some forms of contemporary embroidery.

Start as an ordinary Stem Stitch, working upward (Figure 139). Bring the needle and thread out at A. Holding the thread *down* and to the right, insert at B, coming out at C. Pull the thread through. (With pearl cotton in size 5, BC will be about ⅛ inch.) With the

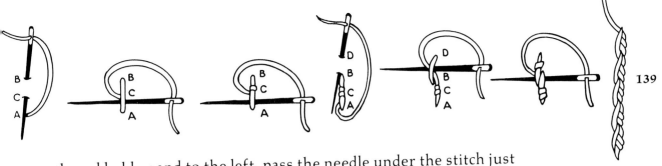

thread held *up* and to the left, pass the needle under the stitch just made, from right to left, without picking up any material. Pull the thread through firmly. A second time, with the thread held up and to the left, pass the needle under the same stitch from right to left, just below the first coil. Pull through firmly. The two small coils should rest neatly one below the other. Keep an even tension.

Continue with the thread held down and to the right, going in at D, and out at B (DB should be the same size as BC). Pull the thread through. With the thread held up and to the left, pass the needle under the new stitch DB from right to left as before. Pull through firmly. For the second coil, pass the needle under two threads, the lower part of the last Stem Stitch you made and the top of the first Stem Stitch. Pull the thread through firmly.

Each succeeding Stem Stitch is made with the thread held *down* and to the right. Each succeeding two coils should be close together, made with the thread held *up* and to the left. For each pair of coils, the first coil passes under one thread, and the second coil passes under two threads. The resulting effect is much like a knotted rope. Try it with heavy crochet cotton such as eight-cord cable twist; it looks quite different.

I like to work individual Portuguese Stem Stitch, going down at D after the second pair of coils. It makes interesting thorny growths on the sides of a stem. Work it also in a circle as petals.

Flat Stitch

The Flat Stitch is a simple way to fill a shape. Made with six strands of stranded cotton, it has a rich, undulating texture. Work from left to right (Figure 140, 141). Bring the needle out at A and insert at B. Go under and out at C, back in at D, under and out at E, in at F, out at G, and so on. Continue going back and forth, filling the shape; keep the needle pointing from the inside out. The stitches should be close together, folding into one another; each new stitch crosses over the bottom of the previous stitch.

In the countries of Southeast Europe, the Flat Stitch and the Double Flat Stitch are used a great deal in vivid colors to adorn national costumes. The shapes are usually outlined first in Chain Stitch and the Flat Stitch worked into the middle of the Chain

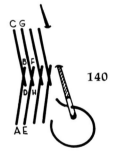

140

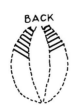

BACK

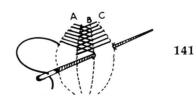

141

Stitch (see Chain Outlined Satin Stitch, page 125). The result is a raised surface. Try making up a design with bands in Flat Stitch, outlined in a darker shade (Figure 142).

142

Double Flat Stitch

To cover larger surfaces, a wider version of the Flat Stitch is used. The overlapping stitches are worked closely together.

First work a stitch inward from the edge, from A to B (Figure 143). Follow it by a similar stitch on the opposite side, from C to D, working outward from the inside. Next work a middle stitch from E to F as close as possible to AB and CD. Return down to the lower edge, at G, close to A.

143

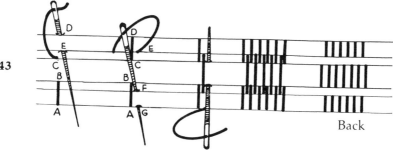

Until the rhythm is established, it may help to draw lines lightly with a blue pencil. Note the pattern formed on the back of the material.

Fishbone Stitch

This is basically a Flat Stitch made with a sharp slant. It is a simple way to fill a shape, especially leaf forms. The stitches can be placed close together or with spaces between them.

144

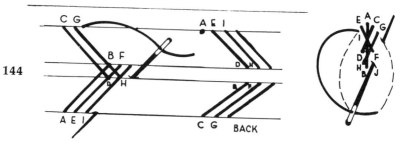

Work from left to right (Figure 144). Bring the needle out at A. Insert it at B, coming out at C (opposite A). Go in at D, below the AB thread, and come out at E. Go in at F, crossing over D, and come out at G. Work back and forth, filling the shape. Practice the stitches close together, folding over one another. Keep the needle pointing outward.

To fill a leaf shape, take a few Running Stitches inside the shape and come out at A, the point of the shape (Figure 144, right). Take a Straight Stitch along the center line to B, coming out at C, close to A. Go in at D across the center line, making a stitch with a sharp slant. Come out at E, close to A on the other side. Go over to F, coming out at G. Work alternately on each side until the shape is filled, with each stitch crossing over the previous stitch at the center.

Raised Fishbone Stitch

This stitch gives a padded effect to the Fishbone Stitch. Work from left to right (Figure 145). Bring the needle out at A. Insert it at B, coming out at C, exactly opposite B. Cross over AB, going in at D. (You have made a Cross Stitch).

The next step will determine whether or not the threads will cross in the center. From D go back under and out at E (the same hole as A). With E starting the next cross, go over to F, close to B, so that no material will show between stitches. Cross under to G, close to C. Go in at H, close to D; cross under to I, close to A, and so on.

For a pointed shape, such as a leaf, start by taking three or four small Running Stitches without a knot, coming out at A. Make a Straight Stitch about half way down the center to B. Come out at C (opposite B). Cross over and go in at D (just to the right of A). Go under and out at E (opposite D). Cross over and go in at F (opposite C). Go under and out at G (the same hole as C). With G starting the next cross, go over to H, going under and out at I. Cross over to J, going under and out at K (just below G). Continue until the shape is filled.

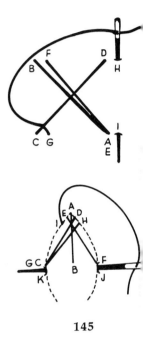

145

Open Fishbone Stitch

This quick and easy stitch curves well. It makes pleasant airy lines suitable for representing grasses and ferns. It is also a useful stitch for the light filling of a shape. The diagrams are only to help you to acquire the rhythm (Figure 146). After very little practice, forget the diagrams and work freely.

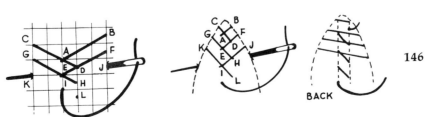

146

Work from left to right or up and down. To practice, use pearl cotton in size 5 or 3. First try the stitch on a large scale, with ¾ or 1 inch between parallel lines, until you have mastered the rhythm.

Insert the needle from back to front at A, on the left of the double center line (Figure 146, back). Go diagonally up and in at B, and under and out at C. (C is not in line with A or B, but halfway between the two.) Go diagonally down and in at D (on the right of the double center line), coming out at E (to the left and below A). Go over and in at F, under and out at G, over and in at H, under and out at I, over and in at J, under and out at K, over and in at L, and so on.

Leaf Stitch

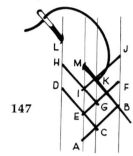

147

This is a good filling stitch, especially, as its name implies, for leaf forms. It can also be used as a border for a light effect.

Work from bottom to top (Figure 147). To practice use pearl cotton in size 5, between parallel lines LHD and JFB which should be about ½ inch apart. (The drawing is enlarged for clarity.) Later practice freely without parallel lines, using finer threads and closer stitches. Insert the needle from back to front at A, to the left of the double center line. Go diagonally up and in at B, keeping the thread above your work. Bring the needle out at C, on the right of the double center line, just below the line AB. Go in at D, coming out at E; in at F, out at G; in at H; and so on. Work alternately left and right until the shape is filled, always keeping the thread above the work.

In filling a leaf form, you might want to outline it with a well defined stitch such as Outline, Pekinese, or Threaded Back Stitch (Figure 148).

148

Fern Stitch

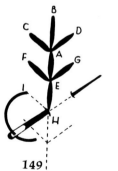

149

The Fern Stitch is a simple stitch, suitable for representing sprays and leaf veins, and for working light edges (Figures 149-151). It consists of three Straight Stitches of approximately equal length, all radiating from one central point. This can be done in a number of ways.

Work from top down (Figure 149). Bring the needle and thread out at A. Insert the needle at B, coming out at C; go back in at A, out at D, back in at A. Continue, coming out at E, back in at A, out at F, and back to E. Come out at G, go back in at E, and come out at H. Go back to E, come out at I, and so on.

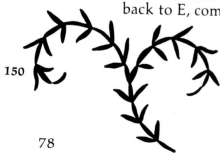

150

151

78

Thorn Stitch

The Thorn Stitch is well adapted to curves and is useful in depicting ferns, grasses, stems, and leaves. It gives a flowing effect because of the continuous central line, a long, loose central thread which is tied down with crossed stitches (Figure 152).

Work from top to bottom or right to left (Figure 153). Cut the center thread a few inches longer than the line to be covered. Bring it out at A and let it lie over the line to be covered. With another thread, come out at B, cross the loose thread, and go in at C. Come out at D, and go in at E. Come out at F, cross over and go in at G. Come out at H, go in at I, out at J, over and in at K, out at L, and so on. When the desired length is reached, bring the long center line through to the back and tie without pulling.

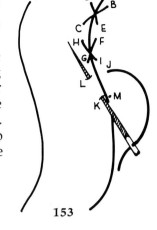

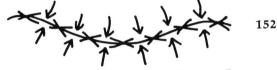
152

153

Detail of THE LAST SUPPER by Giotto. Fresco, Arena Chapel, Padua. (Photograph by Alinari.)

154

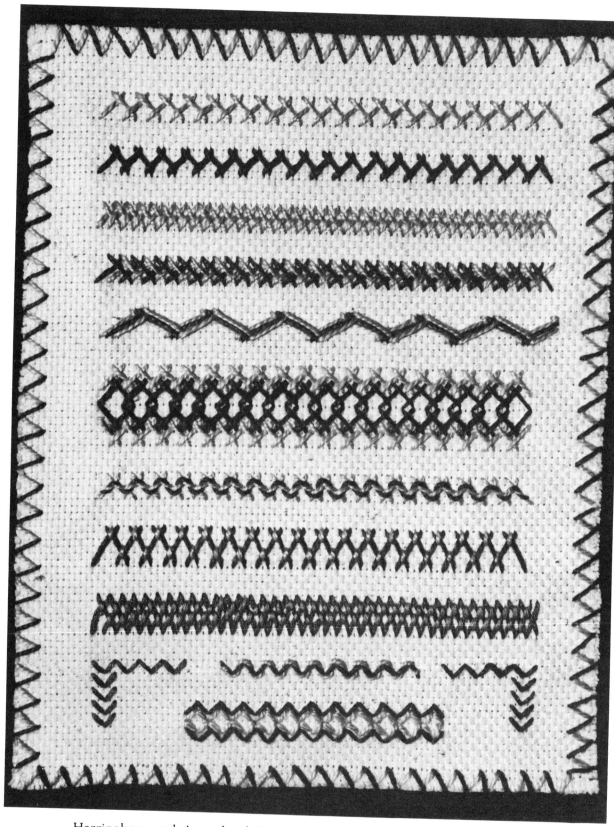

Herringbone and Arrowhead Stitch sampler worked by Sharon Rosebury, eighth grade, Holy Names Academy, Seattle, Washington.

Herringbone Stitch

Just as the Double Running Stitch is called the Holbein Stitch, the Herringbone Stitch should bear the name of the fourteenth century Italian painter Giotto. In his paintings illustrating the life of Christ in the Arena chapel in Padua, Giotto's beautiful Herringbone Stitch borders, worked in gold with great precision, enrich the clothing of many of the figures. Both the single Herringbone Stitch and the Double Herringbone Stitch are represented. Particularly interesting is the way Giotto breaks up what would otherwise be a monotonous pattern in a border depicted in "The Last Supper" (Figure 154). This design would look very effective, for example, around the center of a tablecloth.

A versatile stitch, the Herringbone has so many variations that a whole sampler can be made to illustrate them. Experiment with threads in varying weights. Work from left to right between parallel lines. Later, when you have acquired the rhythm of the stitch, you can work between irregular lines and cover varied shapes.

If this is your first attempt, pull two threads ⅜ inch apart on your doodling cloth and use pearl cotton in size 5. Or use a canvas-type material such as a finegrained monk's cloth with a firm finish. Think in terms of squares between parallel lines.

Bring the needle and thread out at A, at the bottom left corner of the first square (Figure 155). Go over to B, diagonally across the square. From B go under horizontally to C, halfway back to the left. From C go diagonally down to D, halfway across the next square. From D go under to E (opposite B), from E over to F, and from F under to G (opposite D).

For a different effect, pick up smaller stitches with larger spaces between them (Figure 156).

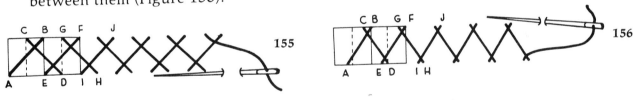

155

156

Closed Herringbone or Double Back Stitch

This stitch is beautifully illustrated in a number of Fra Angelico's paintings. It is worked with the needle coming out in the same hole as that of the previous stitch. This makes a beautiful border or frame. The character of the stitch varies according to the angle at which you cross your stitches. Once you have mastered the rhythm, it goes very quickly.

For regularity, E should be halfway between CB, and D halfway between BF (Figure 157). Watch your start; A is not opposite C but to the left. If C were directly opposite A, the result would be a slanting Herringbone. You might want a slanting effect, but at first work it straight.

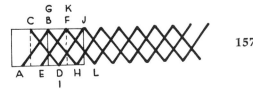

157

SAINT STEPHEN by Fra Angelico. Detail of fresco, Chapel of Nicholas V, Vatican. (Photograph by Alinari.)

Closed Herringbone Sampler. The border on the sleeve of St. Stephen inspired Sister Bernard Marie S.N.J.M. to embroider this sampler. She used the Closed Herringbone edged with a row of Back Stitches, framed with a single row of Square Stitches on each side.

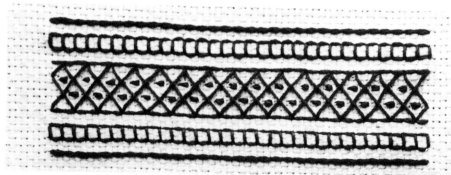

Try the Closed Herringbone with three or six strands of stranded cotton. Three strands with small Back Stitches in rows about ¼ inch wide make a handsome border, an outline for a bold shape, or a filling. The Closed Herringbone is useful for filling irregular shapes. It takes a curve easily. Accentuate the edges with a fine Outline Stitch (Figures 158-160).

160

The Closed Herringbone is also called the Double Back Stitch, because its back shows a double row of Back Stitches. Used for shadow work on transparent material, such as organdy, it shows delicate color through the fabric. This stitch is worked from right to left, with the Back Stitches on the right side of the material, crossing back and forth between the parallel lines. Using stranded cotton, it makes a solid line or filling.

Crisscross Herringbone Stitch

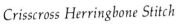

This stitch is useful for covering large surfaces quickly, and is fun to work. Use a heavy thread and a hoop.

Imagine a series of ¾-inch squares, each divided vertically into three ¼-inch sections (Figure 161). In the first square make a large cross, from A to B, B to C, and C to D (Figure 162).

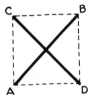

162

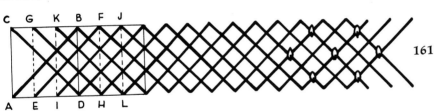

From D, go back two sections to E. Cross over diagonally to F (one section to the right of B). From F go back three sections to G. From G cross diagonally down to H. From H, go back two sections to I, and from I cross over to J. Go back three sections to K, cross down to L, and go back two sections to D, the right hand corner of the first square. From then on, you will be "joining hands" with previous stitches, which will make your work go quickly.

After a little practice, you will develop the freedom enabling you to cover many different shapes. This is a useful stitch for spontaneously creating with a needle.

You can add to the crisscross effect by working over four sections instead of three (a 1-inch square instead of a ¾-inch square). If your stitches are very long, they may need to be tied down with Straight Stitches or Detached Chain. This in itself adds a decorative element (see Tied Herringbone, below).

The Crisscross Herringbone can also be worked as a border between straight or curved lines, with the stitches close together and no material showing. To see the effect, use pearl cotton in size 5, working between parallel lines ¼ inch apart.

Double and Triple Herringbone

Try using several shades of the same color, or two contrasting colors (Figures 163-165). The second color is laced under on the way up, and over on the way down; ab passes under CD, cd over EF, ef under GH, gh over IJ.

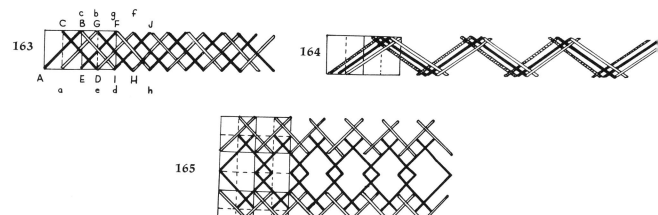

163

164

165

Threaded Herringbone

For the lacing, use a thread of a contrasting color. To achieve a crisp look, use a firm thread. Metallic threads look well.

Lace over the Herringbone crossed threads and under the slanting stitches, without going through the material except at the beginning and at the end. Watch the tension; do not pull too tight (Figure 166).

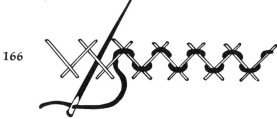

166

Tied Herringbone

Work a foundation row of Herringbone Stitches either open or closed. The tying stitch can be a Straight Stitch taken vertically, or a Detached Chain Stitch. Tie from inside out (Figure 167, 168).

A rich border is made by Closed Herringbone Stitches tied down with Straight Stitches or Detached Chain Stitches (Figure 169).

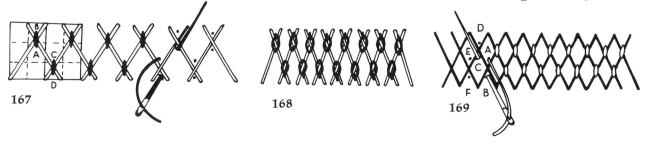

167

168

169

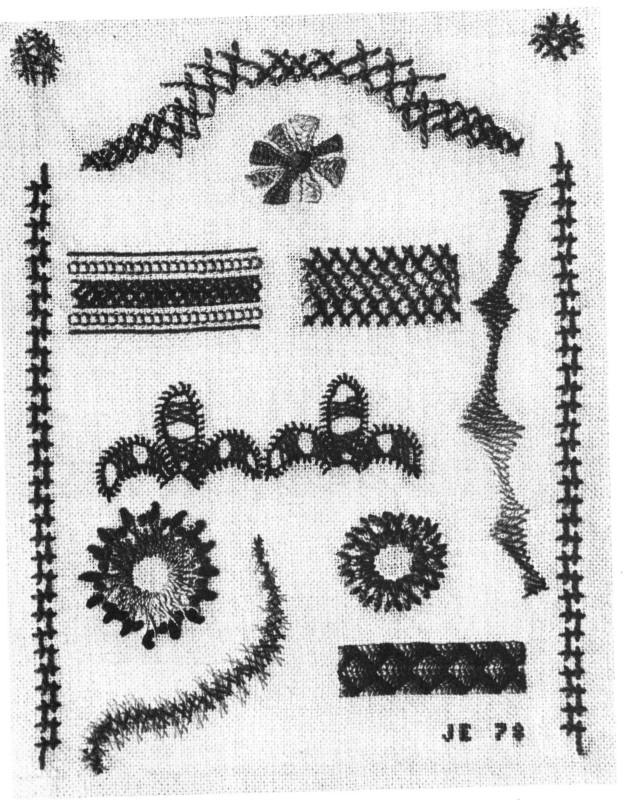

Herringbone sampler worked by the author, with variations and free use of stitches. (Photograph by the author.)

Make the border ½ inch wide or more. For a striking effect, try a border of Closed Herringbone Stitches made with six strands of red stranded cotton, tied down with the same thread, on white cloth, or embroider in white on a colored cloth.

Another way to work the Tied Herringbone is with the Coral Zigzag Stitch (see page 154). Start with a foundation row of Herringbone and work from right to left (Figure 170). Place the needle under the cross, from outside in, without picking up material. Loop the thread over and then under the point of the needle. Snug up your thread around the needle and pull the needle through, forming a knot. Continue from outside in, under each pair of crossed threads.

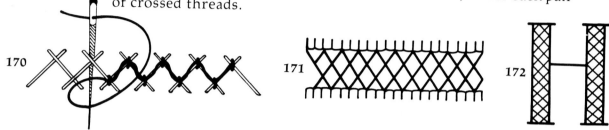

Any of these borders can be edged with Back Stitch, Outline, Chain, Buttonhole, or any other linear stitch (Figures 171, 172).

A wide band can be worked with two rows of Closed Herringbone separated by rows of solid filling, made with Darning Stitch, Chain Stitch, or any other filling stitch (Figure 173).

The Portuguese use combinations of Herringbone and Buttonhole effectively. The two borders shown in Figures 174 and 175 were embroidered in white on a red skirt.

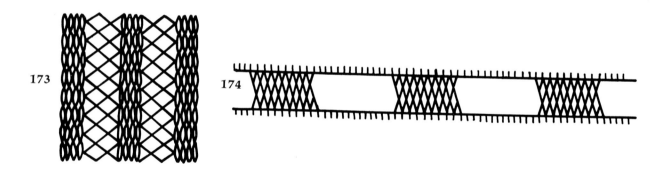

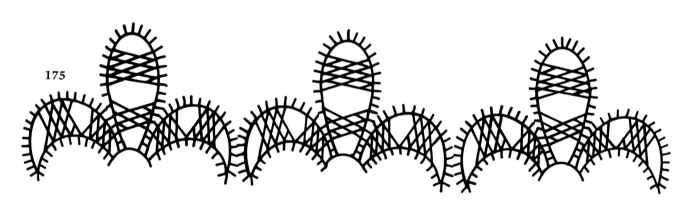

Mexican apron from Erongarícuaro. The outline of the bird is worked in Closed Herringbone Stitch in bright colors; the border is worked in Feather Stitch. (Courtesy of Vicki, La Tienda, Seattle.)

176   177

Herringbone Variation

This Herringbone variation is often found on embroideries from India. Single units, sometimes as small as ⅛ inch, are scattered between shapes (Figure 176). The borders worked in two journeys are effective (Figure 177). In working the last stitch of each unit of four stitches, slide the needle under the first stitch marked x.

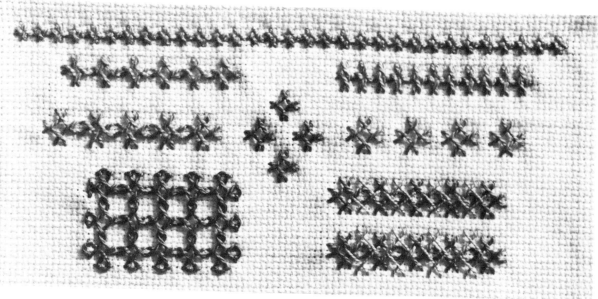

Herringbone variation. (Photograph by Robert McClellan.)

Double Herringbone Interlaced

This beautiful border is well worth the effort involved in mastering it. At first glance, you may decide that it is impossible to achieve, but if little girls in India and Pakistan do it easily, surely so can you. They are often helped by wood blocks which they use to stamp the foundation pattern. When necessary, I mark my cloth every ¼ inch with pencil dots the color of my thread, or I may alternate ¼ inches with 3/16 inches every other dot. The lower row repeats the upper one, a ½ inch below it (Figure 178). You can also use a piece of canvas as a template, marking the dots through holes in the canvas.

178

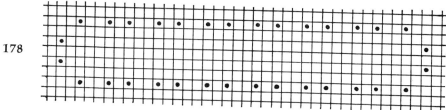

The success of interlacing lies in the correct placement of the base stitches; otherwise the interlacing cannot be worked in proper sequence, over and under. The base stitches are laid slightly differently from traditional Herringbone Stitches. Once you understand the importance of a correct foundation, the actual interlacing is easy and covers ground quickly.

Use two needles: a sharp needle for the foundation, and a tapestry needle for the interlacing. If the top and bottom rows are a ½ inch apart, the equivalent of a pearl cotton size 3 would fill and cover the foundation. To practice, use a finer weight of thread such as pearl cotton size 5. This will make the work easier. In learning the stitch, it is helpful to work with three different colors, one for each Herringbone row and one for the interlacing.

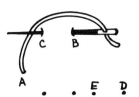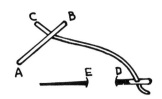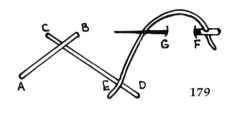

179

Work the first row of Herringbone with stitches relaxed. Come up at A, a third of the way up (Figure 179). Circle the thread *UP*. BC is worked with the needle *OVER* the thread from A as if button-holing. This is the important difference between Double Herringbone Interlaced and regular Herringbone: the thread from C *MUST* be under AB. With the CD thread held *UP* clockwise, go down at D and up at E with no buttonholing. EF goes over CD and FG as in BC, the needle *OVER* the thread. End the row a third of the way up at P (Figure 180). As you work the first foundation row, see that all upward Herringbone Stitches lie on top; all downward stitches should be underneath. Check back from time to time. Even I get absentminded.

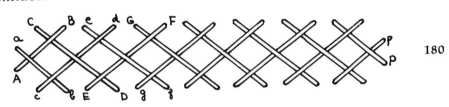

180

For the second row of foundation stitches, follow the lower case lettering. Come up at a, a third of the way down, and work bc as in DE. From c, slide the needle upward *UNDER* cd to d. Work the top crosses as in BC, c under d. Go down to f over EF, and so on to the end of the row. Go down at p. The result is a foundation alternating over and under. Before interlacing, recheck the accuracy of the foundation.

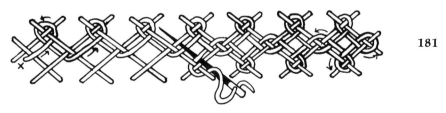

181

To interlace, use a tapestry needle. Start at X (Figure 181). The working thread goes over, under, over, under, over, then *UNDER* itself, and also under the cd foundation. Although the thread goes under twice instead of the usual once, these two threads will be separated on the return journey. Follow the arrows. When you reach the end of the row, start the return journey from right to left. Notice that again you go under twice. If your interlacing is tight, the needle will have to poke around to lift up the "under" thread. End at the starting point X.

Breton Stitch

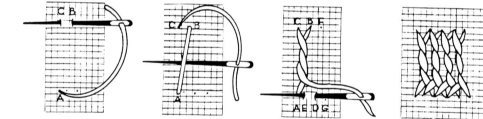

Breton Stitch variation *Point de Veuve.* (Worked a▮ photographed by the author.)

The Breton Stitch, characteristic of the embroidery of Brittany, reminds me of the rows of open work spindles often found in the carved furniture of this area (see the Breton cradle, page 194). This little-known stitch is beautiful and easy to work. An attractive feature is the grillwork effect which lets the background material show through. Traditionally, it was worked with deep blue threads on white cloth, or in white on blue linen, but any color combination can be used.

It is based on the Closed Herringbone Stitch, with stitches close together between parallel lines; the heavier the thread, the greater the distance between the lines. A thread with a definite twist is most effective. Use a hoop to keep the lines from drawing together.

To practice the stitch, use coarse linen or cotton homespun; draw two lines or pull out two threads ⅜ inch apart. Use pearl cotton in size 5, working from left to right (Figure 182).

182

Bring the needle and thread out at A on the lower line and insert at B on the upper line, two threads over, with the thread slightly relaxed. Come out at C, two threads to the left. Pull through. C is opposite A. BC must always be small, otherwise the grillwork effect is lost.

The next step differs from the plain Closed Herringbone Stitch. With the thread from C held above your work, pass the needle under the AB thread from right to left, without picking up any material. Gently snug the thread down. Insert the needle at D on the lower line, three threads to the right of A. (This is the only time you insert three threads over.) Come out at E, two threads to the left of D. (E is opposite the midpoint of CB.) This completes the first stitch. Cross over to F, two threads to the right of B. From F go under to B. Pull through gently. Pass the needle under EF, inserting at G, two threads to the right of D, and so on.

With pearl cotton in size 3, try the lines about ⅝ inch apart, working over four threads instead of two, looping the thread gently twice instead of once. Keep the material very taut in the hoop frame.

One of the most beautiful borders I have ever made was worked with two rows of Breton Stitches in deep royal blue using pearl cotton in size 8, between parallel lines ¼ inch apart. The second row was made by turning the work around, and working the base stitches in the same holes as the base of the first row. By adding a row of Outline Stitches on each side and spacing them about one or two threads from the upper part of the row, I created what looked like a lace insertion.

The stitch can be used on a curve. On a straight line, such as on each side of a place mat, drawing a thread for each parallel line makes the work not only easier but adds to the lacy effect.

Breton Stitch Variation

The Point de Veuve (Widow's Stitch), later called "Vous et Moi" was at one time used exclusively on the little caps worn by widows in Brittany, hence its original name. These small caps were made of fine linen dyed ochre. Until the end of the nineteenth century the color was obtained by boiling together fresh limpets and brown seaweed. Later, strong tea leaves and linden blossoms were used for dye, making a lighter beige with a blush to it. The stitch itself was embroidered with white "coton à broder". Toward the end of World War I, as widows' caps stopped being used, the stitch became known as "Vous et Moi"—You and I.

It is worked between parallel lines which were originally 1 centimeter apart (roughly 1/3 inch). The stitch is now worked any size. Come up at A on the lower line (Figure 183). With yarn held clockwise, go down at B, not quite opposite A, and up at C. With the yarn under the point of the needle, pull through gently. Now circle the yarn counterclockwise and slide the needle under AB, go down at D opposite B, slightly diagonally from A, taking a very small stitch, and come up at E on the lower line. E should be opposite the middle of BC. With the yarn under the point of the needle, pull through.

With the yarn circling clockwise, continue from F in the same hole as C, to G. Occasionally, the stitch is worked with a small space between C and F.

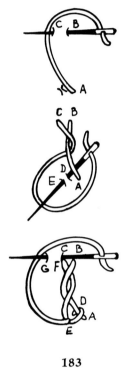

183

Chevron Stitch

The Chevron Stitch is used for lines, borders, and fillings. It is worked from left to right, between two parallel lines, much in the manner of the Herringbone Stitch. To avoid making the stitches too large, place your parallel lines ¼ inch apart or slightly less. Use pearl cotton in size 5 or 8 for practicing.

Bring the needle and thread out on the left of the lower line at A (Figure 184). Insert at B, a little to the right. (If you are working on heavy material and can count threads easily, try leaving four threads between A and B.)

184

Holding the thread down, bring the needle out at C, halfway between A and B. With the thread still held down, insert the needle diagonally on the upper line at D, coming out at E. With the thread held up, go in at F, back and out at D, down diagonally and in at G, with the thread held down, out at H, in at I, out at G, and so on.

E can be opposite B and H opposite F, or they can be spaced further apart for a different effect.

Rows of Chevron make an attractive filling. On your sampler, try a design with pearl cotton in size 8, with lines 3/16 inch apart, with a Double Back Stitch in the center of some of the diamonds (Figure 185).

The Chevron Stitch can be laced like the Herringbone.

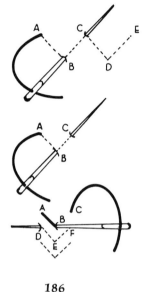

185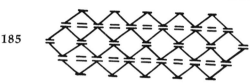

Arrowhead Stitch

This stitch is used in groups for either line or filling, or detached as a powdering. It is worked between parallel lines, horizontally from left to right, or vertically from top down.

Bring the needle and thread out at A (Figure 186). Go in at B, out at C, and over back in at B. ABC should form a right angle. For a continuous line, bring the needle out at C; go in at D, and out at E, making stitches of equal size.

Figure 187 shows a flower design in the Arrowhead Stitch. On the island of Taiwan, beautiful embroideries are made by working rows of Arrowhead close together. Three strands of six-stranded cotton are used, with three rows of one color, following three rows of another color. I like to work two rows in a light shade, followed by two rows of the same color in a medium shade, then two rows in a dark shade. This, too, can be very effective (Figure 188). In working several rows with spaces between, a heavy cotton in pearl size 5 goes quickly (Figure 189).

186

188   189

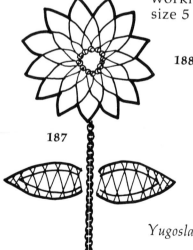

187

190

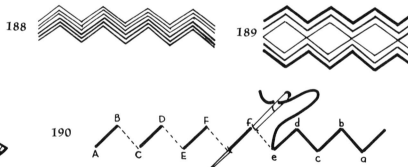

Yugoslav Border Stitch (Double Running Zigzag)

A variation of the Arrowhead Stitch, the Yugoslav Border Stitch is worked in two movements: first from left to right, then from right to left on the return (Figure 190). After practicing the traditional

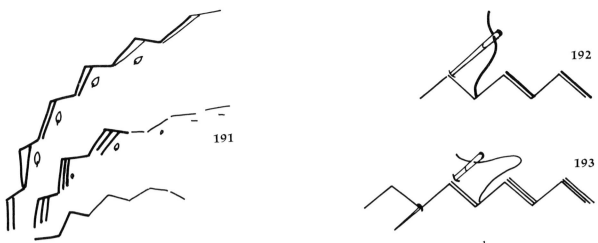

191

192

193

Yugoslav Border Stitch, try to achieve a personal interpretation by using the stitch in free flowing lines (Figure 191). Motion and speed can be expressed by varying the angle and the length of the stitches.

Adding diagonal stitches to one of the movements is effective. Try to create variations by changing the texture and color (Figures 192, 193).

Interlaced Yugoslav Border Stitch

In Southeast Europe, the Yugoslav Border Stitch is used on national costumes in lines interlaced with contrasting colors, such as red interlaced with blue (Figure 194). In some villages of Slavonia, young girls wear white linen costumes which they embroider and interlace with gold thread. In other villages, they embroider in red on white linen—very elegant and eye catching. After they are married, they wear black!

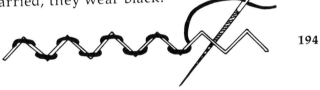

194

Wave Stitch Filling

This is an Arrowhead Stitch worked with horizontal stitches on the back. It can be worked either from left to right or right to left. When used as a filling, each successive row is worked in the same holes as the previous one (Figures 195, 196).

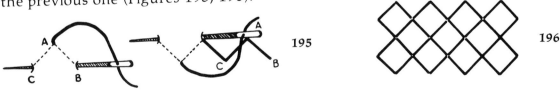

195

196

Insertion Wave Stitch

This is my version of a Wave Stitch with an added stitch. I use it to anchor a plain braid, rickrack, or ribbon on material. It provides a particularly useful trimming if you are adding a length of material to a child's dress or to a skirt. It turns a vexing problem into an

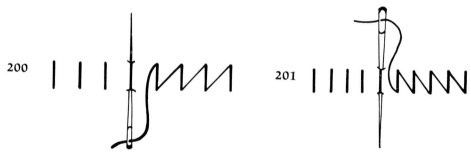

197   **198**

199

attractive decoration. First stitch the two materials with wrong sides together so that the open seam is on the right side. Press it open and flat. Baste the braid over the seam and embroider with the Insertion Wave Stitch (Figures 197, 198).

Bring the needle and thread out at A (Figure 199). Go over and in at B, under to C, over and back to B, and under to D. From D go over and in at A, under to E, and over and back to A. From A go under to F, out and over to D, and in and under to G. From G go over and back to D, under to H, and so forth.

This can be made into an attractive all-over stitch by working several rows touching each other.

Bosnia Stitch

Embroideries of Yugoslavia frequently use the Bosnia Stitch as a filling. It is similar to the Yugoslav Border Stitch, with the first movement straight up and down instead of slanting. I enjoy working it as a line stitch, using two values of the same color such as medium and dark blue, or a different weight of thread for the return journey.

The French call this stitch the Barrier or Fence Stitch but on the return journey, the pickets are joined from the bottom up instead of from the top down (Figures 200, 201).

200   **201**

Huichol Zigzag

The Huichol Indians of Mexico embroider most of their men's clothing in Cross Stitch and Long-Armed Cross Stitch on muslin, 66 threads to the inch. It is all worked precisely on counted thread— a remarkable feat. They sometimes use a stitch I have not seen in other countries, except for a slightly more elaborate French variation. It looks much like a fine rickrack. The Huichol Zigzag is about ¼ inch high but can be worked any size.

On the man's shirt I own, the ¼ inch stitch is worked with an emerald green fine wool. A similar effect is obtained with nine strands of six-stranded cotton or fine orlon. The stitch goes quite quickly once you understand the rhythm. The back looks like two rows of Arrowhead Stitch (Figure 203).

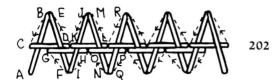 

202

203

Back

To avoid counting threads, use a pencil the color of your yarn to mark your cloth. Along two parallel lines ¼ inch apart, mark dots every ¼ inch; the dots of the lower row alternate with those of the top row, giving you the points of the zigzag (Figure 202). Between the points, draw a line along the middle. This line will be covered by stitches. You can also practice the stitch on canvas.

Come up at A, go down diagonally at B, and come up at C above A, halfway between A and B. Go down horizontally at D. D will be opposite point F, on the other side of the zigzag. Come up at E in the same hole as B, go down at F, and come up at G opposite B and under CD on the same line. Go down at H, come up at I in the same hole as F, and go down at J, opposite H. Come up at K in the same hole as D, above GH, go down at L, and so on. Watch your horizontal lines so that they weave evenly over and under the diagonal ines. CD, GH, and KL are on the same line.

On each side of the zigzag, the Huichols work two rows of Long-Armed Cross Stitch (Figure 204), with two stitches between each point, in an orangy red next to the green and in a warm yellow on the outside—a beautiful color combination. The whole band is ¾ inch wide.

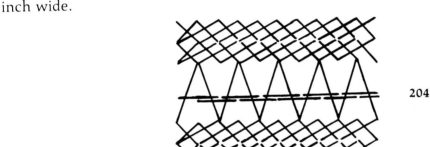

204

Sleeve by a Huichol Indian using their special Huichol Stitch. Notice the turned back edge which shows all the Cross Stitches worked with vertical back. (From the author's collection; photograph by the author.)

French Zigzag band

The French work a band similar to the Huichol Zigzag. It was used in France before woven rickrack was manufactured and called "galon en zigzag". Today it is seldom seen yet it makes a beautiful, rich border when heavy threads are used. In the past, it was worked on little girls' aprons made of checkerboard fabric, using the squares as a guide.

Much of the beauty of the stitch lies in its regularity. Practice it on counted thread fabric easy to count, on aïda-type cloth, or on canvas to learn the rhythm. When this is mastered, you can use fine cloth, marking the points of the upper and lower zigzag with a pencil the color of your yarn. The height must be divisible into three equal parts, each containing an equal number of threads. On fine cloth, a thread can be pulled to mark each side of the middle third to fascilitate the work. This will be hidden by the stitches. If you use pearl cotton size 3 or one strand of crewel yarn, a height of about ⅜ inch would be suitable. The points of the zigzag would be ¼ inch apart, top and bottom alternating. Your work will be easier if you keep in mind that C is opposite A, and F is opposite D (Figures 205, 206).

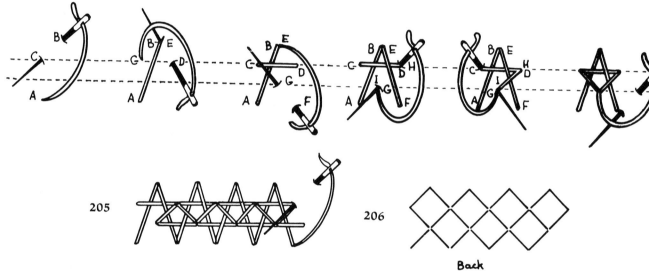

205

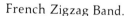

206

Back

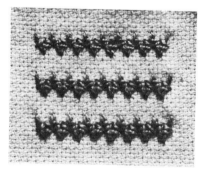

French Zigzag Band.

Triangle Stitch

Two rows of the Bosnia Stitch, worked up and down, facing each other, form the Triangle Stitch. This can be used to create interesting patterns. It can be enriched with a Holbein Stitch down the center, or detached Chain Stitches, or any combination you may prefer (Figures 207-209). First work the horizontal stitches, then the slanting stitches. Work first in one direction, then the other.

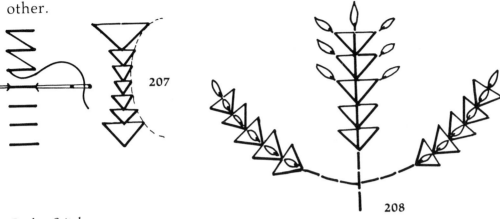

207

208

209

Basket Stitch

The Basket Stitch, one of the most effective border stitches, is well worth learning. Once the rhythm is established, it is done easily and quickly. Practice on coarse material or canvas with threads that are easy to count. The stitch resembles the Herringbone Stitch but is richer looking. You can tell them apart immediately by examining the backs; the Herringbone back shows a series of parallel Back Stitches, while the back of the Basket Stitch shows vertical stitches, alternately straight and slanting. It is worked from left to right.

Not knowing how to start has discouraged people from using the Basket Stitch. After the first five stitches which set the pattern, the work becomes easy. It is simple if you follow each step as illustrated (Figures 210-212). The needle alternately makes a stitch forward and then goes backward over two stitches.

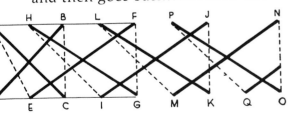

210

211

212

Since the stitch has a tendency to draw the material together, the use of a hoop is advisable. This stitch can be worked either open or closed.

Open Basket Stitch

Think in terms of squares between parallel lines (Figure 210). Bring the needle and thread out at A and insert at B, diagonally across. From B go straight down, coming out at C; then back over and in at

D. You now have a cross. From D bisect the base line of the square, AC, coming out at E. Then go over diagonally and in at F, the upper right corner of the next square. Go straight down and out at G; then back over and in at H, bisecting DB. Go diagonally out at I, bisecting CG; over across to J, and so on. Once the pattern is established, the stitch becomes easy. Try working the stitch closer (Figure 211).

Closed Basket Stitch

Close the stitches, making each new stitch in the holes of the previous stitch (Figure 212). If your material has threads that can be counted, make the width of the first cross, from D to B, over four threads, bisecting at E under two threads. Go over to F, two threads to the right of B; straight down to G; and diagonally across over to H, halfway between DB. Go down to I in the same hole as C; over to J, two threads to the right of F; straight down to K; over and back to L in the same hole as B; and down to M in the same hole as G.

The Closed Basket Stitch is sometimes confused with the Plait Stitch (see page 69). You can tell them apart by the backs. In any Basket Stitch, open or closed, the back shows two stitches, one straight, one diagonal, repeated at regular intervals. The Plait Stitch back shows parallel pairs of stitches at regular intevals.

Sheaf Stitch

The Sheaf Stitch is used in rows for borders, and in groups for fillings. It is made of three or four vertical Straight Stitches of equal size, side by side, with small spaces between them; they are tied together horizontally in the middle (Figures 213-215). First work three vertical stitches A to B, C to D, and E to F (Figure 213). From F, bring the needle out at G, left of the midpoint of DC. Slip the needle under and to the left of AB. Without picking up material, wrap the thread around the three stitches twice; snug up your thread, and insert the needle again at G.

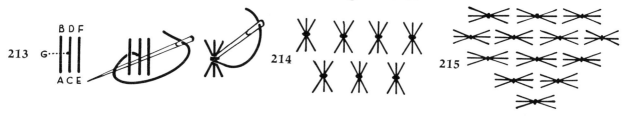

I found a delightful variation of the Sheaf Stitch on a garment from Guatemala. It looks like little tassels (Figures 216, 217).

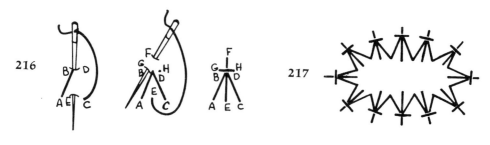

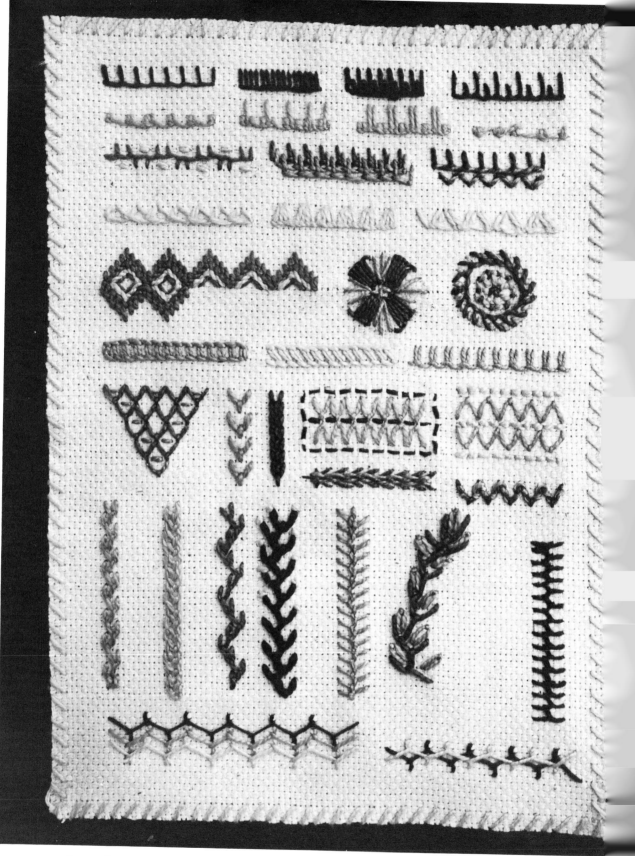

Looped Stitch sampler worked by Lisette Roozen, ninth grade, Holy Names Academy, Seattle, Washington.

LOOPED STITCHES

Introduction

Looped stitches form the second major group of stitches. A looped stitch is formed by curving a Straight Stitch, holding it down with the left hand, and drawing the needle and working thread out over it. I find working looped stitches particularly relaxing, especially when they are worked in the hand rather than with a hoop. This is possible when the material is firm and the stitches are relaxed.

In the nineteenth century, looped stitches were used to decorate household linens. Long rows of scallops were worked in Buttonhole Stitch on the edge of tablecloths, napkins, sheets, pillow cases, and so forth. These were not usually worked on a frame or hoop. Instead, the material was basted to a temporary backing, which was both firm and supple. This kept the work from puckering; the embroideress was able to hold it in her left hand, with the needle and thread sliding between the two cloths. When the work was completed, the basting threads were cut off, and the backing was removed. Oil cloth was—and still is—used a good in Europe as a temporary backing; it could well be used for working freehand stitcheries. Some of the medium-weight flexible plastics, and even plain brown paper, are also well-suited for this purpose.

Spaced Buttonhole or Blanket Stitch

The basic and best known looped stitch is the Spaced Buttonhole Stitch, also known as the Blanket Stitch. A versatile stitch, it can be used for making edges and borders, as well as for outlining and filling shapes.

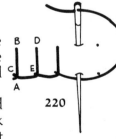

220

It is worked from left to right (Figure 220). Bring the needle and thread out at A. (If you are working over a turned-up edge, work the knot inside the hem.) Holding the thread down with the left thumb, insert the needle at B. Come out above A at C, drawing the needle out over the thread coming from A to form a loop. (When used to bind an edge (Figures 221, 222), the needle inserted at B goes from the back of the material over the thread coming from A.) Go in at D and come out at E, drawing the needle out over the thread coming from C to form a loop, and so on.

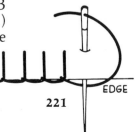

221

222

Buttonhole Stitch

223

This stitch is the same as the Spaced Buttonhole Stitch except that the stitches are worked close together (Figure 223). Variations are endless. Work as many as you can on your sampler, each 1½ to 2 inches long. It will prove to be a very useful reference. Vary the distance between stitches and the length of each stitch (Figure 224). With three successive rows on top of each other, try using three values of the same color, light, medium, and dark.

224

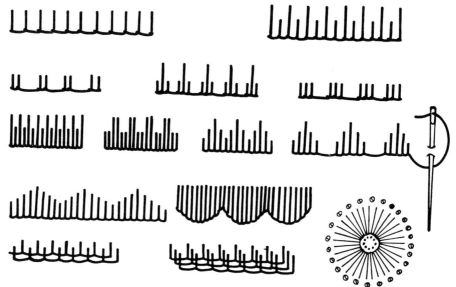

Closed Buttonhole Stitch

This is a Spaced Buttonhole Stitch with pairs of stitches worked from the same hole, first left, then right, to form triangles (Figure 225).

225

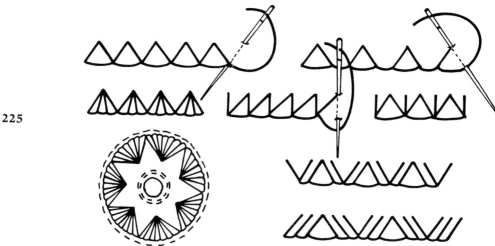

Crossed Buttonhole Stitch

Pairs of Buttonhole Stitches are worked at an angle so that they cross each other (Figure 226).

226

Outline Buttonhole Stitch

For a textured outline of borders, the Outline Buttonhole Stitch is taken either on one side, or on alternate sides (Figures 227, 228).

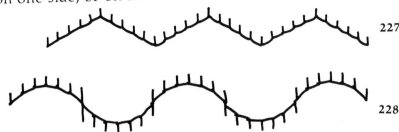

227

228

Two Buttonhole Stitches on alternate sides, with French Knots or detached Chain Stitches in the spaces, make a lively border (Figure 229). This can be worked into sparkling little Christmas trees (Figures 230, 231). A flower design can be made up of rows of Outline Buttonhole with added stitches such as Outline, Running, and Satin Stitches (Figure 232).

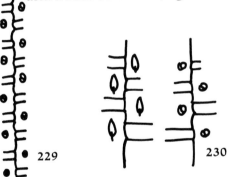

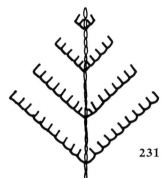

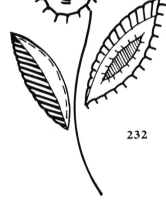

229   230   231   232

Single Feather Stitch

Instead of working stitches at a right angle as in the Buttonhole Stitch, the Single Feather Stitch is taken slanting (Figure 233). It is skillfully used in the revival of English Dorset stitchery.

233

Spiral Stitch

Two rows of Single Feather Stitch facing each other, worked in the manner of the Double Buttonhole Stitch, form the Spiral Stitch (Figure 234). It takes well to curves. With heavy thread, it gives a bold effect; with fine thread, it results in an interesting textured line (Figure 235).

234   235

Double Buttonhole Stitch

This stitch, formed by two rows of Buttonhole Stitches facing each other, makes an attractive outline or edging. Work the first row from left to right. At the end of the row, turn your work around and work the second row, fitting it between the arms of the first row (Figures 236, 237). This makes a simple, effective border with countless uses. It looks well in any weight of thread, curves well, and is a good way to follow line designs.

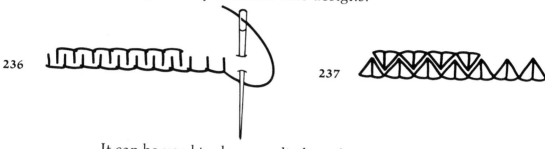

It can be used to decorate little girls' dresses. An embroideress I know in Monaco buys inexpensive white blouses for her little girls and transforms them into lovely creations with a few rows of stitches in bright colors around the collar and down the front. Try making up a border design with the initials of a child's name. Most letters can be treated this way (Figures 238-240). For fine designs, use three stands of six-stranded cotton or pearl cotton in size 8 with lines ⅛ inch apart.

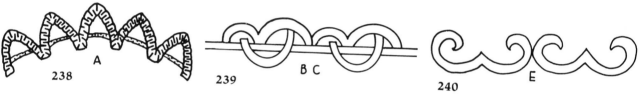

I like to make line designs in the center of colored linen tablecloths and embroider them in white with Double Buttonhole Stitch. I use pearl cotton in size 5 between lines about ¼ inch apart, or if the linen is heavy, pearl cotton in size 3 (Figure 241). It is quick and very satisfying to work. A hoop should be used.

Whipped Buttonhole Stitch

A single edge of Buttonhole Stitches can be whipped with contrasting color (Figures 242, 243). This is a good way to join edges. Work a row of Buttonhole Stitches on each edge; then whip them together (Figures 244, 245). It is an effective way of joining the seams in a child's bonnet.

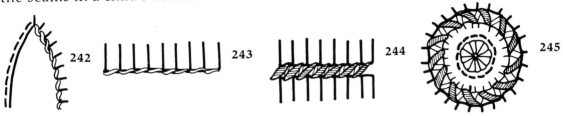

Raised Edge Buttonhole Stitch

This is a useful stitch in creative embroidery. In its closely worked, conventional form, it produces a strong, neat, raised edge for a border. It curves well, and can follow any line.

Used in freehand stitcheries, the stitch can be varied. The arms can be placed perpendicular to the edge or slanting, and can vary in length. They can be worked close together for floral or leaf shapes, or be slightly spaced for line treatment. The stitch looks best when the arms are not too far apart; the spacing depends on the weight and type of threads used. This is a versatile stitch with a distinctive character which will grow on you as you use it.

Work from left to right or from top down (Figure 246). Bring the needle and thread out at A. Go in at B, above A, and come out at C, next to A. Before pulling through, hold the thread from A to the left and up with your left thumb. Pass the thread leading from the eye of the needle from left to right under the point of the needle; sung up and pull through. Repeat, holding the thread from C to the left and up; insert at D, come out at E, and so on. When the stitch is worked so that B is close to C, a rich textured outline is produced. Done in this way it is an excellent stitch to work over the very edge of materials.

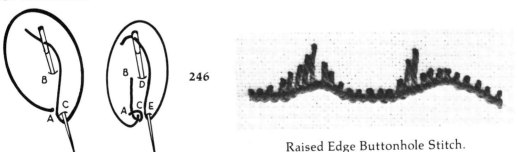

Raised Edge Buttonhole Stitch.

Buttonhole Filling

In filling shapes, the Buttonhole Stitches can be worked solidly or spaced in overlapping rows. They can be worked horizontally, diagonally, or can follow the movement of the shape (Figures 247-253). Successive rows are worked just above the middle of the edge of each stitch of the previous row.

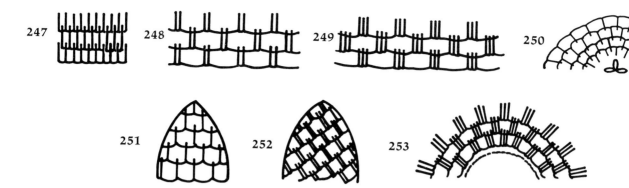

247   248   249   250

251   252   253

Up and Down Buttonhole Stitch

This is a Buttonhole Stitch with an accent (Figures 254-260). It makes a rich looking edge. When worked in a circle or semicircle, the result is an effective and quickly worked flower or design. Using pearl cotton in size 5, start as you would a regular Buttonhole Stitch at A (Figure 254). Holding the thread down with the left thumb, insert the needle at B. Come out near A at C, with the needle over the thread coming from A to form a loop. Pull through. Insert the needle at D, close to C, and take a straight upward stitch coming out at E, close to B. Pull through gently. Slip the point of the needle downward under the small horizontal bar between CD, and draw through. This constitutes the first pair of parallel stitches.

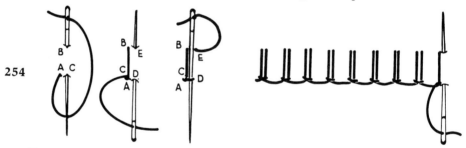

254

From now on, you will be working parallel pairs of stitches with a space between the pairs. For the second pair—a little farther to the right—hold the thread down with the left thumb and insert the needle downward as you did for the first pair from B to C, with the point of the needle over the thread coming from under CD. The second stitch of the pair is worked upward as you did from D to E. Slip the needle under the small horizontal bar just before drawing it completely through and give a slight pull to the thread which comes out at E. The little horizontal bar will fall neatly in place.

In Spain, the stitch is used as a lacy edging, with a loop between the parallel stitches (Figure 255).

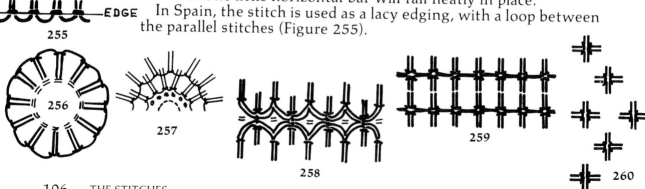

255   EDGE

256   257   258   259   260

Double Up and Down Stitch

You will find many uses for this stitch (Figure 261). It makes a neat edge over a small hem, around place mats, or on the edge of a collar. Several rows with intervals between them, worked with heavy threads, would make a beautiful band around a skirt. You might slip a gold cord under the pairs of stitches.

261 262

Up and Down Buttonhole Filling Stitch

Overlapping rows are used to fill a shape (Figure 262). The spaces between the pairs of stitches can be filled with a variety of stitches in contrasting colors.

Feather Stitches

This is a large family of stitches with countless variations. The stitches can be single, double, triple, interlaced, taken straight, or at a slant. They can be used for borders, outlines, light filling of shapes, and to represent grasses, ferns, and leaves. Long a popular form of embroidery, Feather Stitches are widely used to adorn clothing, especially children's clothes.

Straight Feather Stitch

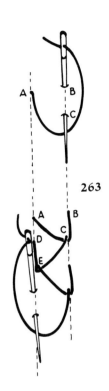

263

The Straight Feather Stitch is basically a Buttonhole Stitch taken alternately from one side to the other.

Work from the top down, or if you find it easier, from right to left between two parallel lines (Figure 263). Bring the needle and thread out at A on the left line. Holding the thread down with your left thumb, insert the needle at B on the right line, slightly higher than A. Come out at C in a straight line. Loop the thread under the needle from left to right and pull through.

Looping the thread toward the left side and holding it down with your thumb, take a stitch opposite C at D, and come out at E, straight down. Loop the thread under the needle from right to left, and pull through. Repeat this stitch from side to side. For borders, aim at regularity with stitches of equal size. For the last stitch, anchor down with a small stitch below the loop.

Closed Feather Stitch

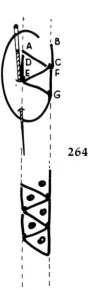

264

This stitch makes an attractive border with great decorative potentials. Start as in the Straight Feather Stitch, but insert at D, very close to A (Figure 264). Come out at E; insert at F, very close to C, and come out at G. Plan your distances so that C is opposite the midpoint of AE, and E opposite the midpoint of CG. Try a French Knot or a Seed Stitch in the triangles formed, using a different value or a contrasting color.

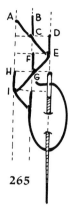

Straight Double Feather Stitch

Work on three parallel lines (Figure 265). Two stitches are taken to the right, alternately with two to the left. Your work will be easier and more regular if you insert the needle exactly opposite the spot where it last came out (D opposite C, F opposite E), and pick up equal amounts of material.

265

Straight Triple Feather Stitch

Work on four parallel lines, and take three stitches alternately to the right and left (Figure 266).

266

Slanted Feather Stitch

This stitch is also known as the Thorn Stitch and the Briar Stitch. It is worked on the same principle as the Straight Feather Stitch, but with a slanting stitch from B to C, D to E, and so forth (Figure 267). Different angles will produce different effects.

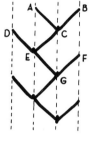

Work on four parallel lines. Try it with the three spaces of equal size, and also with the center space smaller than the other two. Note that D is opposite C, F opposite E, and so forth.

When the Slanted Feather Stitch is worked in a heavy thread, with small stitches close together and no material showing, the result is a decorative braid.

267

Slanted Feather Stitch Variations

268

The Slanted Feather Stitch can be used as a foundation for wheat ears or grasses (Figure 268). In the intervals between the stitches, place Detached Chain Stitches with the anchoring stitch pointing out.

In some provinces of Hungary, an attractive variation of the Slanted Feather Stitch is called the Rosemary Stitch. It is worked between two parallel lines of Chain Stitch, with each Feather Stitch going through the center of each chain. The result is a beautiful border. Feather Stitch over Herringbone works well, too.

There is no limit to where your imagination can lead you. After you have acquired freedom by working between parallel lines, try curving lines and interlacing rows (Figure 269). Start with a row of Slanted Feather Stitches, then interlace a second row with a thread of a different color or a lighter value of the same color. Six-stranded cotton creates a rich effect.

Lace ac over CE, ce under EG, eg over GI, gi under IK, and so on. You may want to add a few Straight Stitches or Detached Chain stitches in the first shade used, or in a third shade. Or you might place berries of individual French Knots, or several small knots, inside the V shapes.

269

Double and Triple Slanted Feather Stitches

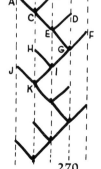

Instead of taking one slanting stitch on alternate sides as in the regular Slanted Feather Stitch, try taking two or three stitches (Figure 270). Note that D is opposite C, F opposite E, and H opposite G.

270

Long-Armed Feather Stitch or Spine Stitch

This is a Slanted Feather Stitch worked on three lines with both the left and the right stitch coming out on the center line forming a spine. It is an easy and effective way of filling leaf shapes, the spine becoming the center vein of the leaf (Figure 271). Make sure that D is opposite C, F opposite E, and so forth.

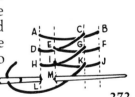

271

Cretan Stitch

The Cretan Stitch is full of surprises. It is an easy, relaxing stitch, which lends itself to completely different and elaborate variations. Once you have acquired the rhythm, you will have fun experimenting with different threads. Although it can be worked as a border, the Cretan Stitch is most frequently used to fill shapes, as it adapts easily to varying widths. If the shape to be filled is large, several rows can be worked side by side.

In English-speaking countries, the Cretan Stitch is named after the island of Crete where, for centuries, bright embroidered skirts have been worked in it. It is also widely used in Persian embroidery and is called the "Persian Stitch" in France.

The basic Cretan Stitch is worked with straight horizontal stitches evenly spaced (Figure 272). It can be worked from top down or from left to right. Bring the needle and thread out at A on the left side. Insert the needle at B; take a small horizontal stitch and come out at C, with the thread from A looped under the needle. Pull through. Insert at D on the opposite side, and come out at E, with the thread looped under. Continue from side to side with the needle always pointing from the outside edge inward.

For a leaf form, bring the needle and thread out at A, at the apex of the shape (Figure 273). Insert at B, on the right side. Take a small horizontal stitch to C, with the thread looped under the point of the needle. On the left side take a stitch from D to E, with the thread looped under. The stitches taken from B to C and from D to E are always about the same size. The distance from B to F and from D to H should also be equal.

272

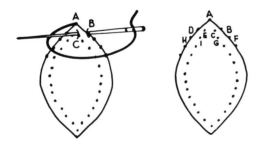

273

Closed Cretan Stitch

This is the form of Cretan Stitch most frequently seen on seventeenth and eighteenth century Cretan skirts. It gives a compact effect. To work it, follow the steps of the Cretan Stitch (Figure 272), but with stitches close together. There should be no open space between BF and AD.

274

Slanted Cretan Stitch

When the Cretan Stitch is worked slanted and spaced, it becomes a Slanted Feather Stitch or Long-Armed Feather Stitch. It is sometimes referred to as Cretan Feather. Take even slanting stitches from B to C and D to E, leaving a small space between rows (Figure 274).

To work Cretan Stitches slanted and closed, make rows of stitches close together, with no spaces between B and F, or D and H.

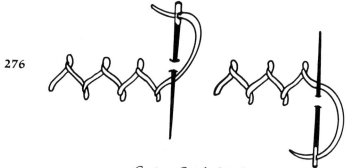

275

Cretan Stitch Filling

Large shapes can be filled with Cretan Stitches by working diagonal rows of horizontal, spaced stitches (Figure 275).

Open Cretan Stitch

This form of Cretan Stitch is useful for borders, using one or several rows. It is worked from left to right (Figure 276). Whatever side you are working on, the needle always points from outside in, passing over the thread to form a loop. Try three rows worked in dark, medium and light values of the same color. Rows can also be worked so that they cross each other. (See Cretan Stitch sampler, page 112.)

276

277

278

Cretan Catch Stitch

In the Cretan Catch Stitch, a vertical stitch alternates with a horizontal Herringbone Stitch (Figure 277). It lends itself to endless variations. In Figure 278, the top edge outlines a shape.

Laced Cretan Stitch

This stitch is also known as the Interlaced Band Stitch and the Double Pekinese Stitch. The Cretan Stitch is interlaced over two parallel rows of stitches such as Back, Holbein or Running Stitches. The stitches of these two rows must be of equal length, and be placed so that the midpoints of the stitches in one row are opposite the ends of the stitches in the second row (Figure 279).

279

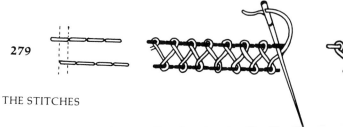

Border detail of an eighteenth century skirt from the island of Crete. It is embroidered in bright colored silks on handloomed cloth of linen warp and cotton weft. The stitches used are the Closed Cretan, Closed Herringbone, Outline, Chain, Square Chain, and Satin. The double-tailed mermaid with her dogs, the scrolls, the carnations, and the birds are typical Cretan designs of the seventeenth and eighteenth centuries. (Courtesy of Textile Museum, Washington, D.C.)

The interlacing is usually worked from left to right. The lacing thread should not be pulled too tight and no material is picked up. The needle picks up the Back Stitch from outside in and is pulled over the thread.

If the Back Stitches are small or if several stitches are taken in each Back Stitch, the effect is a solid braid; if they are larger, a more open effect is obtained. Try using two values of the same color.

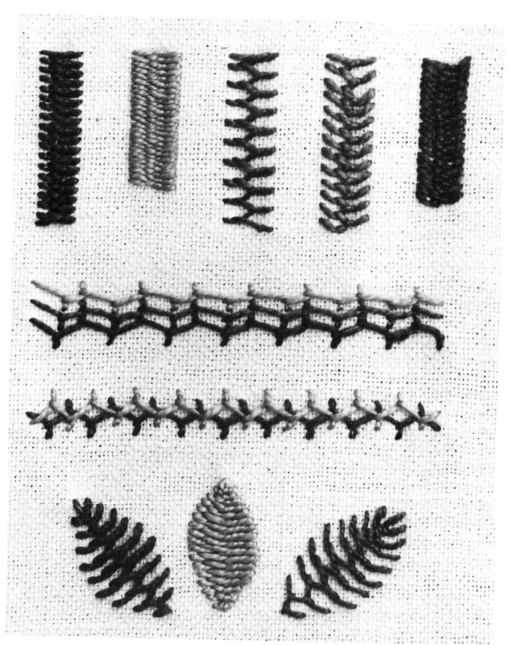

Cretan Stitch sampler worked by Pat Beaver, ninth grade, Holy Names Academy, Seattle, Washington.

280

Fly Stitch

The Fly Stitch is sometimes called the Tied Stitch or the Y Stitch (Figure 280). It is a useful versatile stitch for borders, filling, powdering, and representing plant forms.

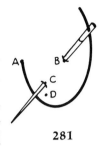

Bring the needle and thread out at A (Figure 281). Hold the thread down with the thumb. Insert at B, coming out below at C. Pull through over the loop. Anchor the thread down at D.

281

The stitch can be worked in single detached units, horizontally "holding hands," or vertically. The anchoring stitch can be very small or quite long. For a solid filling, the anchoring stitch is small and the stitches are close together. The stitch can also be anchored with a Chain Stitch, a French Knot, or a Bullion Knot. If three small stitches are used instead of one, it becomes a Crown Stitch (Figure 282).

   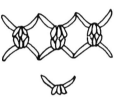

282

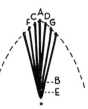

For a leaf filling (Figure 283), start with a Straight Stitch from the apex at A to B, coming out at C. Insert at D, forming a loop, and come out again at B. Anchor the loop just below B at E. Start again, coming out at F, going in at G, coming out at E, and so on. The anchoring threads form the vein of the leaf.

283

Whipped and Interlaced Fly Stitch

The Fly Stitch can also be whipped or interlaced with a thread of a different color or with metallic threads, around the arms and around the anchoring stitch (Figures 284, 285). It is a good stitch for enlarging borders, and works well in conjunction with other stitches, with or without variations in color. There is an affinity between the Fly Stitch and the Detached Chain Stitch (Figures 286–289).

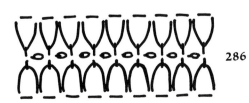 284

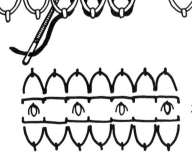

285

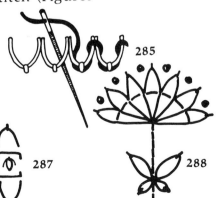

286

287

288

289

Try a border of two rows of Fly Stitches almost "holding hands," with the stems of the Y touching; use a light shade. Work a horizontal row of Detached Chain Stitches between the rows, in a dark shade of the same color. Outline the border with a row of Running Stitches in the dark shade. Worked in pearl cotton in size 5 on cotton homespun, it makes an attractive border for place mats or cushions (Figure 290).

290

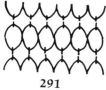

291

Fly Stitch Filling

First work a row of regular Fly Stitches, spaced close together (Figure 291). Reverse the second row, with the tying stitches touching those of the first row. The third row repeats the first, the fourth the second, and so on. Rows of Fly Stitches can be worked on top of each other, using different weights of thread (Figure 292).

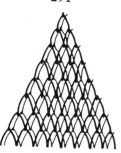

292

Fly and Two Ties

The French call this stitch "Point Etrusque", after Etruria, a province of ancient Italy where Tuscany is now. Researching the name opened a new door for me; it led me to the talented, sophisticated Etruscans whose civilization flourished between the 8th and 5th centuries *B.C.* The stitch, a Fly Stitch variation, can be seen in designs on old Etruscan pottery. I named it Fly and Two Ties because of its structure.

Start with a Fly Stitch, A to B to C (Figure 293), but instead of a straight anchoring stitch, go down diagonally to D under B, then up at E under A, and back down at F. This can be repeated as independent units. It can be worked horizontally (Figure 294), going from F up at B, with the stitches joining arms and legs. It can

293

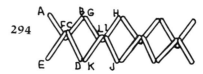

294

be worked vertically (Figure 295) going from F up at G, and so on. I like to overlap vertical rows (Figure 296), using several values of one color for each row or for each two rows. In freehand stitcheries, the stitch can be distorted in one direction or another, joining arms and legs. You can start with nine strands of floss in your needle and gradually take off one or two strands at a time until you are working with only one.

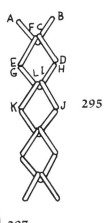

295

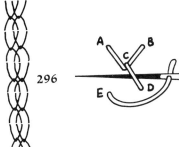

296

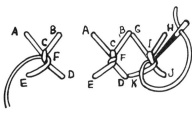

297

I found a twisted version of the Fly and Two Ties on a piece from Sri Lanka (Figure 297). After coming up at E, the needle slides under CD; the thread then twists around CD and goes down at F. Try elongating it, overlapping it or having the legs closer together (Figure 298). These stitches are sometimes further enriched by adding small Back Stitches, Seed Stitches or little Detached Chains between the arms or legs.

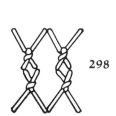

298

Zigzag Fly Stitch

I found this Zigzag Fly Stitch on a Palestinian blouse of closely woven black cotton bought in Haifa in 1918. It is embroidered with twisted silk of a weight similar to pearl cotton size 8, in eight colors with fascinating stitches and motifs. On the blouse, the Zigzag Fly is very fine, only ⅛ inch wide, about seven points to the inch, the colors changing about every two inches. I had not seen the stitch before. It is effective, especially when worked wider with heavier threads. Depending on the effect you want, use pearl cotton size 5 or size 3, working between two lines ¼ inch apart. There is a distinct rhythm which works up quickly.

Work downward. Come up on the left line at A (Figure 299). With the thread circling to the right, go down at B on the same line above A, with a space between AB. Come up at C, diagonally on the right side. With the thread looped from left to right under the point of the needle, pull through. Circle the thread to the left, go down at D, above C, over the two previous arms, and come up at E on the left line. With the thread looped from right to left under the point of the needle, pull through, and so on. The back looks like a Herringbone Stitch.

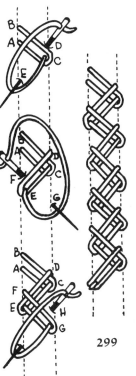

299

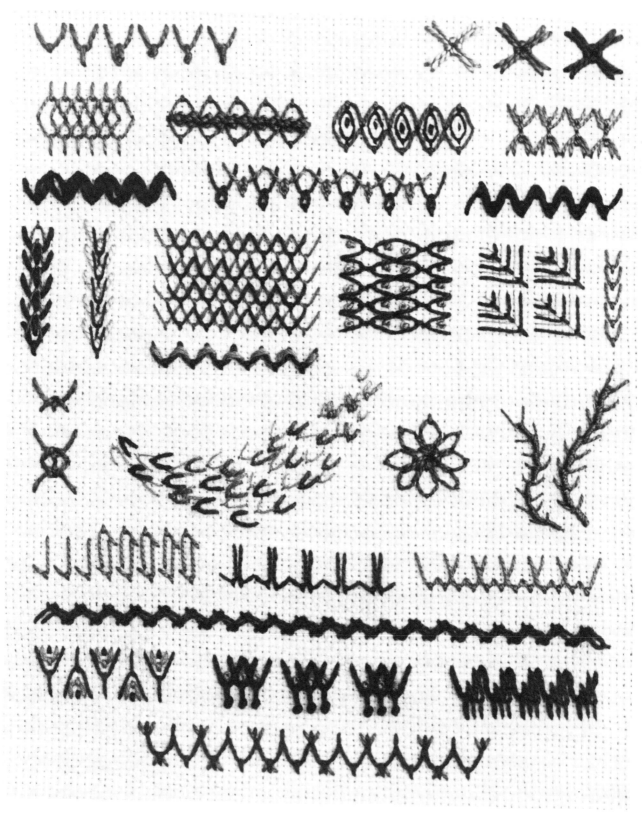

Fly Stitch sampler with variations. (Worked and photographed by the author.)

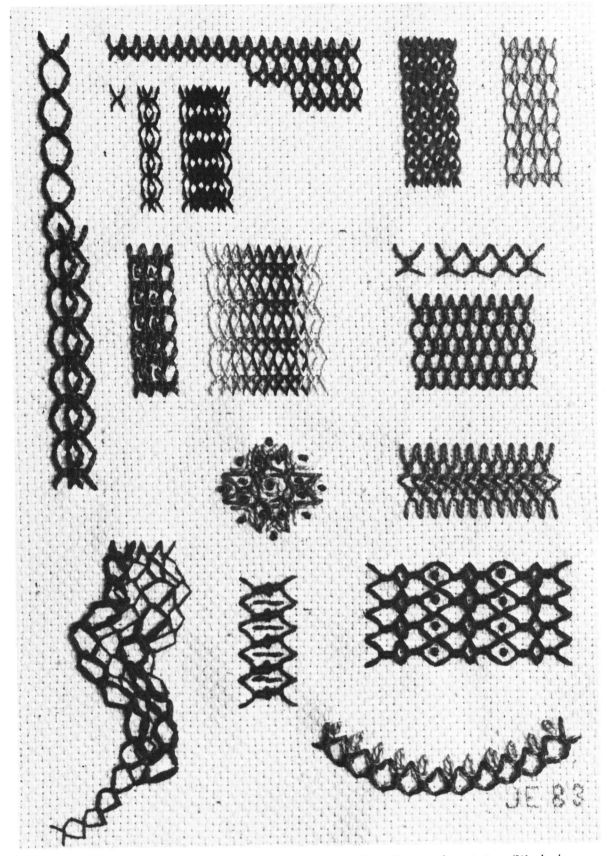

Sampler of Fly and Two Ties and of Twisted Fly and Two Ties, with variation. (Worked and photographed by the author.)

Loop or Centipede Stitch

The Loop Stitch is a relaxed stitch with interesting texture well suited to spontaneous fillings. It is worked between two parallel lines for a border, or within the outlines of various shapes, such as a leaf. In Italy, it is called the Sienese Stitch because it is used a great deal by the women of Siena to fill shapes which are then outlined in Stem Stitch.

The Looped Stitch has a raised spine in the middle. It makes wonderful centipedes. You may not want to make centipedes, but think what fun a little girl might have embroidering a tray cloth for her mother with centipedes in bright colors scattered over it. The result might look like some contemporary paintings!

Use a hoop so as not to pucker the material. Work from right to left. Start in the center between parallel lines, and bring the needle and thread out at A (Figure 300). Insert the needle at B above and to the left of A, coming out at C below B, and pull through. Holding the thread to the left with your left thumb, and circling it up, slide the needle under AB, from right to left, without picking up material, and over the loop coming from C. Snug up gently. Insert at D, come out below at E, and pull through. Holding the thread to the left with the left thumb, slide the needle under the thread coming from D, from right to left, and then over the loop coming from E.

300

Ladder Stitch

The Ladder Stitch is used for filling shapes of varying widths (Figures 301-304). Work from the top down, using a hoop so as not to draw the material together. The rungs of the ladder can be worked very close together for a solid filling or, as far as practical, for a lacy effect.

To learn the stitch, use pearl cotton in size 5, with the rungs spaced about 1/16 inch apart. When you have acquired the rhythm, try using different weights of thread, and vary the distance between rungs.

Bring the needle and thread out at A on the left (Figure 301). Insert at B, about ½ inch from A on the right, and come out at C, just above AB and to the left of B. Pull through. Insert again at D, about 1/16 inch below B, and come out at E, 1/16 inch below A. Pull through. Slide the needle under the thread coming from A, pointing it downward and outward. Next, on the right, slide the needle upward under the two crossed threads coming from C and B. Pull through gently. Insert at F, and come out at G. Slide the needle behind the two crossed threads between E and A. On the right, slide the needle behind the crossed threads between F and D. Continue inserting the needle from right to left and sliding it behind crossed threads, first on the left and then on the right, to form a braid on each side of the ladder. End on the left side with a small stitch crossing the last stitch.

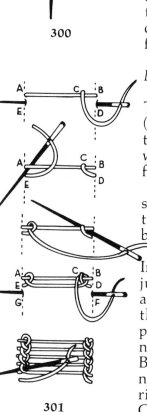

301

302

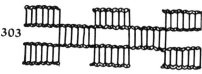

303

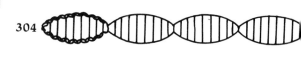

304

118

Vandyke Stitch

The Vandyke Stitch is versatile and fun to work, once you have mastered the rhythm. It is useful for outlines and makes a good edge for a furry animal. Well adapted to borders or fillings, it is especially good for leaf shapes, branches, and stems. It is most effective when worked with heavy soft cotton threads. A hoop is advisable to keep the material from puckering.

Learn first to work it symmetrically with arms on both sides. Then work it with arms on one side only, or on alternate sides, with the length of the arms varying according to your needs. Or you can have no arms at all, at which point the Vandyke Stitch becomes a raised braid, useful for line effects.

It is worked from top down. Bring the needle and thread out at A (Figure 305). Insert at B, about ⅜ inch higher, to the right. Taking a small stitch under, come out to the left at C. Pull through. Insert at D, opposite A. Bring the needle out at E, below A. Without picking up the material, slide the needle from right to left under the crossed threads AB and CD. Snug up the thread very gently, pulling it up. If you pull too tight, the braid loses its beauty.

Insert at F, below D, coming out at G, below E. Slide the needle under the last two crossed threads coming from E and F, and so on. If the slant starts to flatten out, pick up a small amount of material behind the crossed threads. However, you may like the effect of horizontal arms. Try working the stitch with arms on one side only and also without any arms for a raised braid. In the latter case, instead of taking a long horizontal stitch under the material from D to E, make the stitch the same width as CB and directly below it. C would be in line with A and D in line with B.

305

306

Scroll Stitch

The Scroll Stitch lends itself to imaginative uses. It is suitable for borders, outlines, and fillings. In addition to single textured lines, varied effects can be obtained by working several rows close together. Staggered knots at regular intervals give a feeling of motion, and may be used effectively to express flowing water. I used Scroll Stitches on the mural "Indians and Buffalos" as a filling for the buffalos to express jerky running (see pages 230-231).

Different patterns are obtained by varying the space between rows. The knots can be placed evenly under each other, staggered, or facing each other (Figure 306). Use twisted type theads such as pearl cotton in size 3 or 5. Single strand soft-twisted embroidery cottons with no sheen create interesting textures. Stranded cottons are not effective for this stitch.

Work from left to right. Bring the needle and thread out at A (Figure 307). With the thread to the right and above the line to be covered, insert the needle at B, and come out at C, taking a small slanting stitch just above and below the line. The thread from A circles around the needle, first from left to right behind the eye of the needle, then from right to left under the point of the needle. Snug up the thread and pull through. The stitches should be taken at even intervals.

307

Chain Stitch sampler worked by Katherine Johnson, ninth grade, Holy Names Academy, Seattle, Washington.

CHAINED STITCHES

Introduction

Chained stitches, the third main family of stitches, are basically closed loops. Most chained stitches are formed with the working thread looped under the needle from left to right; some are worked with the thread looped from right to left, and others with the thread twisted over, then under the point of the needle.

Stitches of the chained family can be used with equal success for lines or for fillings. They are not only beautiful but are also quick to work and economical of thread since the larger part of the thread stays on the surface of the material.

The people of Asia have long used these decorative stitches with great skill and artistry. However, instead of working the basic Chain Stitch with a needle, they frequently use a fine hook. This is called "Tambour embroidery," a technique introduced into Europe in the middle of the eighteenth century, probably from China. The material is stretched on a tambour frame (these round hoops originated in China) or a rectangular frame, and the working thread is held below the hoops in the left hand. The thread is brought through to the surface of the material from below with a fine hook called an ahri, held in the right hand. Some craftsmen hold the material in their hands and use the ahri without a hoop. Many of India's and Pakistan's Chain Stitch embroideries, from rugs to fine veils, are worked in this manner.

Experienced craftsmen can work rows of simple Chain Stitch very quickly, using a continuous thread. The use of a hook in place of a needle makes frequent starts with a new thread unnecessary. This explains why the backs of Chinese and Indian embroideries show a continuous thread. Smaller, more regular stitches are possible with a hook, as well as great speed. The use of a hook, however, is limited to the basic Chain Stitch. The many other beautiful chain stitches must be worked with a needle. Some of them look complicated, but they are not, once you understand the technique of each particular stitch.

Chain Stitch

The basic Chain Stitch is one of the simplest and most effective ways to follow an outline, or to make a filling worked in close rows. It is worked from top down.

Bring the needle and thread out at the top of the line at A (Figure 308). Holding the thread down with the left thumb, insert again in the same hole at A and come out at B. Loop the thread under the needle from left to right. Draw through.

308

121

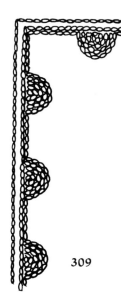

Insert at B inside the loop in the same hole, keeping the thread down to the left. Come out at C, loop the thread under the needle, and draw through. In some countries, the needle is not inserted in the same hole, or is sometimes inserted just above or to the right of A, B, C—which gives the stitch a character all its own. They also work the stitch away from the body rather than toward it. The beauty lies in even stitches; too much tension causes puckers, and too little is untidy. The back should present a row of even Back Stitches.

The Chain Stitch is effective whatever thickness of thread is used, from heavy pearl cotton down to the finest thread. Try using pearl cotton in sizes 3, 5, and 8. The border in Figure 309 was worked in pearl cotton in size 8. For a very fine outline use two threads of six-stranded cotton; for a dainty effect on a colored material, try fine white crochet thread or even white sewing thread.

309

Chain Stitch Variations

There are countless variations of the Chain Stitch. Try the following:

1. Vary the length of the stitches (Figure 310).

310

2. Work a row of Back Stitches over a row of Chain Stitches in a contrasting color (Figure 311). 311

3. Work one row of Chain Stitches on top of another, using heavy thread for the first row and fine thread in a contrasting color for the second row (Figure 312). 312

4. Work a row of Chain Stitches in heavy thread and add a Detached Chain Stitch inside each chain in a contrasting color. To further enrich the texture, in the center of each Detached Chain add a Seed Stitch in a third color or in the first color (Figure 313). 313

Whipped Chain Stitch

A row of Chain Stitches can be whipped in a contrasting color. The whipping thread does not go through the material except at the beginning and at the end. The whipping can be on one or both sides of the Chain Stitches, or the whole Chain can be whipped (Figure 314).

Two close rows of Chain Stitches whipped make a beautiful border. Try whipping pearl cotton in size 5 with a heavy gold thread or cord for a rich effect (Figure 315). You can add width to the whipped rows by working Fly Stitches on each side (Figure 316).

314

315

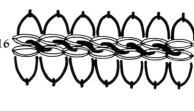

316

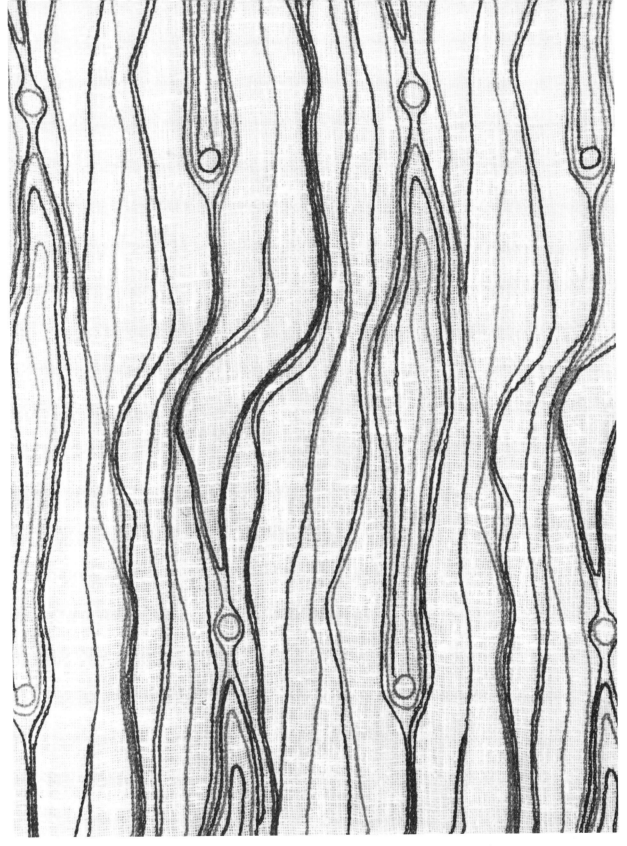

Detail of embroidered curtain in Chain Stitch by Bodil Weyde Anderson. The curtain was awarded a prize at the 1962 Danish Handcraft Guild's embroidery competition in Copenhagen. (Courtesy of Danish Handcraft Guild.)

Threaded Chain Stitch

A row of Chain Stitches can be threaded in one direction from right to left, or in both directions by turning your work around when you reach the end of the row, and threading back to the starting point (Figure 317). The lacing thread should be heavier and darker than the chain thread for contrast; it should be gently relaxed and not pulled tight.

317 ⟨image⟩ 318 ⟨image⟩

Chain and Buttonhole Band

Work three rows of Chain Stitches close together. Over these work two rows of Buttonhole Stitches, without going through the material (Figure 318). The buttonhole headings meet in the center. This produces a wide band that is useful in heavy types of embroidery. The Chain and Buttonhole Band is used frequently in Italian Parma embroidery.

Interlaced Chain Stitch

There is an interesting story behind this little known Chain Stitch variation. It was taught to me as a child by an old embroideress in Brittany. I have come across a description of it only once, in an English publication. The writer attributed the stitch to Mary Queen of Scots because it is found in some of the embroideries she worked in the sixteenth century during her long imprisonment. This stitch, however, is not typically English or Scotch but is characteristic of Breton embroidery.

In all probability, Mary Stuart learned this variation at the French court where she lived for 14 years as a young girl. We know that her mother-in-law, Catherine de Medici, an expert with the needle, personally taught Mary to embroider. In those days, embroidery played an important part in the education of girls, and was the favorite pastime of the ladies of the court. The royal ladies not only embroidered their clothes lavishly, but also turned out elaborate church vestments.

A generation earlier, Anne Duchess of Brittany had married the King of France and come to live at the French court. Fiercely attached to the traditions of Brittany, Anne brought with her, among other things, the embroidery so typical of that Duchy. I have no doubt that this beautiful stitch was treasured and taught at the court, and that Mary Stuart learned it there. Although it looks elaborate, the stitch is quite easy and quick to work. You will find it well worth the effort to learn.

Start with a row of wide Chain Stitches, worked somewhat loosely. In pearl cotton, size 5, the size of the stitches measured on the back should be from 3/16 to ¼ inch in length.

When this row is completed, start again at A, with a thread of a different shade or value, or with a gold cord, working from top down or from left to right (Figure 319).

Lace this thread loosely from outside in, from B to C, under the right side of the second chain, without going through the material, and with the lacing lying just outside the first chain. Then go back

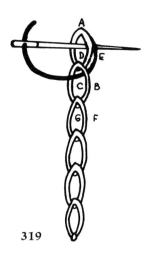

319

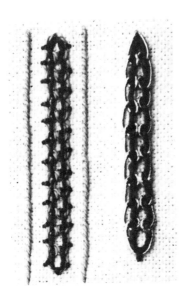

Interlaced Chain Stitch. One is interlaced with two shades of pearl cotton in size 5; the other with gold metallic cord.

320

under the first chain from inside out, from D to E, under both the chain and the previous lacing. Go over and behind the third chain, fro F to G, from outside in; then go back to the second chain from inside out, going under both the chain and the lacing. Go over to the fourth chain, and so on.

Start again at A and repeat on the left side (Figure 320). The interlacing thread should not be pulled tight but should lie against the center chain. Make sure that the two center stitches of the lacing lie side by side, not one on top of the other.

At the end, bring the lacing thread to the back, behind the last chain. The braid looks beautiful just this way, but you may want to anchor down the lacing thread, especially if the article has to be laundered. Using a thread of the same shade as the lacing thread or the center chain, take small anchoring stitches at E, B, F, and so forth.

For a complete border, a row of Outline Stitches or fine Chain Stitches can be worked on either side.

Chain Outlined Satin Stitch

In Hungarian embroidery, the shapes to be filled with Satin Stitch are often first outlined in Chain Stitch (Figure 321). The Satin Stitch is then worked through the middle of the Chain Stitches which raises the Satin Stitches from the surface of the material. The outside of the Chain Stitches provides an attractive, finished edge.

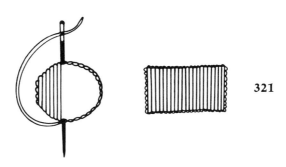

321

Zigzag Chain

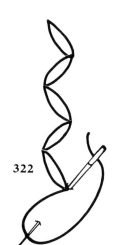

322

A Zigzag Chain is an ordinary Chain worked between two imaginary parallel lines, with each Chain Stitch slanting at an angle to the previous one (Figure 322). It is worked from top down, or right to left. As the needle starts each chain, pierce the previous loop so as to anchor it.

323

324

This stitch makes a rich border, especially with other stitches added (Figures 323, 324), and takes well to a curved line. For example, work it in wool at the base of the neck of a child's sweater. On a royal blue sweater, work the Zigzag in red wool, adding a row of Outline Stitches in red at the inner edge, a yellow Seed Stitch inside the loops, and a green Seed Stitch in the triangles between (Figure 325).

325

Worked between lines very close together, the Zigzag Chain creates a beautiful textured line stitch with a knotted appearance. Try the Zigzag Chain in pearl cotton in size 5 between lines 1/16 inch apart, and also with three strands of six-stranded cotton.

Detached Chain (Single Chain)

326

As its name describes, the Detached Chain is a series of individual Chain Stitches, each one anchored separately with a small stitch just below the bottom of the loop. Another name for the Detached Chain is the Lazy Daisy Stitch. The stitch has many decorative uses (Figures 326-330). Worked very small and tight, it takes on the appearance of a knot which it replaces to advantage in objects which must be frequently laundered. Try anchoring the chain with a knot (Figure 331).

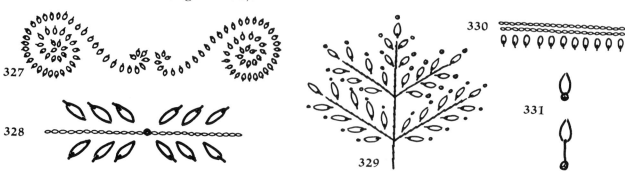

327

328

329

330

331

Detached Chain Filling

The Detached Chain Stitch is especially well suited to filling shapes (Figure 332). For a quick filling, work Detached Chains followed by a Running Stitch. In the second row, make Running Stitches, and in the third row, Running Stitches followed by a Detached Chain, alternating with the first row. Repeat the second row, and then the first row (Figure 333).

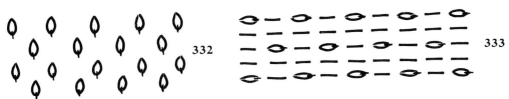

Slipped Detached Chain

This simple stitch has many decorative possibilities, especially when heavy threads are used. Little girls enjoy working it and often call it the "tulip stitch." Try it in a heavy royal blue thread such as pearl cotton in size 3, with a red Seed Stitch in size 5 in the center.

Start with a Detached Chain. As you anchor it at C, come out at D (Figure 334). Slip the needle through the anchoring thread. Pull through and go in at E. The slipped stitch can form a right angle, or it can hug the chain for a different effect. Try slipping two stitches under the anchoring thread. For a continuous vertical line, go from E to C.

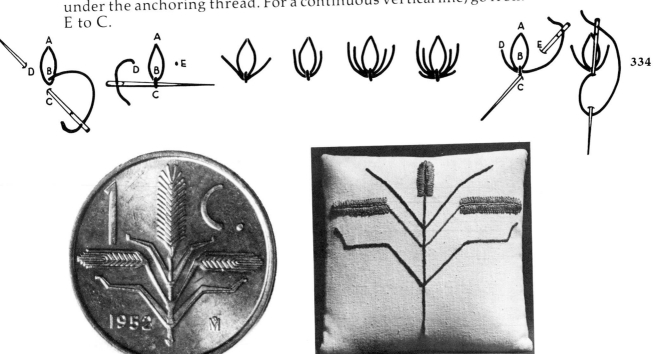

Cushion by Susan Weber (right). On her first attempt at designing after finishing her Chain Stitch sampler, ninth grade Susan Weber used the stylized wheat design she found on a Mexican coin (left). She worked it in heavy dull gold Detached Chain Stitch for the ears and two shades of green Outline Stitch for the stalks on off-white cotton homespun. (Photograph of coin by Colonel Martin D. McAllister.)

Slipped Detached Chain Filling

Work the Slipped Detached Chain with the slipped stitch at a right angle in alternating rows (Figure 335). Think how cheerful it would look on the yoke of a little girl's dress.

335

Long-Armed Detached Chain

When the anchoring stitch is long instead of short, the stitch becomes the Long-Armed Detached Chain (Figure 336).

336

Russian Chain

337

In Russian embroidery, Detached Chains are used in groups of three, both vertically and horizontally (Figure 337). The design shown in Figure 338 was found on an old Palestinian blouse. The lower chain is worked first; it is anchored by the upper middle chain and followed by the side chains.

338

Single Threaded Detached Chain

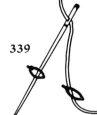

339

Detached Chains can be used instead of Running Stitches or Seed Stitches for lacing in and out (Figure 339). For an interesting effect, use threads of different weights and color.

Double Threaded Detached Chain

After the Detached Chains have been laced one way, turn your work around and lace back (Figure 340). For variety in texture, I like to add French Knots, Seed Stitches, or Cross Stitches between the Detached Chains.

340

Detached Chain Flowers

Detached Chains can be worked various ways in groups to form the petals of a flower, seed pods, and leaves (Figure 341). Remember to vary the weight of the threads you use.

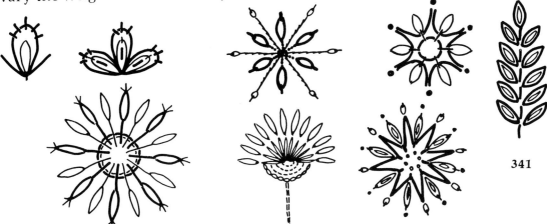

341

Tête de Boeuf Stitch

This stitch is described by its French name which means ox head. It is started by a Fly Stitch which forms the horns (Figure 342). The anchoring stitch is a Detached Chain. It can be used detached in groups, or in rows "holding hands." It can also be worked into little rabbits (Figure 343).

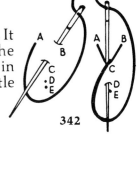

342

343

Tête de Boeuf Filling

An attractive filling is made by rows of Tête de Boeuf Stitches which should be worked alternately (Figure 344).

344

Chain and Fly Stitch

The Chain and Fly Stitch starts with a Tête de Boeuf. As the chain is anchored, the needle comes out to the side, ready for the next Fly and Chain (Figure 345). The stitch can be whipped or laced. Although worked differently, it resembles the Slipped Detached Chain and the Wheat Ear Stitch. Try the various ways of working the stitch and see which texture looks best for your purpose.

345

Long-Stemmed Zigzag Chain

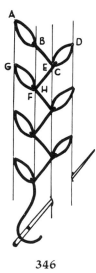

346

The Long-Stemmed Zigzag Chain is formed by a series of Long-Stemmed Detached Chains anchored diagonally. Work the chain between parallel lines, straight or curved. This is a good border stitch; work it from the top down.

Start a slanting chain at A (Figure 346). Anchor the chain from B to C. Work a second chain starting opposite B, at D. Slant from D to E, and anchor at F. A third chain starts opposite E at G, and so on.

Try it with more slant, with D halfway between A and B, and G halfway between D and C (Figure 347). After you have practiced between straight parallel lines, try working between curved lines (Figure 348).

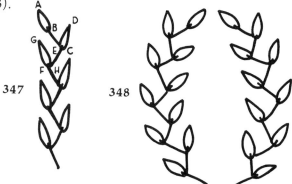

347   348

Petal Stitch

The Petal Stitch is useful for floral or leaf shapes and other growing forms. It curves easily and can be worked in a circle to create flowers.

Work from right to left. To learn the stitch, practice between parallel lines about ¼ inch apart, using pearl cotton in size 5.

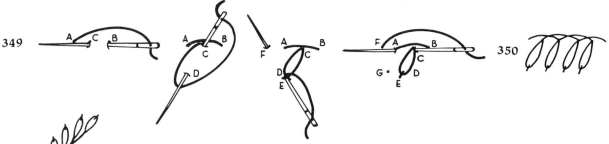

349   350

351

352

Bring the needle and thread out at A (Figure 349). Holding the thread up with the left thumb, insert at B (about ¼ inch from A) and come out at C (halfway between A and B). Pull through. Holding the thread down with the left thumb, insert again at C and come out at D (directly below A). Pass the thread under the point of the needle from left to right, making a chain. Pull through. Anchor the chain from D to E, coming out at F (about ⅛ inch to the left of A). Holding the thread up, insert at C and come out at A. Pull through. Make a chain from A to G, and so on (Figure 350).

After you have mastered the stitch, practice on curved lines, varying the weight of the thread and the size of the chain (Figure 351). Size 8 creates a dainty pattern, size 3 a bold, striking effect. Worked in a circle, Petal Stitch makes effective sun flowers (Figure 352).

Tray cloth designed and worked by the author. This typical Basque design, worked in Basque Stitch with scrolls and "cross," was inspired by eighteenth-century chests in the Musée Basque in Bayonne. The Basque Knot is used for the edge.

Basque Stitch

This stitch is a delightful, quick way to embroider scrolls, and to outline designs and floral shapes. It has a light and airy feeling. The stitch is found in old embroideries of the Basque country, as well as those of Spain, Portugal, and Southern France. It probably dates back to the days when the Moors were established in Spain.

The Basque Stitch resembles the Petal Stitch but it is lighter and quicker to work. It is particularly effective worked in white on colored cloth. Traditionally, it is worked in white on a blue-green cloth, or with red thread on green cloth.

The women of Ninhue, Chile, whose picturesque embroideries of village scenes are becoming well known, were taught the Basque Stitch by Carmen de Orrego-Salas from an early printing of this book. They devised an ingenious variation, using it spaced around edges much like a Blanket Stitch.

Work from left to right. Bring the needle and thread out at A (Figure 353). With the thread towards the right, insert the needle in front of the thread coming from A, from B to C. In pearl cotton in size 5, BC should be about ⅛ inch. Before pulling the needle through, take the thread from behind the needle; cross it over the needle, and then under the point from left to right, forming a loop. Snug up the thread and pull through. Insert the needle at D below the loop; come out at E (to the left of B), just under the thread between A and B. Pull through. Repeat, inserting the needle in front of the thread a little farther to the right, from F to G. The distance between E and F is determined by the thickness of the thead; it can vary from ⅛ inch with size 5 to ¼ inch with heavier threads. Circle the thread from behind the needle, crossing it over the needle and then under the point from left to right, and so on.

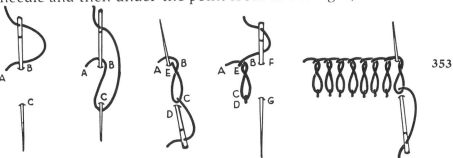

353

131

The Basque Knot, very similar to the Palestrina Knot, is frequently used in conjunction with the Basque Stitch. After considerable research, I found that some Basque people give the name of "Basque Stitch" to the chained stitch described here; others to the knotted stitch. One French magazine gives the name to the former, another to the latter. The Curator of the Musée Basque in Bayonne, France, confirms that the true Basque Stitch is the chained stitch and that the Basque Knot, of more recent origin, is a variation of the Palestrina Knot.

Checkered Chain Stitch

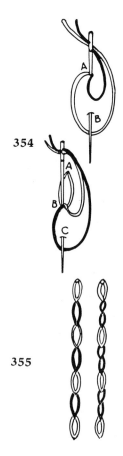

Children call this stitch the Magic Chain. It is worked with two threads of contrasting colors in the needle at the same time, from top down.

Start as an ordinary chain, but instead of looping both threads under the needle, loop them alternately one at a time. Bring the needle out at A, with both threads together (Figure 354). Insert again at A, come out at B, but loop only one thread under the needle to make the chain. The other thread stays above the needle. Pull both threads through.

Reverse for the next chain, inserting at B and coming out at C, with the other thread under the needle making the chain.

Try different patterns and different sizes (Figure 355).

Checkered Chain and Chain sampler by the author. This border is inspired by skirt borders from northeast India. A red and white Checkered Chain is used in the center, followed by regular Chain Stitch on each side in royal blue, yellow, red, and white.

Square Chain or Open Chain

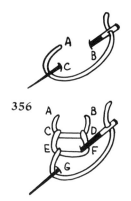

This versatile stitch is useful for borders and fillings, and is particularly well suited to lines and shapes of graduated widths (Figures 356, 357). However, it is advisable to work between parallel lines while you are learning the stitch. It can be filled with contrasting Flat Stitches, fine Chain Stitches, or French Knots, or a Running Stitch can be worked over it (Figure 357). Use it also for couching threads, tapes, cords, and so on.

Work from top down. Instead of making a chain with a vertical Straight Stitch as in a regular chain, take the stitch diagonally.

Bring the needle and thread out at A (Figure 356). Holding the thread down with the left thumb, insert the needle at B, to the right of A. Bring the needle and thread out diagonally at C (a little below A) at whatever width the stitch is to be. Loop the thread under the needle, and pull through, leaving it a little loose. Insert at D inside the loop, below B. Snug up the thread gently around the needle. Come out diagonally at E, below C, and loop the thread under the needle. Pull through, leaving it a little loose. Insert at F, and snug up the thread. Come out at G, and so on.

To end, make a small anchoring stitch in the last two corners, or one stitch in the center.

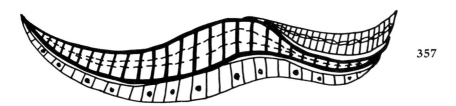

357

Detail of a pillow top from west Pakistan. The stylized floral motif is embroidered with silk in grayed shades of yellow and orange, worked in Square Chain. The stems and leaves, in grayed green, are outlined in black. The background is red silk with a grayed blue cast to it. (Courtesy of Costume and Textile Study Collection, University of Washington.)

Threaded Square Chain

In a number of cultures, the Square Chain is worked threaded, which I prefer to the regular Square Chain. It can be more easily increased or decreased in length and width. Work it in whatever direction is easiest for you—from left to right—from right to left, upward, or downward. Establish the most natural rhythm for you. On the back, the stitches should slant in the same direction for even tension.

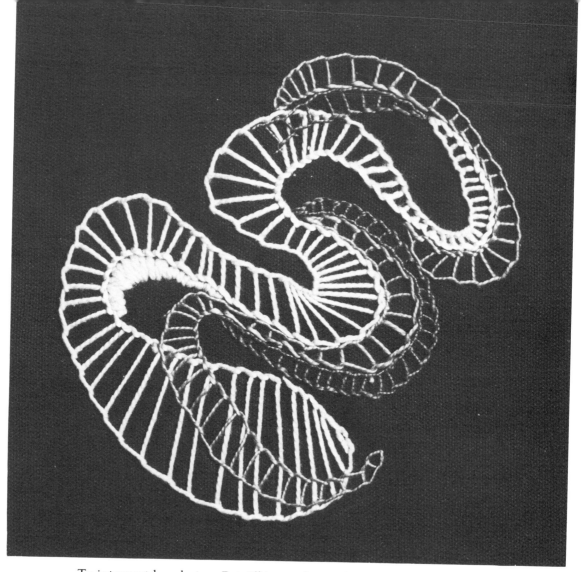

To interpret her design, Pat Albiston chose Threaded Square Chain because it follows curves easily and changes widths with great freedom. She used pearl cotton size 3 in several values of pink to plum on a midnight blue background.

Start with two small parallel stitches, one above the other, A to B, C to D (Figure 358). The distance between them determines the width of the chain. With pearl cotton size 5, try 3/16 inch. Come up at E and pull through. The distance CE determines the depth of the chain and whether or not cloth shows between stitches.

Slide the needle downward under DC and BA, without going through the cloth. Pull through. Go down at F, up at G. Pull through. Slide the needle under EC and FA. Go down at H, and up at I. If the cloth shows between stitches, the space can be filled with other stitches, knots, Single Chains, or Satin Stitches.

358

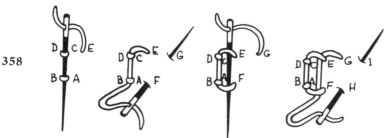

Closed Square Chain, Closed Threaded Square Chain

A characteristic stitch of India and Central Europe, the Closed Square Chain is worked with the bars close together so that the ground material does not show. It is sometimes mistakenly labeled a close Buttonhole Stitch (Figure 359).

Central Europeans call it the Small Writing Stitch or the Large Writing Stitch, depending on the width of the chain and the thickness of the thread. They work it very effectively to follow linear designs, using a soft cotton with no twist or shine. On a number of ethnic pieces that I have seen, the Closed Threaded Square Chain does not show slanting stitches on the back. Instead, they have minute stitches on the back of the edges that barely pick up the cloth. These were made by stitching away from the worker and threading the stitches alternately from side to side (Figure 360). It is much easier this way.

Yugoslavian pillow cover. Worked with red embroidery cotton on natural linen, it is embroidered on one side only in Closed Square Stitch (Large Writing Stitch). The size is 15¾ by 18½ inches. (Courtesy of Smithsonian Institution.)

359

360

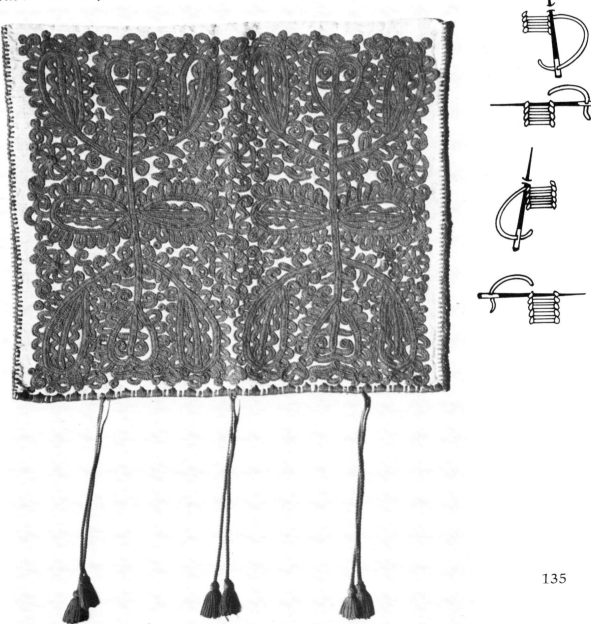

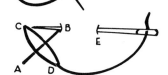

Chained Cross Stitch

This is a Cross Stitch with added texture. Work it over ¼ inch squares in pearl cotton sizes 3, 5, and 8. Each weight of thread creates a different effect.

Bring the needle and thread out at A (Figure 361). Insert diagonally at B, coming out at C. From C, make a Chain Stitch to D. Start again from D to E.

Chained Cross Stitch worked with pearl cotton in sizes 3, 5, and 8.

361

Double Chain, Closed Double Chain

The Double Chain is very similar to the Closed Feather Stitch, except that the needle is inserted inside rather than outside the loop. It makes an attractive border or wide outline; it can also be used to fill shapes of varied widths. Under different names, it is found on some of the earliest textiles—from Peru to India. Among the Turkoman nomads of Asia, the chain is worked so compactly as a ¼ inch wide outline that no cloth shows between the stitches, which appear to be horizontal. It is a Closed Double Chain. The Turkomans use a silk with a tight Z twist instead of the more usual S twist; this gives the embroidery its unique character.

Detail of a Turkoman coat.
(Courtesy of Kundus Gallery.)

Detail of cattle trapping embroidered by women of Gujarat, India, on silk cloth with silk threads. It is used to cover cattle during weddings and religious festivals. Note how the shape is filled with closely worked Double Chain. Other Chain Stitches are used, with Back Stitches for the outline. The body of the cow is grayed yellow; the saddle is dark blue-green and cream. The outline is black with a cream Back Stitch edge. (Courtesy of Costume and Textile Study Collection, University of Washington.)

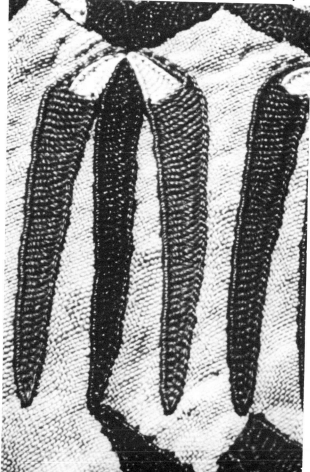

While in European and English-speaking countries Double Chain is normally worked toward you, many other cultures—including the Turkomans—work it with the needle pointed away from them. If you would like to try this method, follow the diagram with the book turned around. Otherwise, working from the top down (Figure 362), bring the needle and thread up at A, on the left side of two imaginary parallel lines. Insert at B on the right line, coming out at C, with the thread looped under the needle. Pull through. Holding the thread over to the left, go down again at A, and come up at D, in line with A, looping the thread from right to left under the needle. Pull through. Go down at C inside the loop and come up at E below C, this time looping the thread under the needle from left to right. Continue, looping alternately from right to left and from left to right, inserting the needle inside each chain. To end, anchor with a small stitch. Texture and interest can be added by working a small Back Stitch or French Knot in the middle of each chain in a blending or contrasting color.

362

Twisted Chain

This is a useful stitch for lines and borders with a textured look. Work from top down as a Chain Stitch, but instead of reinserting the needle in the same hole, insert it slightly to the left of the previous stitch, crossing over the thread. Bring the needle and thread out at A on the line to be covered (Figure 363). Holding the thread down with the thumb, insert at B, to the left of A. Slant downward and come out at C, below A. Loop the thread over the needle, and then under the point of the needle from left to right. Pull through. Insert at D, to the left of the loop, coming out at E, and so on. Close parallel rows of Twisted Chain create interesting textures (Figure 364). They can also be twisted in alternate directions, or a spine can be added (Figure 365).

363

364

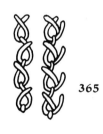

365

Detached Twisted Chain

This stitch is used in the same way as the plain Detached Chain and is well suited to textured powdering. Each stitch is anchored with a small stitch (Figure 366).

366

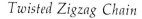

For rich, beautifully textured lines (straight or curved), this stitch, sometimes called Spanish Stitch, has no equal. One of my favorite stitches, it may well become one of yours too. Once you understand the mechanics, the work goes very quickly and looks like appliquéd braid. However, remember not to pull the thread too tightly or the material will pucker.

Heavy twisted threads such as pearl cotton in size 3 or 5 create the best effect. The stitch looks beautiful worked in cotton, silk or wool around the neck of a pullover or down the front of a cardigan.

Work from top down. To practice draw three parallel lines with a blue pencil on your doodling cloth. The distance between the lines will vary according to the thickness of the thread you use; the heavier the thread, the greater the distance. With size 3, the distance between the outside lines would be about ⅜ inch; with size 5, ¼ inch.

Using size 3, bring the needle and thread out at A, to the right of the center line (Figure 367). Holding the thread down and to the left, insert at B, on the center line. Come out at C, on the left line, ⅛ inch lower. Draw the thread from A over the needle, and then under the point as in a Twisted Chain. Snug up and pull through gently.

Insert the needle at D, just to the right of B, coming out at E on the right line, ¼ inch lower. (From now on, the points will be ¼ inch apart if you use size 3 or about 3/16 inch with size 5).

Before pulling the needle through, twist the thread from C over and under the needle as before, and pull through. Insert the needle at F on the center line just above the CE thread and come out at G, ¼ inch below C. Twist the thread over and under, and pull through.

Insert at H, just above the EG thread, coming out at I, and so on. Continue alternately from side to side, remembering not to pull the thread too tight.

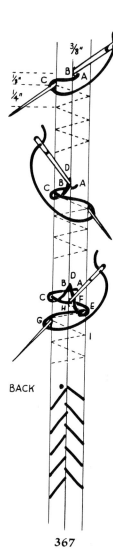

BACK

367

Twisted Zigzag Chain. Both examples are worked with pearl cotton in size 3, one with stitches 1/4 inch apart, the other with stitches 3/16 inch apart.

Rosette Chain

The Rosette Chain is a decorative line stitch based on the Twisted Chain. It creates a textured, knotty-looking line, good for edging curved geometrical shapes such as circles or for outlining small flower shapes.

Work from right to left. Try to keep the distance between B and C under ¼ inch. When using pearl cotton size 5, the best results are obtained when the distance is not over ⅛ inch. The heavier the thread is the greater the distance can be. Too great a distance tends to make the loops slip a little, in which case they should be anchored with a small stitch.

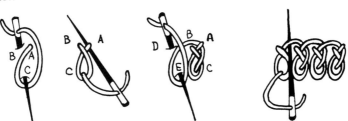

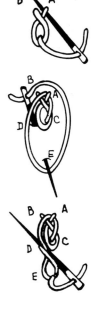

368

Bring the needle and thread out at A (Figure 368). Hold the thread to the left with the left thumb; insert the needle at B, to the left of A above the thread, and come up at C. Loop the thread over the needle, then under it from left to right. Pull through the loop. You have completed a Twisted Chain.

Pass the needle and thread upward under the thread coming from A, without piercing the cloth. Pull through. Holding the thread down to the left, insert the needle at D, above the thread, coming out at E. With the thread over, then under the needle, pull through. Pass the needle under the thread to the left of B, and so on. The most effective results occur when DB and BC are close enough that the rosettes touch each other.

I found a beautiful variation of the stitch on a seventeenth century Spanish bodice. It was used as a nubby edging, heavy silk on linen. The Rosette Chain was worked snug, vertically (Figure 369), with stitches close together. BC was ⅛ inch. The silk was about the weight of pearl cotton size 5. D was opposite C and under B; E was under C.

On another Spanish bodice, small square flowers worked with Rosette Chain were scattered closely over the yoke. Each had four petals made up of two rosettes ⅛ inch each (Figure 370). The petals can also be worked in a circle (Figure 371). The diagrams are greatly enlarged. The flowers are barely ½ inch in diameter.

369

370

371

Cable Chain

For line and filling, the Cable Chain is an attractive variation of the plain Chain Stitch. It has great decorative possibilities, and is well worth learning (Figures 372, 373).

Work from top down. Bring the needle and thread out at the top of the line at A (Figure 372). With the left thumb, hold the thread straight down. Pass the needle from right to left under the thread, lifting it a little. Then point the needle counter-clockwise towards the right over the thread, so that the thread is twisted around the needle.

Still holding the thread under the thumb, insert the needle just below A at B, coming out at C, the length of a chain. Snug up the thread. Loop it from left to right under the point of the needle, and pull through. You now have a link and a chain.

To make the next link, repeat what you just did from A to B, holding the thread down and passing the needle from right to left under the thread, and so forth. Insert the needle just below C (same spacing as between A and B, Figure 372) and continue with a chain. It takes a little time to master the process of "under, then over" the thread, but it soon becomes as easy as the plain Chain Stitch.

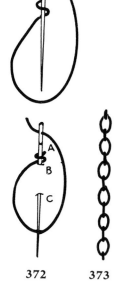

372   373

374

Double Cable Chain

This is worked with two rows side by side with the inner loops whipped together in contrasting color or gold. It produces a rich braid effect (Figure 374).

Slipped Cable Chain

Work a row of Cable Chain, then slip one or two stitches under the links (Figure 375). The result is similar to the Slipped Detached Chain. The advantage of the Slipped Cable Chain is that threads of different color, weight, or texture can be used for the slipped stitch. You can use contrasting colors or three tones of the same color. A second slipped stitch can be worked separately with a different thread. Slipped Cable Chain is beautiful in white, with the slipped stitch a heavier weight. The center of the chains can be ornamented with a Seed Stitch or French Knot. You will find many uses for this decorative stitch.

375

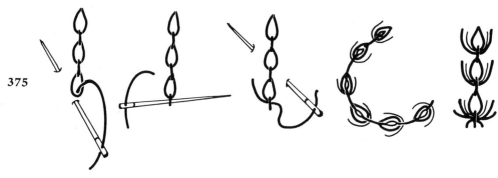

Zigzag Cable Chain

This stitch has decorative possibilities, either in single rows or in several alternating parallel rows. It is effective, whatever type of thread is used.

Work from top down or right to left, as a Cable Chain, but with each chain at a right angle to the last chain, with the small link in a straight line (Figures 376, 377).

Split Stitch

The Split Stitch is useful for fine outlines and delicate fillings. It was used in medieval embroidery for subtle shadings by working silk floss in rows of different shades. An untwisted thread is most suitable because it can be easily split in two by the needle.

Work from left to right, much as a Stem Stitch. Bring the needle out at A (Figure 378). Keeping the thread down, go in at B and come out at C, between A and B on the line to be covered; split the thread in the middle with the needle as it comes out at C. Go in at D, and out at B, splitting the thread. CD is the same size as AB. Continue, going in at E, and so forth.

Nineteenth century Chinese embroidery. It shows a magnificent use of the Split Stitch. The spaced, textured lines should inspire many uses in contemporary stitcheries. (Courtesy of Smithsonian Institution.)

When the Split Stitch is used for fine delicate shading, the direction of the stitch is important. It should be worked in close rows, all in the same direction. For a similar effect, see the Long Stem Stitch, page 72. The Split stitch can also be worked with heavy threads to express textured stems.

Pueblo Stitch, Split Laid Work

The full name of the Pueblo Stitch is Pueblo Embroidery Technique. It has been used for centuries by the Pueblo Indians of New Mexico and Arizona, producing embroideries with their own distinctive character. The yarns are kept almost completely on the right side; only small dots appear on the reverse side. It was taught to me at the Institute of American Indian Arts in Santa Fe, New Mexico, by American Indian artist Josephine Wapp. She works the stitch without a hoop to fill large spaces of traditional Pueblo Indian designs, using her own homespun naturally dyed two-ply yarns, which split exactly in two. The rows are worked close to each other as a solid, slightly textured filling. I prefer it to the Split Stitch.

Mrs. Wapp says she likes to work it "usually from bottom up and back down." Perhaps you will too. I find it easier to work from left to right, turning the work around after the first stitch of the next row back. Use a sharp needle. Pearl cottons are easy to work with, as are two-ply crewel or four-ply yarns. For fine work, use two strands of stranded cotton.

Bring the needle and thread up at A and pull through. With your left thumb holding the thread flat on the cloth, go down at B and come up at C, taking the smallest possible horizontal stitch from right to left and splitting the yarn in two with the point of the needle (Figure 379). As you come up, watch the tension so that the cloth does not pucker. Pull through.

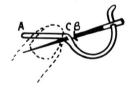

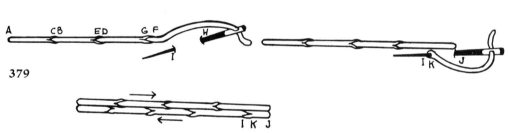

379

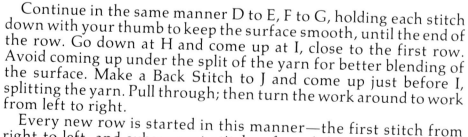

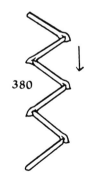

380

Continue in the same manner D to E, F to G, holding each stitch down with your thumb to keep the surface smooth, until the end of the row. Go down at H and come up at I, close to the first row. Avoid coming up under the split of the yarn for better blending of the surface. Make a Back Stitch to J and come up just before I, splitting the yarn. Pull through; then turn the work around to work from left to right.

Every new row is started in this manner—the first stitch from right to left, and subsequent stitches from left to right with the work turned around. Unless you want to create a pattern, vary the places where you split the yarns.

An interesting variation I made up while doodling with needle and thread is to work the Pueblo Stitch zigzag (Figure 380). If you make the zigzags very short, you will get an unusual textured line.

Detached Split Stitch

The Detached Split Stitch has a relaxed, irregular texture which makes it useful in freehand stitcheries. Practice it with stranded or loosely twisted threads. Unexpected effects are obtained by simultaneously threading in the needle two or more strands of different weights or colors, and mixing textures such as cotton and silk.

The appearance of the stitch varies with the way each stitch is tied (Figure 381). The anchoring stitch which comes out at C should be relaxed and not pulled tightly. It can be short or long; it can be placed alongside the Split Stitch or down the center at D. If it is tied on the side, parallel to the Split Stitch and worked in circles, flower shapes with intersting textures result. If it is tied down the center, the tying thread CD should be as long as AB; otherwise the stitch would look like a Detached Chain.

For an interesting textured filling, try working the Detached Split Stitch as you would Long and Short, with the tying stitch down the center.

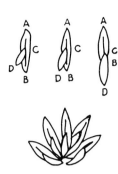

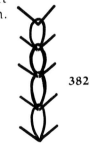

381

Wheat Ear Stitch

The Wheat Ear is a versatile stitch. You can create textured lines and interesting borders with it. Used singly as a powdering, it looks like winged seeds. It can be worked into little rabbits and of course as the name implies, it makes realistic ears of wheat (Figures 382-384).

Work from top down. Start with two Straight Stitches at an angle to each other (Figure 382). Bring the needle and thread out at A. Insert at B, coming out at C. Insert at D, to the right of A. Go under and come out at E. Pass the needle behind the first two stitches without picking up material. Insert at E. Bring the needle out at F. Go in again at E, coming out at G. Go back in at E, then under and out at H. Pass the thread behind the last two Straight Stitches (not behind the chain). Insert at H, come out at I, and so on.

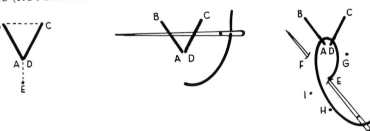

382

For borders, work parallel rows "holding hands," with either Running Stitches between (Figure 385), or detached stitches facing each other (Figure 386).

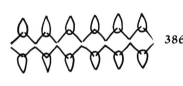

383   384   385   386

Whipped or Laced Wheat Ear Stitch

The Wheat Ear Stitch can also be whipped or laced for added color and texture. Whipping the two sides of the chains with gold thread, or lacing the straight stitches is effective.

Spine Chain

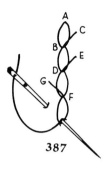

387

The Spine Chain is a useful stitch for textured lines (straight or curved), stylized stems, tree trunks, and so forth. Although it looks like the Wheat Ear Stitch with only one arm, it is worked differently. (See "Beetle," the ends of the legs, page 232.)

Work from top down (Figure 387). Bring the needle and thread out at A. Holding the thread down, insert again at A and come out at B, looping the thread under the needle to make a plain chain. Pull through. Insert at C, coming out at B inside the chain. Make the next chain from B to D. Go in at E and out at D. Make the next chain from D to F. Try the spine on the other side from G to F, and so on. Also work the spines either all on one side or alternating (Figure 388).

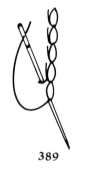

388

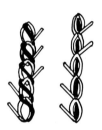

389

A different effect is obtained by placing the spine close and parallel to one side of the chain. It gives an interesting textured chain (Figure 389).

Whipped or Laced Spine Chain

Try other variations, such as whipping or lacing the Spine Chain, or any of the plain Chain Stitch variations. A Seed Stitch inside the chain adds texture (Figure 390).

390

Broad Chain and Heavy Chain

These two stitches are basically the same. For the Broad Chain, the needle takes a step backwards, sliding under the last chain made; for the Heavy Chain, the needle slides under the last two chains made. They both follow curves easily and have a firm braid effect. They are useful in creating pictures with the needle when a heavy but smooth textured line is needed. For instance, in abstract design, a feeling of variation in depth is obtained by combining lines of simple Chain with lines of Broad Chain, using a Heavy Chain for a strong foreground. Try them for stems, organic forms, monograms, and so forth. In their conventional form, Broad and Heavy Chain are worked with a firm heavy thread and the stitches must be small. There is, however, a free-flowing quality to the Broad Chain worked with long stitches, which makes it well suited to spontaneous expression.

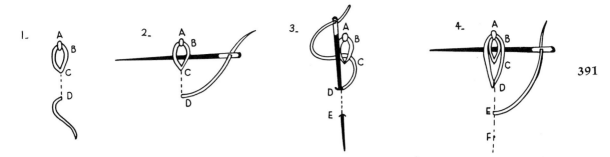

Work from top down. Bring the needle and thread out at A (Figure 391-1). Take a small Straight Stitch, inserting at B. Come out at C. Pass the needle behind the first stitch AB, without picking up the material. (It may be easier for you to use the eye end of the needle to pass behind.) Insert again at C. This forms the first chain. Come out at D. Both stitches are the same up to this point.

For a Broad Chain, pass the needle behind chain BC, going in at D and out at E (Figure 391-2, 3). Pass the needle behind chain CD, going in at E, and so on.

For a Heavy Chain, when the needle comes out from C to D, pass the needle again behind AB, going in at D, and out at E (Figure 391-4). Pass the needle behind chains BC and BD, two chains back, going in at E and out at F. Pass the needle behind the last two chains without picking up material, and so on. The Heavy Chain gives a raised corded effect. The mane of the "Lion" is worked in Heavy Chain (title page).

Hungarian Braided Chain

For a wide, thick textured line, this Braided Chain is more effective than the Heavy Chain. Like all chains, it curves well. Work it with a heavy thread such as pearl cotton in size 3 or a similar weight.

Start as a Heavy Chain, but instead of going behind two chain stitches, go behind the *inside* chain only, without picking up any material (Figure 392). You will find your work easier if your needle picks up the inside chain before pulling the thread of the previous stitch completely through. You may also prefer to use the eye end of the needle to pick up the inside chain.

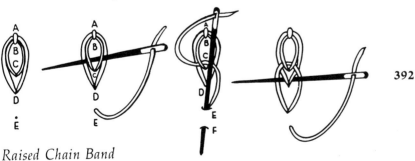

392

Raised Chain Band

This attractive textured band looks elaborate, but is quick and easy to embroider. It is worked with a tapestry needle over a foundation of horizontal Straight Stitches, their size and spacing depending on the thickness of the threads used. With pearl cotton in size 5, the horizontal stitches with be a scant ¼ inch wide and a scant ⅛ inch apart.

Raised Chain Band.

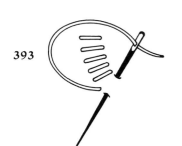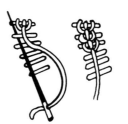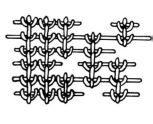

393

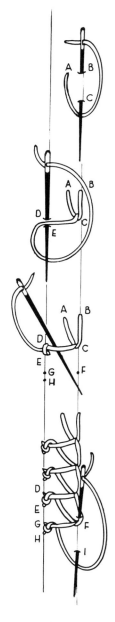

After laying the foundation stitches, bring the needle and thread out at A, just above the first horizontal stitch (Figure 393-1). Slide the needle under the first bar from below, coming out to the left without picking up any material. Pull through. Then slide the needle downward on the right side from above, still without picking up any material and with the point of the needle over the loop. Pull through and snug up gently, straight down the center. Continue, going under the second horizontal stitch, coming out to the left, and so on over every successive bar. Practice on your doodling cloth, varying the width of the horizontal stitches. These can show a little on each side, or they can be completely covered. If the horizontal stitches are wide enough, two or three rows of the chain can be worked side by side. The same principle can be used for a variety of raised stitches over a foundation of Straight Stitches.

Crested Chain

This is an attractive stitch, which looks like a Spanish braid, and is particularly suited to edgings. Well worth learning, it is not difficult. Use a twisted thread such as pearl cotton. Work from top down between parallel lines which can be either straight or curved. The distance between the lines depends on the thickness of the thread; with size 3, the lines are 3/8 inch apart; with size 5 about 5/16 inch; with size 8 about 1/4 inch.

Bring the needle and thread out at A, near the right side (Figure 394). Insert at B, on the line, coming out at C with the thread looped under. Take a small stitch on the left side, opposite C, from D to E. Pass the thread from C over the needle and then under it. Pull through. With the thread up, pass the needle downward under the thread between C and D, without picking up any material. With the thread down and to the left, insert the needle at C, coming out at F. Pass the thread under the needle from left to right. Pull through. Take a stitch from G to H, as from D to E, with the thread passing over the needle and then under it. Pull through. Don't forget to pass the needle downward under the thread between F and G; otherwise the effect would be lost. Watch the stitches on the back of the material to make sure that your lines remain parallel.

Crested
Chain.

394

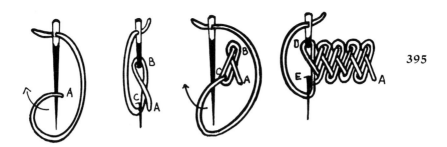

Braid Stitch

The Braid Stitch is best used on material that will not have to be laundered. Unless the stitches are worked close together, the loops tend to slip. Worked compactly, it makes a rich-textured border that curves easily and has a braided look. It has often been used on ecclesiastical embroidery. Use a firm twisted thread. You can draw parallel lines which will be covered, or you can pull a thread out. The width of the braid varies according to the weight of the thread. With pearl cotton size 3 or three-ply wool, the lines would be ¼ inch apart; with pearl cotton size 5, about ⅛ inch apart.

Work from right to left. Bring the needle up at A on the lower line (Figure 395). Hold the thread to the left with your thumb. Slide the needle downward under the thread without picking up any cloth. Turn the needle clockwise, passing over the held thread until you point to 12 o'clock. Hold the twist on the needle with your right index finger, and insert the needle at B on the top line slightly to the left of A, coming up at C on the lower line below B. Pull the thread snug around the needle. With the thread from RIGHT TO LEFT under the point of the needle, hold the stitch with the left thumb and pull through. Repeat, holding the thread from C to the left and so on. Go down at D, up at E. End with a small stitch over the last chain. An extended braid can be made by anchoring down the loops with Straight Stitches or Long-Stemmed Knots. When the spaces between AB and CD and between AC and CE are very close together—about 1/16 inch apart—a beautiful tight braid is obtained. It makes a rich-looking outline that curves easily. If you are working between straight lines with the grain of the material, pulling out two threads 1/16 inch apart not only makes your work easier but adds a lacy touch to the braid.

Detail of embroidered eighteenth century Chinese silk robe. The Chinese Knot is used here as a filling. Note the direction of the rows. The outline is a couched beaded cord. This piece also shows typical rows of couched gold thread. (Courtesy of Smithsonian Institution.)

KNOTTED STITCHES

Introduction

Knotted Stitches differ from all other stitches by their special irregular texture. The best known are two detached knots, the French Knot and the Bullion Knot. These are made by twisting the thread around the needle in series of separate units, either scattered over a surface or close together for a solid filling.

The other Knotted Stitches are worked in continuous rows with series of tightened loops on the surface of the material. They wear and launder better than the detached knots. All Knotted Stitches are useful for linear designs, straight or curved, as well as for filling shapes. Their raised, rough texture is particularly valuable for contrasts and accents.

French Knot

This stitch is used either in rows for lines, massed together for fillings, or singly for powdering. When using it for a line, work from right to left, or whatever direction seems easiest. A hoop to hold the material taut makes the work easier. Practice with a heavy thread, such as pearl cotton in size 3 or two strands in size 5, using a heavy needle.

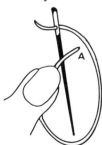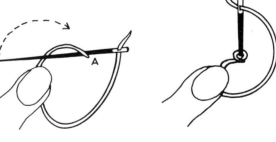

396

Bring the needle and thread out at A (Figure 396). Holding the thread down with your left thumb, about 1 inch from A, slip the point of the needle under the thread, straight down from above. Still holding the thread down, rotate the point of the needle clockwise over the held thread, making a half circle from six o'clock to twelve o'clock. The needle should then be pointing straight up, with the thread twisted once around it. Hold the twisted thread on the needle with the index finger of your right hand, and insert the point of the needle just above—close to A, but not exactly in the same hole. Snug up the thread around the needle gently and not too tightly. Push the needle through to the back of the material, sliding it through the twisted thread. Pull through. This forms a knot on the surface of the material. Repeat wherever the next knot is to be.

149

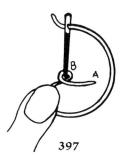

397

The neatest knots are made with one turn of the needle. For a heavier knot, use heavier thread or double your thread. For a fine knot, use finer thread and a finer needle. It takes practice to turn out well-rounded knots. You can circle the needle under the thread two or more times for heavier knots, but these have a tendency to be floppy. For borders, flowers, and stamens, you can also insert the point of the needle at B, a distance away from A, for a Long-Stemmed French Knot (Figure 397).

French Knot Border Stitch

398

This stitch makes a rich-looking and unusual border. Try it with pearl cotton in size 3 or 5. Use a hoop. It is worked from left to right between parallel lines ¼ inch apart. Starting on the upper line, bring the needle and thread out at A (Figure 398). Holding the thread down with your left thumb to make a loop, insert the needle at B—close to A—and come out at C on the lower line, with the thread under the needle from left to right. Pull through. Make a French Knot with a single twist, inserting at D, just outside the loop. Come out at E on the upper line, next to B. Holding the thread down to make a loop, insert the needle at F—close to E—and come out at G. Anchor the loop at H with a French Knot, as at CD, and so on. When the end of the border is reached, start back from right to left, making a French Knot with a single twist between the arms of each loop.

Interesting designs can be worked with the French Knot Border Stitch, either in rows or in circles. Figures 399 and 400 could be used on a place mat, and Figures 401 and 402 on the center of a table cloth. Figure 403 was inspired by a design on an embroidered shawl from Brittany. Figure 404 suggests floral shapes.

399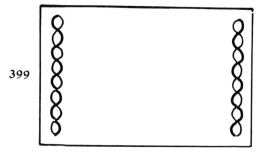

400

401

402

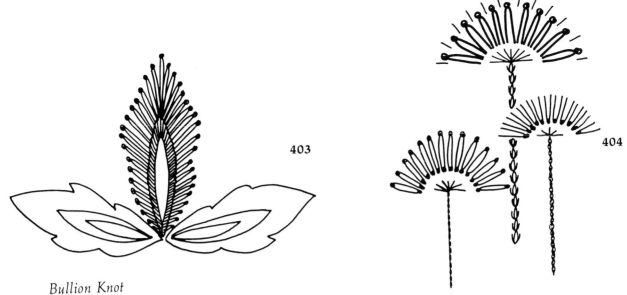

403

404

Bullion Knot

The Bullion Knot is useful for petals, leaves, and raised wheat grains. It is especially effective when massed in groups. When possible, use a long round eyed needle that does not have a bulge; it will be able to slip easily through the twisted thread (Milliner's needles answer this description.) Wind the thread around the heavier part of the needle, not the point; otherwise it will be difficult to pull the heavy part of the needle through.

Bring the needle and thread out at A (Figure 405). Insert at B, and come out again exactly at A, pulling the needle almost but not completely through. Hold the thread from A with the thumb and index finger of your right hand and gently wrap it over the needle from left to right, and then under as many times as are needed to cover the distance between A and B. The number of times depends on the weight of the thread. For instance, to make wheat grains using three strands of six-stranded cotton, you might wind fourteen or fifteen times.

With the thumb and index finger of the left hand holding the twists, pull the needle and thread through; gently ease and coax the thread through towards B, until the twists lie smoothly across AB. This takes practice. You may need to rub the underpart of the twists with the end of the needle to smooth them out. Insert the needle at B and pull through to complete the stitch. Figures 406 and 407 show how the Bullion Knot was used on a French linen table cloth embroidered around 1880.

For a Raised Bullion Knot forming an arched roll, wrap more thread around the needle than will cover the distance AB.

405

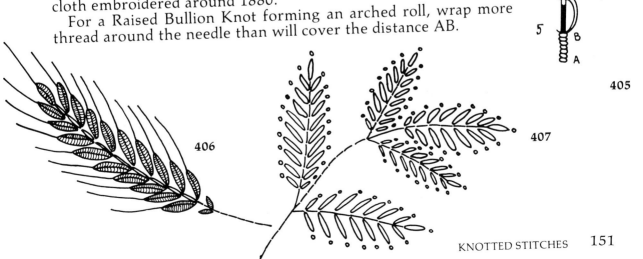

406

407

Long-Stemmed Bullion Knot

408

These have many decorative uses. They are particularly suitable for stamens. Used in a circle, the long stems can serve as a base for Ribbed Spider Web. Instead of going down at B in the last step for a regular Bullion Knot go down at C, farther away (Figure 408).

Chained Bullion

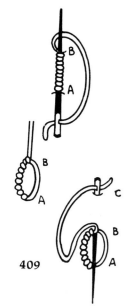

Another interesting variation, found on a piece from Syria, starts as a regular Bullion Knot, with a few more wrappings than needed to cover the distance AB. Once the coils have been lifted into place (Figure 405 1-4) do not go down at B. With the thread from B held up, go down at A and up at B (Figure 409). With the thread from left to right under the point of the needle, pull through, forming a chain. The stitches should be relaxed. Go down at C and come up at B inside the chain, with the needle almost but not quite through. Continue, wrapping the thread from B as many times as you did for the first stitch. There are many possible variations. Try working them in a zigzag (Figure 410), or in a plant shape (Figure 411).

409

410

411

Chinese Knot

The Chinese Knot is characteristic of the rich embroideries of China. It was taught to me by my grandmother when I was a child. Her brother, my great-uncle, worked for many years in China, where his wife learned the stitch. She taught it to my grandmother who taught it to me. This is the very way stitches were taught in the Middle Ages before books were printed; travelers passed them on to relatives at home who recorded them on samplers. I have come across only one description of the Chinese Knot, in an old issue of the English magazine, *The Embroideress.*

The Chinese Knot is similar to the French Knot, but on examining it closely you will see that each knot has more of a little stem coming out of it. This gives the stitch its own special character. In some of the most beautiful Chinese borders, the stitch is worked exclusively in close, continuous rows in the same direction, with variations in color intensity for delicate shading. It is used to fill shapes, with continuous flowing lines, much as the Chain Stitch is used, but the resulting texture is quite different.

The Chinese also used their knot to fill shapes outlined with couched threads or cords. When used this way, the stems are not as visible and are not as much part of the design.

The Chinese worked the stitch with silk. The British make a soft, twisted embroidery silk which is very similar to the Chinese silk with which I was taught the stitch.

In addition to providing an understanding of the nature and texture of Chinese Knot embroidery, the stitch should prove useful in contemporary embroidery. It is easier to work, neater looking, and launders better than the regular French Knot; it does not flop. An added advantage in working knots the Chinese way is that a frame or hoop is not essential.

Practice with heavy threads such as pearl cotton in size 3. You will find that a shape can be filled quickly. Experiment with the heaviest threads you have; jute string, for instance, creates unusual effects. Try rising vertical rows of knots for delightful growing forms, buds, and seeds.

Bring the needle and thread out at A (Figure 412). Holding the thread down to the left with the thumb and circling it up, pass the needle behind the thread without picking up any material. Take a small stitch inside the loop from B to C. The thread is behind the upper part of the needle but in front of the lower part. Snug up the thread, and pull through. Continue, holding the thread down and circling it up, with the needle going from D to E, and so on. Make each stitch close enough to the preceding ones that the knots lie side by side without space between. The second row is worked under the first row, also from right to left. The knots can be staggered.

Coral Knot

The Coral Knot is used for straight or curved lines—especially for decorative textured outlines—and for fillings. It is usually worked from right to left but can also be worked from left to right.

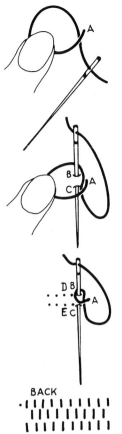

412

413

Bring the needle and thread out at A (Figure 413). Holding the thread down on the line to be covered with the left thumb, insert the needle just above the thread at B; take a small slanting stitch to just below the line, coming out at C. The thread goes over the point of the needle and then under it from left to right. Snug it up around the needle and pull through. Repeat for the next knot, and so on. The knots are usually taken at small, regular intervals. To make a knotted outline, make the knots close together.

In old English books, the slanting Coral Knot is called Snail Trail. The Coral Knot is also worked with BC straight up and down (Figure 414).

To make larger rounded knots, begin as above. After a knot is completed, slide the needle upward under AB; then circle the knot completely around and go down against the knot at D (Figure 415). Come up at E just under BC and pull the thread snug all around. Continue with the knots close to each other. They look like pearls (Figure 416). If you need a single pearl, go down under E.

414

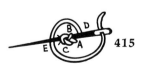

415

416

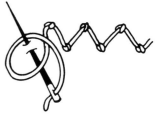
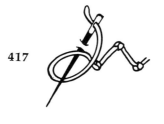

417

Coral Zigzag

The Coral Zigzag, used for borders, is worked in the same way as the Coral Stitch, but between two parallel lines with knots alternating from the upper to the lower line (Figure 417). The needle must always be inserted from outside in, the thread passing over, then under, the point.

Double or Palestrina Knot.

Double Knot or Palestrina Knot

In France, Switzerland and Italy, this beautiful stitch is called the Palestrina Knot after the town of Palestrina in Italy. This is a well-deserved name for the stitch; I would like to see it used everywhere. It is a handsome and easy way of working a knotted line with a beaded effect. Practical as well as decorative, it stays in place and is easy to launder and iron. It can also be used as a solid filling in the same way the Chinese used their knotted stitch.

The women of Palestrina use the stitch for linear designs, working close knots for curved lines and rows of knots outlined in Stem Stitch for straight lines. They also use the stitch to fill shapes. Important motifs such as flowers are filled with straight rows of the larger Palestrina Knots, separated by one line of Bokhara Couching. Smaller motifs such as buds or leaves are filled with the Small Palestrina Knot which is worked slightly differently; they are also separated by one line of Bokhara Couching. All the shapes are outlined in Stem Stitch. Occasionally, for a more solid contrast, the shapes are filled entirely with close Bokhara Stitch outlined in Stem Stitch.

In Palestrina the work is usually carried out in heavy threads, white on colored linen, or blue, dark red, or russet on white linen. A heavy pearl cotton thread produces the best results. The design shown in Figure 418 was inspired by a child's bib embroidered in Italy in white cotton thread on blue linen.

418

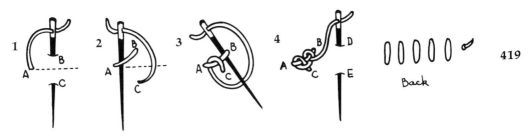

Work from left to right. Bring the needle and thread out at A on the line to be covered (Figure 419). Make a small slanting stitch, inserting at B above the line; come out at C below the line, with the needle straight up and down under the traced line. Pull through. The distance BC should equal AB for well-rounded knots close together. This distance will vary with the thickness of your threads.

Slip the needle from above, under the stitch just formed, without picking up material. Pull through. Keep the thread to the left of the stitch.

Slip the thread from above under the first stitch again, to the right of the first slipped thread which now goes under the needle, making a Buttonhole Stitch. Pull the thread gently so that it encircles the first stitch. Start the next slanting stitch to the right, inserting it at D and coming out at E. DE equals BC. For a single knot, go down at D (Figure 420). The distance between B and C and between D and E can be varied, keeping the thread relaxed, with the knot kept on the line to be covered (Figure 421). If B is well above the knot, it becomes a Long-Armed Palestrina; if C is well below the knot, it becomes a Long-Legged Palestrina. The extensions can vary in length and can also be on both sides, with the knot in the middle (see top of Palestrina Knot sampler).

421

You can make up many variations, as I have, while doodling with your needle. Here are a few:

Triple Palestrina

This is a beautiful thick knot with a third dimension (Figure 422). Repeat steps 2 and 3 of the basic Palestrina three times altogether under AB. Pull snug after the last buttonhole. It can be a single knot or several close together. Worked with a heavy thread such as pearl cotton size 3, the result is like a string of pearls.

Squared Palestrina

Think in terms of a square with ABC in three corners (Figure 423 step 1). Continue steps 2 and 3 as with the basic Palestrina. After the buttonhole to the right, pull the thread snug and go down in the fourth corner, making a knot in the center. For a continuous row, come up again at C.

422

423

155

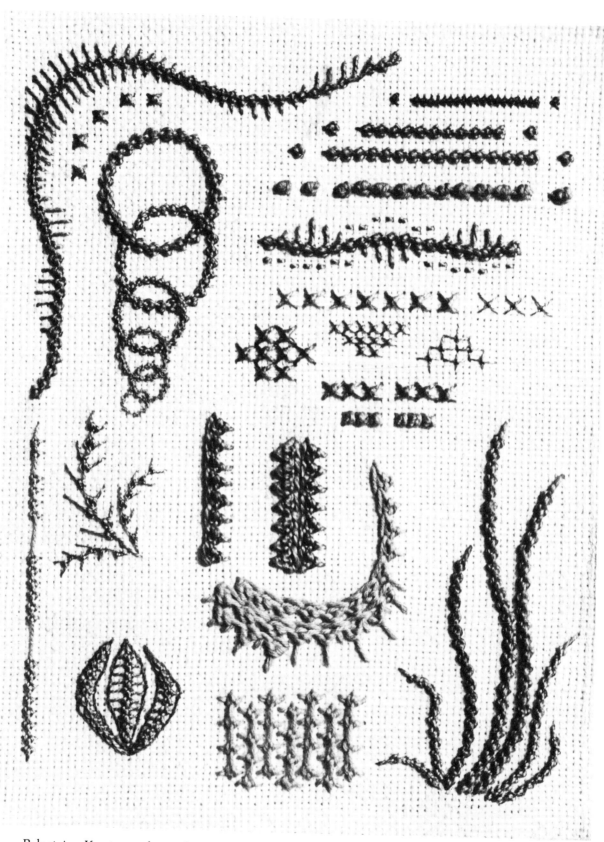

Palestrina Knot sampler with variations. (Worked and photographed by the author.)

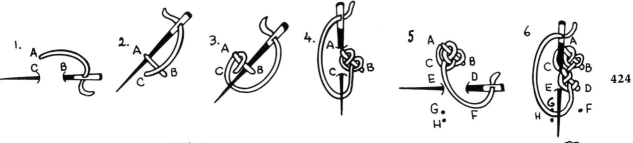

424

BACK

Palestrina Knot and Chain

This is another beautiful variation worked with a heavy thread for a line or border (Figure 424). After steps 1, 2, and 3, circle the thread clockwise. Going down at A, take a vertical stitch coming up at C (Step 4) with the thread under the point of the needle, pull through. Start the next stitch (Step 5) by going down at D and coming up at E, horizontally. Repeat steps 2 and 3 under CD. Circle the thread clockwise (Step 6), go down at C inside the chain and come up at E. With the thread under the point of the needle, pull through. Continue with FG, and so on. To end, anchor the last chain from G to H.

Random Palestrina, Random Palestrina Knot and Chain

After you have mastered the basic stitch, try working both the Palestrina and the Palestrina Knot and Chain at random in any direction—overlapping, in different lengths, or in layers over each other (Figure 425). Exciting effects can be obtained.

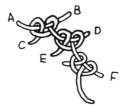

425

Reverse Palestrina Knot (Knotted Pearl Stitch)

This variation is worked from right to left. It starts just as the Loop Stitch, but has a second loop knotted around the first. It is one of the most beautiful stitches you can learn, goes quickly, and stays in place. You will find many decorative uses for it.

Different effects can be obtainaed by using different weights of thread and by varying the distance between B and C, D and E, and so forth. A good distance for practicing is about ¼ inch between B and C if you are using pearl cotton in size 3. Keep the working thread coming from C to the left and slip the needle under BA from above (Figure 426). Slip it a second time for a Buttonhole Stitch to the left, under BA. The second loop should gently encircle the first. The knots can completely cover BC, DE, and so on; or if BC, DE, are longer, the knots can stand up as a spine in the middle.

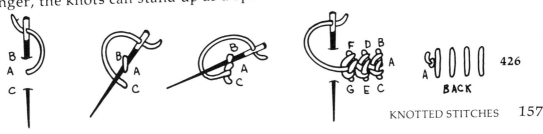

426

BACK

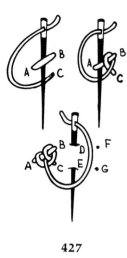

Small Palestrina Knot

This variation of the Palestrina Knot, used by the women of Palestrina, is a smaller knot worked from left to right. It starts as a regular Palestrina Knot but is followed by two Buttonhole Stitches both worked through the AB stitch from right to left, without picking up material (Figure 427).

Basque Knot

The Basque Knot starts exactly like the Palestrina Knot. But when slipping the needle under the AB thread for the second time, instead of slipping the point of the needle to the right of C, slip it under AB between A and C. The effect is slightly different.

427

Sorbello Stitch

This stitch, the specialty of the Italian village of Sorbello (now part of Naples), is very decorative and quick to work. You will find it different from any other stitch and well worth adding to your repertoire. The women of Sorbello used a heavy white cotton on colored or unbleached linen, or a heavy brown cotton on a white background.

The stitch is worked in straight or curved lines for borders. It is also used to fill geometric designs in the same way as the Cross Stitch, but has more texture. Use it for table mats, cushions, curtains, monograms, and so forth; it would also be an excellent overall stitch for a bedspread. You could adapt old quilt, candlewick, or Cross Stitch patterns, using candlewick thread. It is fun and easy to work on checkered material.

Cushion cover from Sorbello, Italy, and detail. It is worked in Sorbello Stitch in a design which is traditional in southern Italy. The background is natural linen. The embroidery is white and blue cotton. (Courtesy of Costume and Textile Study Collection, University of Washington.)

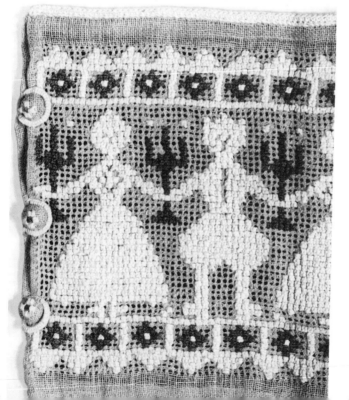

The stitch should be relaxed. To practice, use pearl cotton in size 5, with stitches 3/16 inch or a little less, in both directions. Also try ¼ inch stitches; the effect is that of a knotted Cross Stitch, rather different from the usual Sorbello look. A striking effect is obtained with pearl cotton in size 3 with stitches between 3/16 and ¼ inch. You can also try six-stranded cotton with stitches between ⅛ and ¼ inch.

Bring the needle and thread out at A (Figure 428). Insert at B, making a horizontal stitch, and come out at C, below A. Pull through. AB should equal AC. Slide the needle under AB from above, without picking up material, and come out towards the left. Holding the thread to the left with the left thumb, slide the needle again under AB from above, coming out over the held thread. This thread now goes under the point of the needle from left to right, making a Buttonhole Stitch. Pull through gently. Insert the needle at D and come out at B. Pull through. This completes the first Sorbello Stitch which looks like two loops in a square.

Continue, inserting at E, coming out at D, and so on. Traditionally the stitches were the same size. I enjoy distorting them by setting the four points ABCD at different angles, by making longer, or shorter stitches still joining arms and legs at points B and C, and by using different weights of thread. This freeform Sorbello can be used for Couching, for instance, as illustrated on the sampler. Another possibility I came up with is to work C and D in the same hole for a triangle Sorbello! It is a good stitch for doodling. The Sorbello Stitch was rarely mentioned or used outside Italy when it was described in the early printings of this book. It gives me a great deal of satisfaction to see that it has now received the attention it deserves.

428

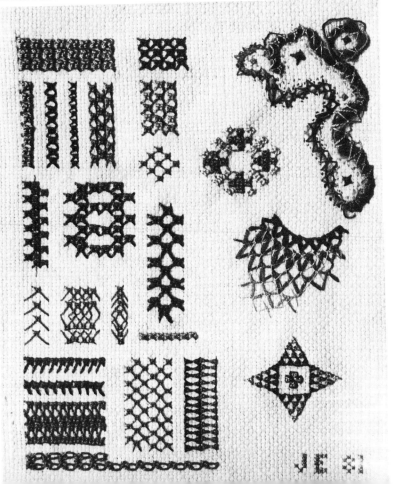

Sorbello Stitch sampler with variations, 7½ by 9½ inches. Worked and photographed by the author.)

KNOTTED STITCHES   159

Knotted Buttonhole Stitch

This is a Buttonhole Stitch with a knot at the end of each stitch. Its obvious use is as an edge, but it can also be used to indicate the stamen of flowers or other growing forms (Figures 429, 430). It is worked from left to right.

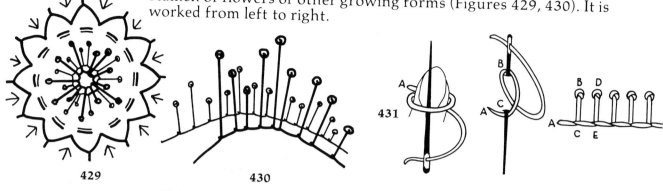

429   430   431

Bring the needle and thread out at A (Figure 431). Holding the thread under the left thumb, wind it around the thumb clockwise (under, over, and under).

With the point of the needle, pick up the loop on the thumb from below and insert the needle at B. Bring it out at C over the lower thread coming from A, making a Buttonhole Stitch. Snug up and pull through. Wind again around the thumb as at A, and so on.

Knotted Cable Chain.

Knotted Cable Chain

The Knotted Cable Chain is one of the most beautiful stitches for lines and borders, straight or curved. It is just as quick to work as the Cable Stitch but is richer looking. A heavy rounded thread shows its full beauty. It is worked from right to left.

Bring the needle and thread out on the line to be covered at A (Figure 432). Hold the thread down with the left thumb on the line. Insert the needle, taking a small vertical stitch from B to C, with the thread from A passing over the needle, then under the point. Pull through. This makes a Coral Knot.

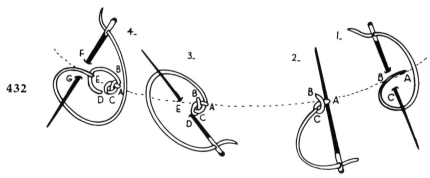

432

Pass the needle and thread under the first stitch between A and B from below, without picking up material. Looping the thread to the left, take a stitch from D (next to the knot at C) and come out on the line at E (above and to the left of D). Loop the thread coming from the right under the point of the needle. Pull through making a chain.

Holding the thread down on the line, take a small vertical stitch from F to G, thread over and under as at BC, and so on.

Try a necklace of Knotted Cable Chain around the neck of a pullover or down the front of a cardigan. It can also be worked in a zigzag.

Knotted Cable Chain Variations:

The Knotted Cable Chain lends itself to many exciting variations closely related to the Twisted Chain and Rosette Chain families. They are especially effective when worked with a tightly twisted thread, which brings out the beauty of the detail. They can be worked in individual units or in vertical instead of horizontal rows, with a number of additional variations dependent on the placement of DE.

Single Knotted Cable Chain

In Figure 433, A and B are on a straight horizontal line. CDEF are on a straight vertical line passing between A and B. The Single Knotted Cable Chain can be anchored with one or three small stitches, one or three long stitches or a French Knot.

In a useful variation (Figure 434), E can be immediately below C, pulling the circle snugly and anchoring it at F, close to E. The result is large, individual, textured knots, the overall effect depending on the thickness of the thread. The length of EF can also be varied. A different placement of DE will make the stitch wider. D can be on the same line as C or higher (Figure 435). An extra threading will turn it into a textured high knot (Figure 436).

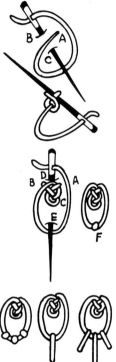

433

434

435

436

The Knotted Cable Chain can be worked into a vertical line. Start as in Figure 433 with DE straight up and down between A and B. The next knot starts from E (Figure 437). Go down at F just below E and come up at G, in a straight line. From E, circle the thread to the left, then over and under the needle. Pull through. Slide the needle under EF. With the thread circling counterclockwise, go down just below E at H and come up at I, and so on.

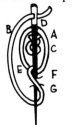

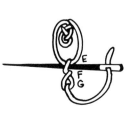

437

KNOTTED STITCHES 161

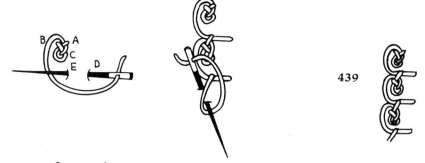

In another variation, D can be placed close to the side of A or at an angle, or perpendicularly, making a buttonhole (Figure 438). In one of my favorite edgings, I work the buttonhole DE close to the knot (Figure 439). You can also use a textured high knot in the same manner. With pearl cotton size 5, the distance between the buttonholes would be about ⅜ inch. With a high-twist crochet cotton, the distance would be ¼ inch.

Knotted Cable Chain sampler with variations, 7½ by 9½ inches. (Worked and photographed by the author.)

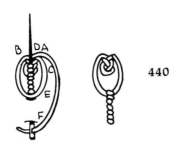

440

Single Knotted Chain with Bullion Knot

In doodling to find new and interesting ways of filling a flower shape, I came up with a Bullion Knot as an anchor. It is now a favorite of mine (Figure 440) (see also Figure 539). Bullion knots are easier to work if you use a milliner's needle which does not have a bulge at the eye. From E go down at F and come up at E in the same hole. Push the needle almost but not completely through. Follow the Bullion Knot directions, wrapping the yarn from E as many times as needed to cover the distance EF and going down at F.

Knotted Zigzag Chain

Although it is possible to work the Knotted Cable Chain in a zigzag, a variation of the stitch, which I found on an eighteenth century Spanish bodice from Andalusia, is very beautiful and a more stable stitch. It is worked vertically with knots just outside the zigzag. The stitch has a great deal of character and can be worked in different sizes. It is easy and quick to work once you understand the rhythm (Figure 441). Watch the back as you go along for correct placement (Figure 442).

Come up at A and pull through (Figure 441, step 1). Go down at B and come up at C in line with B. (The size of the stitches varies with the thickness of the thread. With pearl cotton size 5, BC would be 1/16 inch; with size 3, about ⅛ inch). With the thread over and under the needle, pull through, making a Twisted Chain. Circle the thread up to the left and slide the needle DOWNWARD under A without picking up any cloth. Pull through snugly to make a knot.

Circle the thread counterclockwise (step 2), and go down at D in the same hole as A. Come up diagonally below D at E. Circle the thread from left to right under the needle. Pull through making a chain. Go down at F (step 3), just outside the chain, close to E. Come up at G. (With pearl cotton size 5 the distance FG will be 1/16 inch). Circle the thread from E right to left over and under the needle. Pull through. Slide the needle DOWNWARD under EF (step 4). Pull through firmly to make a knot.

Circle the thread clockwise (step 5), and go down at H in the same hole as E, nudging under the chain. Come up at I, pull through. Go down at J, close to I (step 6), and come up at K. With the thread over and under the needle, pull through. Slide the needle DOWNWARD under I J. Pull through until the thread is snug. Circle the thread counterclockwise and go down at L (the same hole as I, under the chain). Come up at M, and so on. A variation used in Spain works each new chain inside the previous one instead of under it. H is over the side of the chain in the same hole as E; L is over the side of the chain in the same hole as I.

1

2

3

4

5

6

Back

442

Fragment from the Bayeux Tapestry. "Duke William leads his army down to the beach . . . to the invasion fleet with its troops and horse transports." (From *The Bayeux Tapestry*, edited by Sir Frank Stenton, published by Phaidon Press Ltd., London, distributed in the U.S.A. by New York Graphic Society, Greenwich, Conn.)

COUCHING AND LAID WORK

Introduction

Couching, Couched Filling, and Laid Work are closely related ways of tying down threads on the surface of the material.

In Couching, a single thread or groups of threads are tied down at regular intervals on the surface of the material. When these threads are tied in an open trellis pattern of threads crossing each other in regular sequence, the process is called Couched Filling.

In Laid Work, threads are laid closely side by side, with no intervals between them, and then tied down with another thread which is itself couched down.

In another form of Couching, each thread laid is immediately tied down with the same thread. Threads can also be laid like the spokes of a wheel and held down by weaving or whipping a thread from the center outward.

Couching

Couching, from the French *coucher,* to lay down, is an easy, useful and decorative way of filling spaces. It also makes an exciting outline. In Couching, threads laid on the surface of the material are tied down with another thread. It was used a great deal in medieval embroidery to keep scarce and costly threads, especially gold and silver, on the surface of the material. It is still used today to avoid damaging fine materials. For example, sewing through satin with a gold metallic thread, no matter how thin, would spoil the surface of the material. With Couching, a very fine tying down thread and a fine needle will not spoil even the most sensitive surface.

The Couching technique is often used on handmade church vestments, not only to create an unbroken outline or to fill spaces but also to cover the edge of appliquéd shapes. For those dedicated to this work, no stitch is more important or more rewarding.

Rich-looking cushions, screens, purses, caps and so forth, can be embroidered quickly and economically with inexpensive metallic threads.

Couching is an easy solution to the problem of threads that are decorative in themselves but are too heavy for simple stitching. It makes possible the use of a variety of materials from fine nylon net to heavy burlap—materials which would appear to be incompatible with the stitching thread. Thick yarns, string, and even raffia can be couched on the finest net. Jute string now comes in a silky texture in many beautiful colors.

The couching thread itself can be very thin. It can be the same shade as the thread it anchors, and thus be almost invisible, or it can be part of the design with its own pattern of stitches and colors, blending or contrasting.

Couching is particularly good for spontaneous outlining of free shapes. It is a good way to interpret your doodlings. For couching free-form designs without a traced line, pin the yarn, string or whatever you are couching in the design you want. Pull the beginning and the end of the couched thread through to the back of the material, securing it invisibly with the couching thread. The couched thread, or several threads, are held in place with the left hand without stretching. Take small stitches with the tying thread, going over, snugly around, and into the material at regular intervals. These tying threads can form a pattern, using a variety of stitches. To keep the work taut, use a hoop or a frame. In simple Couching the laid thread is tied down with Straight Stitches (Figure 443).

443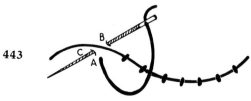

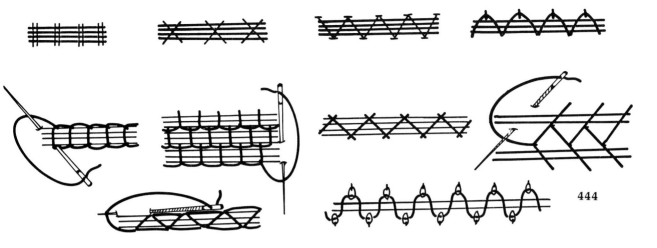

444

Couching Variations

A variety of stitches can be used to tie down the laid threads. Figure 444 shows tying done with groups of two Straight Stitches, with Cross Stitch, Chrevron Stitch, Open Chain, Buttonhole Stitch, Herringbone Stitch, Fly Stitch, Closed Feather Stitch, Slanting Feather Stitch, and with lacing through Detached Chain Stitch.

Several rows can be couched side by side and form patterns with the typing thread (Figure 445).

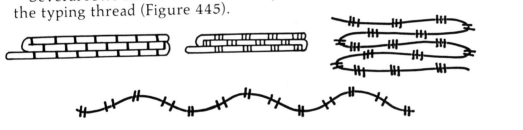

445

Couched Filling

Another form of Couching is Couched Filling, also called Squared or Trellis Filling. It is an easy way to fill large surfaces. A hoop or frame is essential to keep the work taut.

Threads are laid across the shape, first vertically, then horizontally. Each intersection is tied down with a small diagonal Straight Stitch or a Cross Stitch (Figures 446, 447). The laid stitches can also be woven over and under.

You can go a step further for more intricate patterns. Lay threads in one color horizontally and vertically, forming squares. Tie down. Over these, in another shade or a different weight of thread, lay another set of threads, crossing the squares diagonally, and tie down (Figure 448). The squares can be filled with stitches creating designs.

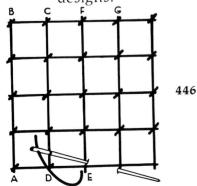

446

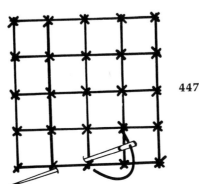

447

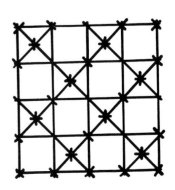

448

449

In Figure 449-1, two rows of parallel Running Stitches cross over, and just outside the laid stitches. These can be tied in the center with a Cross Stitch. In Figure 449-2, the light and the heavy laid threads are tied down with small Straight Stitches. Alternate groups of four detached Chains and four Seed Stitches decorate the squares. In Figure 449-3, laid threads in close pairs are tied down with Double Crosses and the squares are filled with groups of heavy Satin Stitches.

Couched Filling is used in Jacobean crewel embroidery. It is also found in much of European peasant embroidery. In Brittany, for instance, it has been used for many generations to ornament traditional costumes of the province. As part of *Broderie Bretonne*, you can still see it today in children's clothing, especially in the charming children's caps embroidered in white on royal blue or red wool cloth or in blue or red on white wool cloth (Figure 450) (see also Brittany bonnet on page 211).

450

Bayeux Stitch

One of the most fascinating examples of Laid Work handed down to us is the Bayeux Stitch. It is used over all the filled shapes of the famous eleventh century Bayeux Tapestry, embroidered in wool on coarse linen. This is not a tapestry but an epic embroidery, over 230 feet long by 19 ½ inches wide. With the vitality so characteristic of folk art, it tells the story of the invasion of England by William the Conqueror, of the Battle of Hastings in 1066, and of the downfall of Harold. It is really a story with a moral, embroidered almost certainly at the direction of the Norman bishop, Odo of Bayeux for the edification of his flock to be exhibited on the walls of the nave of his new cathedral dedicated in 1077. It could be subtitled "The mission of Harold II of England before he took an oath on the relics of the Cathedral of Bayeux, followed by his punishment when he broke his oath."

The embroidery seems to have always been the property of the cathedral and the town of Bayeux; it is mentioned as far back as 1476 in a manuscript inventory of the Treasures of the Church of Notre Dame of Bayeux. Everyone is agreed that it was embroidered soon after the Norman Conquest in the latter part of the eleventh century, but there is much speculation as to who designed and embroidered it. The English feel, with justification, that it was made in England. I like the French legend which attributes it to Queen Mathilde, wife of William the Conqueror, and to her ladies in waiting, fulfilling the request of their bishop, embroidering the lively story, adorning it with many humorous touches. It is an imaginative labor of love.

Whatever its origin, the Bayeux Tapestry is not only a famous historical document, it is also filled with a wealth of ideas and designs for embroiderers today.

The technique has its origin in Byzantine embroideries. These were brought back to Scandinavia and Iceland in the ninth century by the Vikings, reaching England and France in the late tenth century.

Detail of fragment from the Bayeux Tapestry shown on pages 164 and 165.

The Bayeux Stitch covers ground quickly and economically. It must be worked with the material stretched on a hoop or frame. The laid threads are not treated as Satin Stitch because too much wool would be wasted under the material. They are laid in two movements, from edge to edge, usually starting at the widest point so as to establish a definite direction (Figure 451). The first movement leaves free exactly the width of the same thread which is to be filled by the second movement. The threads are packed tightly with no material showing between them to give a massed effect.

When the shape is filled, the laid threads are tied down perpendicularly with a couched thread that is usually but not necessarily of the same weight and color. (See Bokhara Stitch, page 174.) The vertical couched threads should be about ⅛ inch apart, and so should the tying down stitches. In the Bayeux Tapestry, the direction of the laid and couched threads produces certain calculated effects. The outlines of the filled shapes and the details are stressed with Outline Stitch.

There is no limit to the way threads can be laid and couched. The women who worked the Bayeux embroidery chose to place most of the couched threads at right angles to the laid threads, but the laid threads can be couched in varying patterns, either geometric, or to suggest growing forms such as leaf veins. It is a quick and effective way to fill large shapes. The design shown in Figure 452 was inspired by birds in the Bayeux Tapestry, but was executed in a great variety of stitches.

452

Left:
THE NORMAN CONQUEST OF ENGLAND. This mural, inspired by the Bayeux Tapestry, was designed and embroidered by the pupils of the Potomac School, McLean, Virginia. Caroline F. Seamans, teacher, writes: "In the sixth grade at Potomac School the children study the Middle Ages. The Bayeux Tapestry is examined as a document and as a work of art in the study of the invasion of England by William, Duke of Normandy. One year the children wanted to make their own Bayeux Tapestry, to depict in their way scenes of the historical event. Each child designed what she wanted to portray and then worked her picture in wool on a burlap square. When all were completed they were sewn together to form the large piece." (Courtesy of Potomac School, McLean, Virginia. Photograph by John Hebeler.)

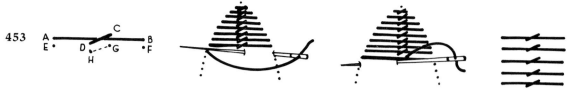

453

Roumanian Stitch

The Roumanian Stitch, sometimes referred to as the Roman Stitch, or the Overlaid Stitch, is found in the embroideries of many European countries as well as the Near East. It is used for broad outlines and fillings, and is an excellent stitch for filling flower or leaf shapes as the tying stitch can be used for the center vein. It is a couched stitch in which the same thread is used for both couching and tying. The thread is worked across the shape to be filled, and then tied down with a small slanting stitch.

Work from the top down or from left to right. Bring the needle and thread out on the left at A (Figure 453). Go in at B and come out at C, not quite halfway between A and B and slightly above the AB thread. Pull through.

Take a small diagonal stitch over the laid thread to D, holding it in place. Come out at E and go over to F, coming out at G (in line with C), and so on. The Roumanian Stitch is usually worked solidly with threads close together, but it can be spaced for a more airy effect. A versatile stitch, it can be used in a number of different ways. (Figures 454-456).

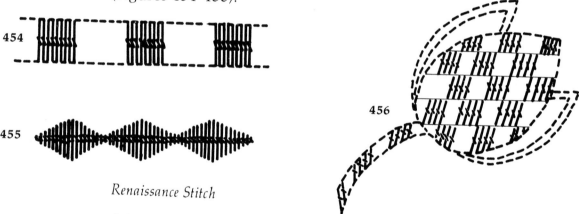

454

455

456

Renaissance Stitch

A beautiful variation of the Roumanian Stitch is the Renaissance Stitch, used in the embroideries of Switzerland, usually white on white. I like to work it in color, as a decorative band, using pearl cotton in size 3 or 5.

The beauty of the stitch lies in its regularity. It looks best when worked over counted threads.

457

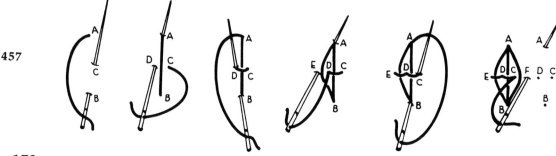

172   THE STITCHES

Bring the needle and thread out at A (Figure 457). Go in at B and come out at C, halfway between A and B and a little to the right of AB. Insert the needle at D, to the left of AB, and come out at A. Go in again at B, coming out at D, with the thread held to the left and under the point of the needle. Make a small horizontal stitch from D to E, the same size as DC. Go from E to A, from A to B, and from B to C, this time holding the thread to the right and under the point of the needle. From C insert at F. The three little horizontal stitches, DC, DE and CF, should be the same size.

From F the needle goes under to the beginning of the next lozenge, either spaced or "holding hands" with the first.

Try using pearl cotton in size 3, making AB ⅝ inch and EF ½ inch or a little less. With size 5, make AB ½ inch and EF ⅜ inch. The Renaissance Stitch can also be worked with stranded cotton but it looks crisper with a twisted thread. Figures 458-460 show some of the ways the stitch can be used.

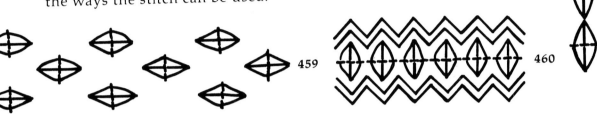

459

460

458

New England Laid Stitch

The New England Laid Stitch is a variation of the universal Roumanian Stitch with a long tying thread on the front, leaving little thread on the back. It was devised by the women of Colonial America when embroidery threads were scarce. At the end of the nineteenth century, in the New England town of Deerfield, a delightful revival of the eighteenth century American designs took place, this time using linen thread instead of crewel. The women responsible for this revival named their group The Deerfield Society of Blue and White Needlework.

The traditional New England Laid Stitch was worked from right to left, the stitches touching one another, usually with no space between, which gives the stitch a distinctive textured surface (Figure 461). Working it downward or from left to right, as with the Roumanian Stitch, gives it a slightly different, smoother texture (Figure 462).

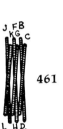

461

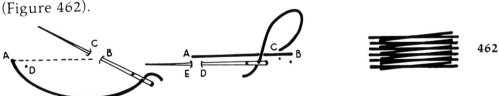

462

Figure of Eight Stitch

The Figure of Eight Stitch resembles the New England Stitch and also is economical of thread, since most of it stays on the surface of the material. The stitch is used in the ethnic embroidery of Central Europe. In Hungary, it is used to embroider petals of flowers and similar shapes. It is a quick and easy way to fill a shape, especially with heavy threads, and produces a raised wavy surface. It is a useful stitch in contemporary embroidery.

Start with an Outline Stitch on the upper part of the shape, and then bring the needle and thread out at A on the lower edge (Figure 463). With the thread over to the right, slide the needle downward under the outline stitch at B, without picking up any material. Pull the needle and thread through. Hold the thread up and go in at C; come out at D, taking a very small stitch close to A. Pull through.

Repeat, holding the thread to the right.

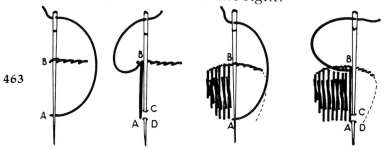

463

Bokhara Stitch

When several tight, little stitches are used at regular intervals to tie down the long stitch, the Couched Stitch becomes the Bokhara Stitch. Decorative patterns can be worked with the tying stitches.

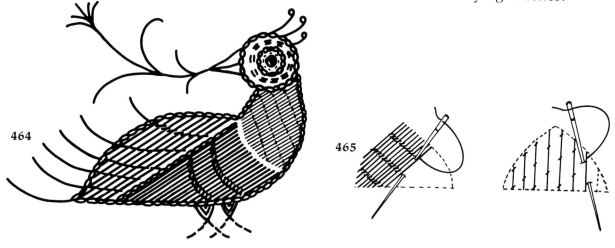

464

465

Figure 464 shows a design adapted from a nineteenth century Slavonic embroidered vest. The Bokhara Stitches can be close together for a solid filling, or slightly spaced for a different effect (Figure 465). In working the mural "Indians and Buffalos," I used one strand of stranded cotton with Bokhara Stitches slightly spaced, so that the background linen would show, to give a light but definite color and texture to the faces of the American Indians (pages 230-231).

In the embroideries of Palestrina, Italy, the spaces between the Bokhara Stitches are filled with knots (see Figure 418).

In the near East, the Bokhara Stitch is used to embroider rugs and wall hangings, a technique from which the embroidery stitch is derived. The couched threads are close together, with the tying stitches worked in regular slanting rows next to each other as in Figure 465, left. But before each tying stitch is anchored down, the needle is slipped downward under the anchoring stitch to its left. This locks the rows together and gives added strength to the surface, which is essential for rugs.

The Colcha embroidery of New Mexico is a happy blending of Roumanian and Bokhara Stitches.

Spider Web Stitch

The Spider Web Stitch produces many different effects according to the number of foundation stitches, the way they are laid, and whether they are subsequently woven or whipped.

The simplest way to lay foundation stitches is to work radiating Straight Stitches, evenly distributed, starting from the center out, like the spokes of a wheel. The larger the wheel, the more spokes it should have. These can be of even lengths for geometric regularity, or they can vary for a more spontaneous effect, as a real spider's web has anchoring threads of varying lengths.

If the web is to be woven, there should be an odd number of foundation stitches. To practice, use pearl cotton in size 5 and make the diameter of the wheel ¾ inch across. Bring the needle and thread out at the center and work outward (Figure 466). Be careful to hold the knot under the material to one side so as not to poke into it as you come up from the center. From A, insert at B, coming out again at A. Insert at C, coming back under to A, then at D, and so on.

466

If the web is to be small, one way to lay the foundation stitches is to make a Fly Stitch (see page 113), with two additional Straight Stitches from the center out, coming back into the center at C (Figure 467).

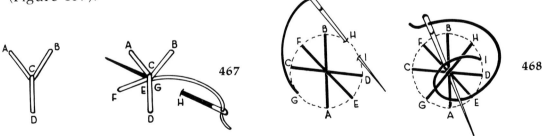

467

468

The foundation stitches can also be laid crosswise without going through the center (Figure 468). If the web is to be woven, one extra half stitch must be added to obtain an odd number of spokes to the wheel. The space between B and D has two spokes instead of one. For this reason CD should not be at a right angle to AB but slanted.

Whether woven or whipped, the threads laid in this manner must be tied in the center, without picking up material. Slide the needle under the foundation stitches between BF and AE and loop the thread from I over and under the point of the needle. Pull gently up to knot the thread in the center. This is the quickest way to work the Spider Web Stitch. It produces an interesting raised surface useful in contemporary stitcheries.

This raised effect can be enhanced by working the foundation stitches slightly relaxed and holding the center up before starting to weave. One way to achieve this is by means of a temporary thread of a different color, about 6 inches long, slid under the center stitches between BH and GA. Hold the two ends of this thread in your left hand and use it to raise the foundation stitches slightly from the surface of the material while you weave in and out with the needle in your right hand. Instead of a temporary thread, I use a thin hair pin.

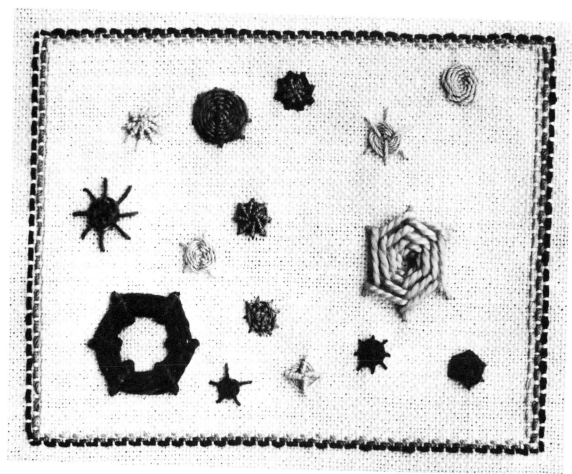

Spider Web sampler worked by the author.

Woven Spider Web Stitch

To weave the web, use a tapestry needle and the same or a different thread. Come out at the center of the wheel (remember to have an odd number of spokes), and weave under and over the spokes—under A, over G, under C, and so forth (Figure 468). Pull the thread snugly at first, relaxing slightly as you work outward. If the wheel is to be large and flat, for added strength anchor the weaving thread once in a while by picking up a thread or two of the base material as you weave under. This is important if the piece is to be laundered.

The same color, or different colors, can be used throughout. Two or three values of the same color can be very effective. The weaving can completely cover the spokes for a solid, circular shape, or the spokes may be left partly uncovered for effects that can be quite exciting.

Ribbed Spider Web Stitch

Whipping the web can be worked two ways with completely different results, and over either an even or odd number of spokes.

For the first way, the Ribbed Spider Web Stitch, start from the center between A and E; work from right to left (Figure 469). Go backward over one spoke, E, forward under two spokes EA, backward over A and forward under AG. Continue round and round, making what really are Back Stitches over one spoke, with the needle under two spokes getting ready for the next Back Stitch. Pull the stitches snug towards the center so that the ridges stand out.

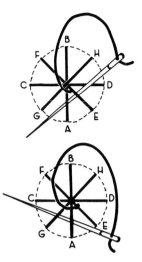

469

Raised Stem Spider Web Stitch

This stitch, the second way of whipping the web, is worked from left to right. Start at the center between A and E (Figure 470). Go backwards over two spokes, ED, forward under one, D, without picking up any material. Snug up the thread towards the center.

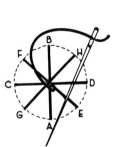 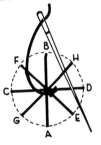

470

Continue going backward over two spokes and forward under one spoke until you have the size web you want. The result is a spiral rosette, not only beautiful in itself but a strong center for shapes.

It is fun to practice all these variations with different weights of thread. The Spider Web Stitch is full of possibilities for creative stitcheries.

Spider Web Lozenge

The Ribbed and Raised Stem Spider Web Stitches can be applied to a simple cross (Figure 471). As you work outward, you may need to pick up a thread or two of the base material from time to time for added strength.

471

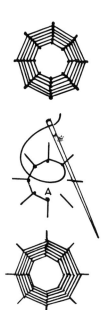

Ringed Spider Web Stitch

Work straight stitches in a ring pattern without going to the center (Figure 472). Use either the Ribbed or Raised Stem Stitches. Working the ring in the Raised Stem Stitch creates a feeling of depth, especially if heavy thread are used. Experiment with new ways of laying the threads; for instance, try working a Buttonhole Stitch ring, with the edging stitches close together at the inner edge.

Any of the Spider Web Stitches can be used for original borders on table linens or on clothes. The webs can be close to each other in rows or they can be separated by designs executed in other stitches (Figure 473).

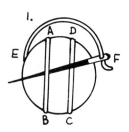

472

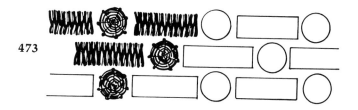

473

Mirror Work (Shisha)

474

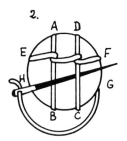

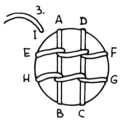

There are a number of ways to attach the little mirrors from India and Pakistan. The traditional mirrors which have so much charm are made from small hand-cut pieces of hand blown-glass balls which explains the little bubble imperfections and irregular edges. They are increasingly being replaced by machine-cut glass: no imperfections but much of the charm is lost.

Mirrors are attached in two steps, a technique which can be used to attach other objects, such as flat stones. The first step is to make a holding frame which can be worked in a variety of ways. I found that the most secure way is what my Indian teacher taught in my college days and called the anchored tic-tac-toe. For a mirror about ½ to ⅝ inch in diameter, use about 36 inches of pearl cotton size 5. Instead of using a starting knot, work two or three small Running Stitches and a Back Stitch. Hold the mirror over them with your left thumb, with your index finger under the cloth. Come up at A right against the mirror (Figure 474-1); go down snugly at B, up at C, then over the mirror and down at D. Note the small distance between AD and BC. All the holding threads should be quite snug against the mirror.

From D, for correct tension, come up at E. As you go toward F, with the working thread *UP*, the needle and thread pass over and under AB, then over and under DC. Go down at F, up at G. As you go from G to H (Figure 474-2), with the working thread *DOWN* for opposite tension, the needle and thread pass over and under DC, then over and under AB. Go down at H and come up at I between E and A (Figure 474-3), a little way from the mirror's edge. Turn your work so that I is at 6 or 7 o'clock, so to speak.

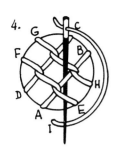

4.

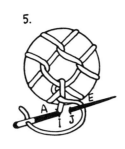

5.

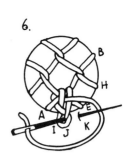

6.

The second step in attaching a mirror consists of stitching around the holding frame. This can be done in a number of ways. You can go around the mirror either clockwise or counterclockwise. Women in India, as in many cultures, tend to work away from themselves, clockwise. We tend to work toward outselves, counterclockwise. On some of the most beautiful pieces from India and Pakistan, Cretan and Chain Stitches are used. With the thread from I circling to the right (Figure 474-4), slide the needle under the intersection ABEF. The needle should point away from the center of the mirror and toward you. Pull the thread snugly over the working thread. Circle the thread counterclockwise (Figure 474-5), and insert the needle at I, coming up at J. With the working thread under the point of the needle, pull through, making a chain. Repeat the Cretan Stitch under the holding frame (Figure 474-6), pulling snugly. Insert at J inside the chain, and come up at K. Continue around the mirror, adjusting the tension to get a round shape. The size of the Chain Stitches should be such that a very small amount of cloth shows through.

Other stitch combinations can be worked, such as Cretan and Herringbone, Cretan and Buttonhole, or Cretan and Cretan (Figure 474-7). You can add many ornamental stitches (see Figure 505).

7.

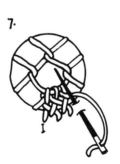

Sampler worked by the author. This is typical of end-of-the-quarter review samplers of over 30 stitches worked spontaneously on striped material by 12 eighth-grade students at Holy Names Academy, Seattle, Washington. There were no prearranged patterns. The samplers were all different and attractive. Each girl used her review sampler as a wall hanging. (Photograph by the author.)

III Creating with Stitches

FINISHING
AND USING THE SAMPLER

Whether you have made one large sampler or several notebook-size samplers illustrating families of stitches, each one should have a finished edge. A large sampler looks well if it has a frame of stitches around it. There should be a certain affinity between the frame stitches and the main part of the sampler.

In planning the border, look at the stitches you have recorded. You might like blocks of Running Stitches, several rows of whipped Running Stitches, Chain Stitches, Chevron Stitches, or others. The sampler often looks better when the top and bottom of the frame are wider than the sides. The long sides might have a single row of Spaced Buttonhole Stitches with a row of Double Buttonhole Stitches for the top and bottom. The Up and Down Buttonhole Stitch looks well used this way.

On my sampler, shown on page 2, I used four rows of Outline Stitches on the long sides. Three of the rows are close together and the fourth a little farther in, framing a row of closed Feather Stitches at the top and bottom (Figure 475). Close rows of Chain Stitches on the long sides might frame a border of Chevron Stitches at the top and bottom (Figure 476).

475 476

The color you use for the border should accentuate or blend with the general color scheme of the sampler. When I am not sure which colors will look best, I lay different colored threads on my work and move them around to get a feel for balance. In finishing my sampler this procedure led me to add small groups of French Knots in two of the secondary colors inside some of the Closed Feather Stitches. They gave just enough sparkle to the border.

You should embroider your name and the date on your sampler. Think how happy you would be to own a dated sampler made by your own great-grandmother! You can use your own handwriting or block letters. Back Stitches are the easiest to use for this; they go around letters better than Outline Stitches and look crisp. For lettering I also often use fine Chain Stitches made with fine thread, as on the baptismal robe shown on page 50.

When all the stitching is done, look at the back of your sampler and make sure that no long, dangling threads remain.

The last step is to hem your sampler. The size of the hem is up to you and depends on the material at your disposal and how you want to display your sampler. If you wish to hang it, the hem should be wide enough to accommodate a brass rod or wood slat at the top and bottom.

TRANSCENDENCE by Mariska Karasz (facing page). In this stitchery, one of her most colorful, joyful, and exciting nonobjective works, the artist gives full rein to her versatile vocabulary of stitches, using every imaginable type of fiber. (Courtesy of Bertha Schaefer Gallery.)

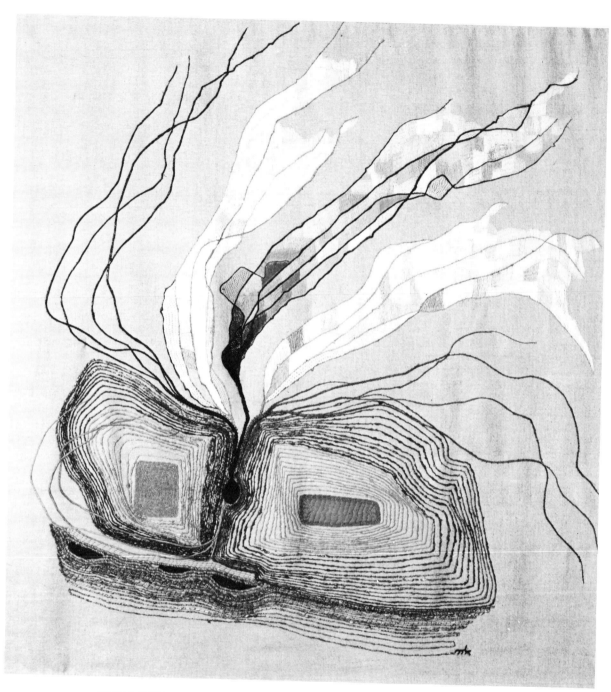

THE MUSTARD SEED by Mariska Karasz (above). Of all the works of this artist, "The Mustard Seed" is perhaps the most moving. It is the very symbol of her legacy to the world. For countless people, she opened a new door to creativity. She gave others the courage to explore an art form she pioneered. She will be remembered as one of the great artists of our time. (Courtesy of Mrs. Solveig Cox and Jefferson Place Gallery, Washington, D.C. Photograph by Victor Amato.)

Mariska Karasz's stitcheries, which were exhibited all over the United States, were inserted between two thin strips of wood slats at the top and bottom. This method was very effective, and also simplified transportation problems since the work could be rolled up without creases. However, you may prefer to frame your sampler; in this case the back might be covered with glass or acetate so that you can refer to it later on. Remember that a sampler is a reference.

If the stitches you were learning were recorded on small samplers of families of stitches or their variations, a good way to finish these is to embroider around them one of the stitches of the family. For instance the Eskimo Laced Edge is a good frame for a sampler of Flat Stitches (see page 32). Any of the Buttonhole Stitches would look attractive around a Buttonhole Stitch sampler.

Place small samplers between sheets *of* transparent acetate. These come in notebook size with holes, ready to insert in ring notebooks (see page 15).

Your completed sampler should not be considered an end in itself, but rather as a record of the possibilities with stitches. When you are thinking of a project, whether it be decorating a child's sweater or creating an original wall hanging, ideas will start coming when you look over the basic stitches and their variations illustrated on your sampler. You will be able to choose the most suitable stitches for your project. If you have learned most of the stitches in this book, you have at your fingertips many more stitch variations than a composer has tone variations. Every artist—musician, dancer, or painter—has to learn the controlled use of his medium by practicing progressive steps. So it is with embroidery. If you have little experience designing in this field, there are definite steps you can take toward acquiring confidence, freedom, and creative ease. You have already taken useful steps in this direction if you have worked out small illustrations on the side of your sampler as suggested previously.

CREATING BORDERS
WITH STRAIGHT AND CURVED LINES

Begin your designing by creating your own simple borders. You don't have to know how to draw in order to design a border. People who cannot draw often produce the best designs. There is great satisfaction in using a combination of stitches that you can call your own. Use your borders right away on place mats, tablecloths, chair seats, cushions, curtains, skirts, children's clothes, and so forth.

The simplest way to design a border is to use a pencil, paper, and ruler. Draw lines at various intervals, working them out first in a simple stitch, and then varying the stitch.

The border I used on the long side of my sampler is worked in an Outline Stitch in three shades of green; the outside row is dark green, followed by a medium green row, and a light green row; the fourth row repeats the dark green. What could be simpler? Yet it is effective (Figure 477). Try different intervals; variations in spacing create interest. Repeat groups of lines, interpreting them in different stitches—Chain, Zigzag Chain, a row of Palestrina Knots. Use variations in color and texture. Practice inventing borders on table mats and napkins, using a different combination for each.

You can make a decorative wall hanging by embroidering lines of different lengths grouped in varied spacings on a piece of cotton homespun, coarse linen, or burlap. Try couching a few heavy yarns or even string, using some of the many Couching variations, and adding rows of wide stitches such as Herringbone and Cretan, or the Vandyke Stitch with its variations in width. Work rows of Running Stitches, plain or whipped. It might be fun to string a few beads here and there along with your Running Stitches, or insert straws, dried grasses, or weeds in the Wave or Bosnia Stitch. You can also choose a striped material, and stitch over or alongside the bands in contrasting shades. This is a fascinating way of reviewing and practicing families of stitches (see sampler, page 180).

Another way to increase your experience in designing bands is to plan a cushion or chair seat. Many dining room chairs are made with removable seats, or have seats that can be covered with a flat cushion. Use upholstery material with good wearing qualities.

477

Chair seat by Elizabeth Moses. Elizabeth embroidered this chair seat for her dining room. She used Holbein, Running, Back, Satin, Detached Chain, and Twisted Chain Stitches.

184

Draw the lines lightly in groups on the material or use a material with printed or woven stripes. Repeat some of the colors in the room or the colors of a painting on the wall. Use sturdy stitches which will wear well, avoiding the Rosette Chain type of stitch or heavy knots which are apt to shift.

You can vary your border by adding circular lines to the straight lines, still using paper and pencil.

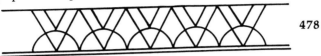

478

As a child, I made up a design for a border by using a small ruler, a pencil and my thimble. We were vacationing in the mountains—far away from any stamped designs. I wanted to embroider a runner for my mother's dressing table. With a straight line as a base, I drew a row of semicircles around my thimble. This seemed a little skimpy, so I drew triangles with each point touching the center of each semicircle, adding smaller triangles with each point touching the top of each semicircle (Figure 478). I worked the design in Chain Stitch—one of the few stitches I knew—in three shades of blue, and was pleased with the result. Not long after, my parents went to Africa and to my amazement brought back as a present a hand-embroidered cap with exactly the same design. The colors were different but the stitch and even the size were almost identical. I have since come across "my design" a number of times. Each time, it brings a deep sense of solidarity with these unknown women in different parts of the world who were undoubtedly motivated to design by the same impulse of using the nearest thing to them, their thimble.

481

479

480

482

There is an infinite number of possible variations of this basic design idea. The design can be doubled, facing the base of the semicircles to make full circles (Figure 479), or doubled the other way for a completely different look (Figure 480). This is easily done by folding tracing paper, a useful designing tool. Circles or semicircles can straddle a center line (Figures 481, 482).

The same design can be curved and would look well worked in fine threads on the edge of a collar or a circular yoke (Figure 483). It can be worked on a larger scale with heavy threads on a round tablecloth, or around a skirt.

483

Instead of a thimble, you can use a penny, a quarter, or a fifty cent piece. Coins, cups, saucers and plates are the tools used by women all over the world to make circles and curves. One of the traditional borders of Brittany is made of semicircles drawn around a thimble, either touching each other or spaced out. It is frequently worked with Chain Stitches in close rows of dark, medium, and light blue.

484

Other designs can be made by varying the shapes of triangles (Figure 484). Borders may be suggested by the designs of many things around you. Is there a design on your dishes? Try adapting it, using the same colors, on table mats, runners, or a tablecloth. A dainty design on a French eighteenth century plate from Marseilles was the source of one of my borders (Figure 485). Train your eyes to be on the lookout for border designs. I have used the ironwork design of an elevator door on a table mat (see page 203, the second mat from the left).

485

BUILDING BORDERS SPONTANEOUSLY

After you have acquired confidence in designing borders with straight and curved lines, try building them spontaneously on the material. First use a pencil to help you to visualize. The next step, and one I particularly enjoy, is to take a doodling cloth and experiment with stitches directly on it.

Try starting with a row of Chain Stitches, or Double Threaded Running Stitches. If you feel the need for a guide line, draw a light line with a blue pencil or draw a thread out of the material. A short distance away, perhaps ⅜ inch, work a parallel row (Figure 486). Think of detached stitches you can place between the two rows— Detached Chains in groups (either horizontally or vertically), Zigzag Chain, Slipped Chain and Fly, Arrowhead, Feather Stitches, and so forth.

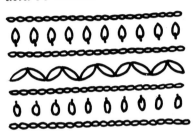
486

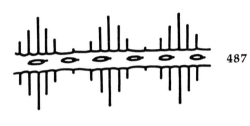
487

Many variations are possible with the Buttonhole Stitch. Work two rows, base to base with a space between (Figure 487). Think of a pleasing stitch to fill the space. By varying the positiion or the direction of one stitch, you can obtain entirely different effects (Figures 488-490).

488

489

490

The basic principles of design apply to stitches as they do to everything else. Many of the stitches described in this book have existed for centuries. What varies is the way in which they are used. Each culture has its own interpretation. Try your own and see what you can do. Remember that stitches influence each other. Find out which ones go well together.

Take the Fly Stitch, for example. Repeat it pointing up or down; vary its size. Add other stitches for balance or contrast; Detached Chain, Back Stitches and Running Stitches go well with Fly Stitches (Figures 491-493).

491

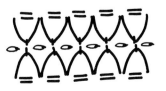
492

493

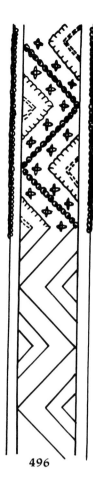

 494

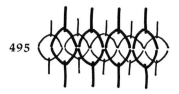 495

One of my favorite borders is made by overlapping Fly Stitches, using a light shade for the first row. A second row in alternating spaces is made with a darker, dominant color. A row of Palestrina Knots accentuates the center (Figure 494). Figure 495 shows another variation.

Groups of stitches worked close together create textures. Make up your own groups in varying combinations of favorite stitches, colors, and threads. Try various widths. If you use your imagination, there is no end to what you can create. Building your own borders or bands will be a big step towards acquiring confidence in your own ability to create. Pekinese, Outline, Back, and Buttonhole Stitches are combined with Cross Stitch Flowers and Palestrina Knots in Figure 496.

Figures 497-500 are stitch suggestions for building borders based on sketches I made during an exhibit of Yemenite embroidery at the Skirball Museum in Los Angeles.

496

Detail of a shirt worked by the author. The band was designed by Margalit Adi-Rubin, a native-born Israeli of Yemenite descent. The Yemenite Jews are a talented people who brought with them to Israel their distinctive traditional crafts. They embroidered their clothes with great precision in recurring combinations of simple stitches in parallel strips or in geometric shapes, relieved on the edges by charming little details. On this shirt, the vibrant, exciting color combination is royal blue, peacock green, chartreuse, and grass green.

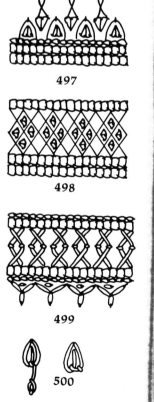

497

498

499

500

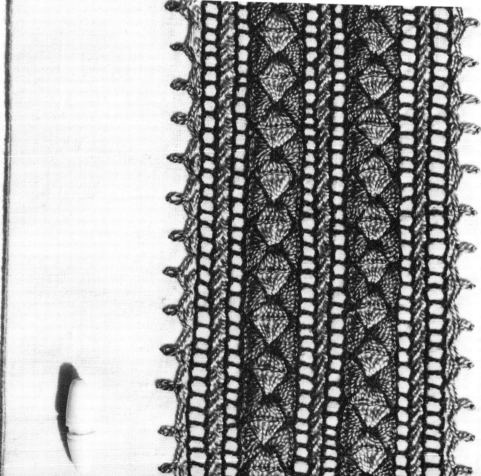

WORKING WITH GEOMETRIC DESIGNS:
CROSSES, STAR SHAPES, AND MEDALLIONS

After working border designs of your own, a further step in developing confidence in your ability to create is to use stitches in geometric forms. Crosses, star shapes and medallions provide a good foundation for exercises in creating with stitches. It may be helpful to first draw the basic line with a pencil the color of your thread.

A simple cross can be made with parallel rows of stitches, using the Buttonhole Stitch for example (Figure 501). Add a square in a different textured stitch, such as the Double Threaded Back Stitch. A second square close by could be in a lighter stitch such as Outline (Figure 502).

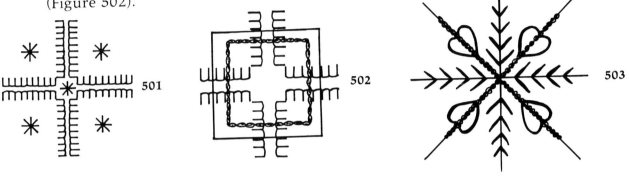

501   502   503

Try the same idea with two circles, worked in a solid stitch such as Satin or Flat Stitch or in rows of Surface Darning.

Two crosses at an angle to each other, as in Figure 503, can be the start of many designs. One cross might be worked in Fern Stitch increasing in size towards the center, and the other cross in close Coral Stitch or Small or Large Palestrina Knot, depending on the size of the cross. Hearts in a variety of stitches might be worked over the second cross. This type of design would look attractive enlarged and repeated at intervals on curtains.

A very simple star shape can be enriched and enlarged to become a beautiful motif for a cushion or the center of a tablecloth. It can also be expanded into a wall hanging, using a coarse material, heavy threads, and large stitches.

The core of Figure 504 is pictured in Figure 504A. The size of the circle and the length of the radiating lines determine the size of the star. Draw the outline of your star on tracing paper and transfer it to your doodling cloth with dressmaker carbon paper. Then start creating! What would be a good stitch for outlining the star? Your star might be more exciting if the two sides of each point were worked with a different stitch as in Figure 504. For example, you could work Coral Stitches going up one side of the point, and small Closed Buttonhole Stitches going down the other; small Running Stitches going up and Threaded Back Stitches going down; or plain Chain Stitches going up and fine Buttonhole Stitches going down.

On your doodling cloth, interpret each point of your star a different way to find which is most pleasing to you. You might want a small circle in the center of the star. Look at your sampler to find a suitable stitch. How about a row of Fly Stitches "holding

504

504A

hands" or Zigzag Chain? Inside the points try a Feather Stitch or a center row of Seed Stitches.

Outside the star, the design can be augmented. A Basque Stitch might follow the outline of the star. A large circle could enclose it, or two circles, one in Palestrina Knot and the other, lighter, in Double Threaded Back Stitch. The circle could be the base of overlapping triangles as shown in Figures 483 and 484.

Between the points of the star, you can extend lines and work a floral shape at each end, interpreting each flower as the spirit moves you (Figure 504). Contrast open spaces with spaces worked in solid filling, such as the New England Laid Stitch and the Closed Cretan Stitch. These are the decisions that make creating with a needle a stimulating experience.

When you have worked out your design, why not embroider it on a piece of material for a cushion? Use different weights of thread, perhaps white or cream on a dark material, or varying shades of the dominant color of your room. Your design could also be used on a tablecloth, repeated nine times in Hungarian style (see Figure 526).

There are many forms of stars. You can, for example, vary the number of points. The American Indians have star shapes of their own. In the Middle Ages star designs were sometimes asymmetrical. Investigate snowflake patterns. Experiment with squares and rectangles, varying their sizes and overlapping them, outlining some, filling others with solid stitching. One of the most beautiful round tablecloth designs I have ever seen was embroidered for Marie Antoinette—a compass rose with the lines embroidered in close rows of Outline Stitch.

Cushions by Susan Ayrault. The square design and the exotic bird were Susan's first attempts at design, after completing her sampler. The outside row on the round cushion is made up of Basque Stitches.

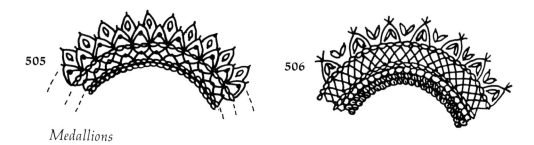

505   506

Medallions

In designing medallions, small or large, a compass is useful to give accurate stitching lines. Use erasable colored pencils the color of your threads. The overall size can be increased or decreased, according to your need, from 1 inch to many inches. The size in turn determines the weight of threads you should use. It could be pearl cotton size 3, 5, or 8, depending on the diameter of the medallion.

Some stitches lend themselves to outside edges such as the Crested Chain, the Basque Stitch, combinations of Fly Stitches, and Zigzag Chains (Figures 505-509). The centers can be open, flat, or raised. Repetition of a limited number of stitches and colors looks best. Figure 505 may look complicated and time consuming, but it is much simpler than it appears. Start with a Crested Chain on the outside compass line. Add a Back Stitch of a complementary color inside. This is followed by two rows of Fly Stitches, stem to stem, which are then interlaced. Continue to draw compass lines as needed, making up your own exciting combination of stitches and playing colors against each other.

I like to collect medallion designs from other cultures and have often embroidered medallions four inches wide on T-shirts or the backs of blouses, adding rays of different lengths in a variety of stitches extending from the circle. I have several skirts from India covered with many repeated medallions from 1½ to 2½ inches in diameter. You will enjoy creating your own stitch combination.

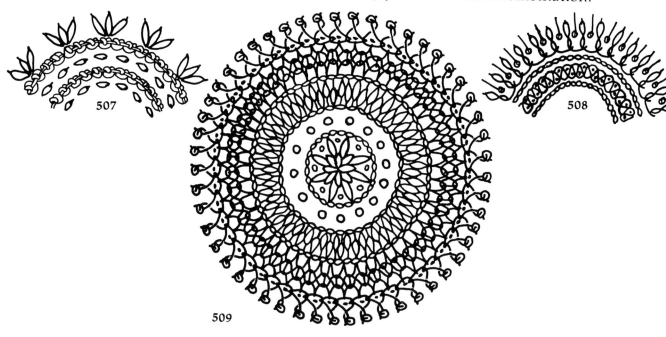

507   508

509

FROM GEOMETRIC DESIGNS TO VARIATIONS IN SHAPE

When you have achieved facility with geometric designs, try variations in shapes, such as the heart shape so frequently found in European embroidery, flower, and leaf shapes. Use a pair of scissors and paper. Great artists often use this technique; the famous Matisse leaf shapes were cut freely out of paper. You can feel the quick swift strokes of the scissors in Genaro's wall hanging shown on page 202. Cut out your own shapes; vary their size. Place them on a piece of textured cloth and move the shapes around—try overlapping them. When the arrangement pleases you, pin it on the cloth and leave it for a few hours or overnight. A new day with a fresh outlook may bring new ideas.

It took me several weeks to be completely satisfied with the size and placement of the tree shapes cut out of paper for the mural "Indians and Buffalos," shown on pages 230-231. When the distribution of the shapes satisfies you, trace around them with an erasable pencil the color of your thread, and stitch the outline in bold stitches.

One little girl made a delightful tray cloth with five scattered oak leaves from her garden. She outlined them in Chain Stitch, with one side whipped, and worked the veins with a finer thread in Double Threaded Back Stitch.

Stylized shapes of birds, fish, and animals are stimulating to play with. Look in children's books for inspiration. The Mexicans do wonderful things with whimsical animal shapes, frequently outlined with a fine Closed Herringbone Stitch as on the apron shown on page 87.

THE ELEGANT ONION, by Joan Bunata, an artist making use of stitches recently learned. It is white and creamy white; the silver frame is 21 by 21 inches. The piece is an excellent illustration of the principles of design: it uses balance, reversed repetition (to avert monotony), variation in the stitches used, contrast of texture, unity, harmony, graceful and restful lines whose rhythm flows and reaches upward, and a stabilizing symmetry in the circles and anchoring roots. (From the author's collection; photograph by the author.)

Joan Bunata's embroidery, The Elegant Onion, shows a variety of curved shapes. One way to experiment with an Elegant Onion-type design is to think of a simple vegetable, fruit, or flower shape (for instance, a magnolia blossom). Take a sheet of paper roughly the size of the design you want and, without drawing a line, cut bold strokes with a large pair of scissors, outlining the shape. Holding the base, cut petals freely from side to side almost to the base, leaving a center core. Spread the cut shape on another sheet, so that the petals spread apart, rounding them out if you like. Repeat the exercise several times until the design satisfies you. Place a piece of drafting paper over the cut shape and outline it. With the transferred design as a record to guide you, pin your paper shape onto the background cloth, and with basting stitches outline each petal. You are now ready to fill the petals with stitches.

Backgrounds can remain plain or they can also have groups of stitches. Sometimes the texture of the material will help to determine whether or not stitches should be added. There should be a definite rapport between the material, the threads, and the design. For example, on very coarse linen, small dainty stitches may look lost and out of place, and small circular lines may also be difficult to work. The most successful design is likely to be developed from congenial materials. However, in the case of wall hangings that do not have to be laundered, exciting results are obtained by mating unlikely companions such as heavy yarns couched on fine net. Use your sampler for ideas just as you would a reference book. Stitches are your vocabulary; increase your vocabulary, and you will find that you have more to say.

Breton cradle, eighteenth century. (Courtesy of Musée Breton de Quimper, France. Photograph by Etienne Le Grand.)

Although you may not have learned all the stitches described in this book, you will have discovered one of the side benefits of mastering even a limited number of unfamiliar stitches—a new awareness of stitcheries, contemporary and past. You will enjoy more fully the designs and embroideries of other nations, each with its own distinctive character.

Today, with easy travel and rapid exchange, with art books available from all over the world, there is an immense wealth of design material for those who seek it. Designs are not necessarily born spontaneously; more frequently they are derived consciously or unconsciously from some existing form. Take a look at designs with embroidery possibilites; they might be on a textile, on dishes, or in a book. Adapt them to your need; design is born of a need.

Adaptations of the design on an eighteenth century Breton cradle in a museum in Quimper, France, were made for a head board panel, a wall hanging, a cushion, and a floral spray (Figures 510-513).

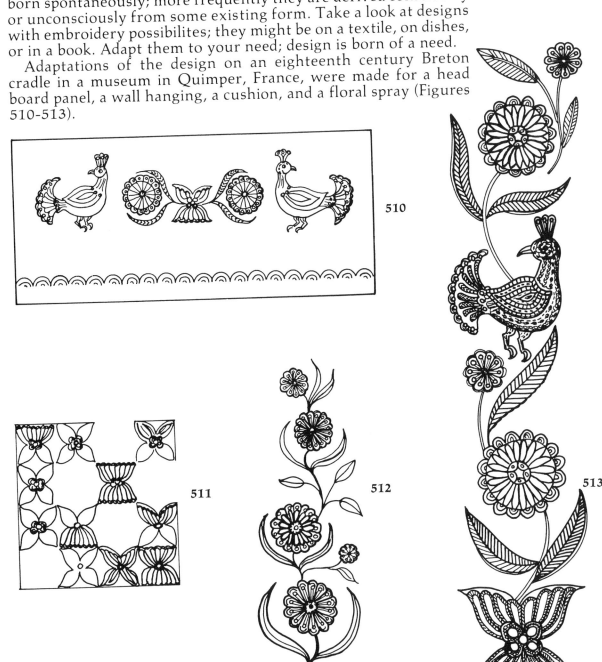

510

511

512

513

WORKING ON PRINTED AND PLAIN MATERIALS

Working on printed materials is an easy, relaxing way to create with stitches. It is fun and does not take much time. Look for materials with embroidery possibilities such as stripes and all-over prints. There are excellent decorator materials, as well as yardage for clothing, which you can use for cushions, seat covers, head boards, room dividers, and so forth. Place mats, tablecloths, bedspreads, and curtains with unusual conteporary designs are also available. Use the print as a guide, and accent the design with stitches, or better still, use it as a background for new shapes. If you are unsure of where to place a shape, trace it on tracing paper and move it over the design until you find a position you like.

You might find a print which would benefit by an additional color. Here is the opportunity to introduce it. There are printed linen wall hangings for children's rooms, which are attractive but often a little flat; give them an individual touch by adorning them with bold stitches.

Give a print blouse or dress a smart individual look by stressing part of the design with stitches. In an hour or two, you can transform a little girl's print dress into an original creation.

In addition to printed material, plain material can be used for spontaneous creating with stitches. On plain material you can create *pictures which tell a story,* such as a mural of Noah and the Ark for a child's room, taking the outlines of the animals from a child's book, and filling them with a pure fantasy of stitches. In the same manner, a fairy tale or favorite story might be illustrated on a bedspread.

At a child's birthday party, you can outline each child's hand on a plain cloth, producing an unusual design by repeating the shape, varying the size, position, and color; you can interpret the shapes as the spirit moves you in a variety of stitches. With the date and the names added, this could be a treasured birthday cloth, and one that you could add to every few years.

You can also create *pictures with a theme.* For example, make a sampler of leaf shapes with each leaf illustrating a new stitch interpretation. Embroider flowers and plants in a new way, avoiding attempts at realism. If you cannot draw your own simplified outlines, look through old herbals, botany books, or old crewel embroidery pictures. With tracing paper, outline the design, eliminating all but the basic lines. Children are good at these simplifications; so were European peasants and pioneer American women.

You can go a step further and create *freehand abstract* embroideries. Painting with threads can be a stimulating and joyful experience. It is a good way to acquire a feeling for what stitches will do for you, for what they can express—motion, speed, quiet, depth.

Choose a textured material such as one of the homespun varieties for your background. Drop a length of yarn, cord, or jute on the material. It will probably fall into curves. If your string was wound on a tube, it will naturally fall into loops. Nudge the patterns into pleasing shapes. Try strings of different textures and colors. Use pieces of black string for accents. Observe the designs created in this way. Some will be relaxed spontaneous patterns like a skier's

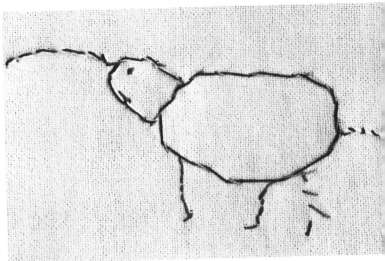

Eleanor Enthoven, at age 3, is completely absorbed in freehand stitchery. Her work is stretched out on a hoop. A hoop or light frame is indispensable for young children in order to keep the material taut.

ELEPHANT by 4-year-old Eleanor Enthoven. A spontaneous stitchery after a visit to the zoo.

THE SEATTLE SPACE NEEDLE AT NIGHT by Eleanor Enthoven, at 3½. Only a child could achieve such delightful simplification. The background she chose is a dark cobalt blue. The line on the right is the orange elevator going up. Above it, a plane is circling the needle. There are pink stars above and inside the restaurant two orange people are dining.

The Seattle Space Needle. (Courtesy of Century 21 Center, Inc., Seattle, Washington.)

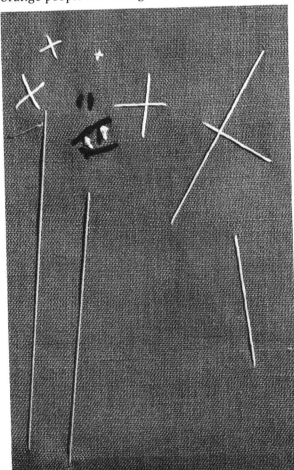

tracks on the snow. Select the pattern you want to use. The direction of the line may be due to chance, but your judgement is not. You are the one to decide whether the accident is something to be retained and developed or to be rejected. The process of rejecting and accepting plays an important part in creating freehand embroideries.

The string or yarn, unless it is unusually limp, is apt to fall raised in places. This creates shadows that can give you ideas for stitches or a new set of lines. Mark these lightly with sharp-edged chalk, noting the width of the shadow. This is a good start for your design. Pin the strings or yarns into place, disturbing the pattern as little as possible, and couch them with some of the many couching variations.

If you are interested in the shadows, work these with close rows of stitches, or with a stitch of variable width such as Herringbone, Loop, or Vandyke. You might want to mark the line made by a string with your chalk, remove the string, and interpret the line in a stitch of your choosing. You might choose a light, dainty line; a quick, running line; the corded effect of the Portuguese Stem Stitch; or the Hungarian Braided Chain.

This is one of the times when a complete sampler of stitches is an invaluable help. At a glance you can see the stitch most likely to express what you feel. Select threads congenial to the design you have started, in shades which blend or contrast with one another.

At this point, you may find it helpful to pin your cloth to a wall or curtain and look at it from a distance. A different angle of vision often brings new ideas, and may be the starting point of new forms and accents. Fill some of the enclosed areas, such as those formed by loops, with blocks of stitches. These might be solid stitches, such as the Closed Cretan, the Figure of Eight Stitch, or the Bayeux Stitch. Or you might use more open filling stitches like the Ladder Stitch; rows of overlapping Buttonhole Stitches; a variety of couched fillings, such as Bokhara with Palestrina Knots; rows of Open Chain, worked side by side; or light airy groups of detached stitches, such as Twisted Chain, Tête de Boeuf, and Cross Stitch Flower.

Divide large areas into smaller areas. For example, if you have teased heavy cotton string into the stylized shape of a bird, the head, wings, and tail form separate areas which you can either fill or sprinkle with stitches. The body can be irregularly divided with patterns created by stitches. Backgrounds can be left free or enriched with rows or blocks of stitches.

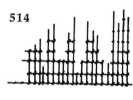

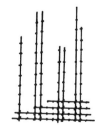

514

Study the use of stitches on the mural "Pastoral" shown n page 36. Patches of color can be treated as a wash in watercolor; they can have interesting broken edges, worked in couched threads of irregular lengths (Figure 514).

Freehand embroideries can be purely abstract or can have a theme. Use nature as a source of inspiration for forms, lines, textures, color. Train your eye to translate what you see in terms of stitches. If you are in a plane, notice the patterns formed by the fields and the earth, the roads, cities in the daytime, cities at night, clusters of houses here and there. If you drive or walk in the country, look up at the cliffs with the different layers of soil in waving patterns and subtle variations of texture and color. At the beach watch the scalloped curves created by the tide. If you go to the seashore or to the country, bring back a stitchery with vacation impressions. It is fun and much easier than you think. Enjoy the experience of creating with a needle, without worrying about what other people might say. Look at the suggestions on page 184 for such accents as couching weeds or grasses. Beads, shells, and seeds present endless decorative possibilities.

With freehand embroideries, let your imagination guide you; let the design unfold as you proceed, and invent new ways of using the stitches you have learned. You will find this to be most absorbing and exhilarating.

Lassie Wittman's interpretation of "Water flowing around two obstacles." (Photograph by the author.)

HOW TO CREATE SPONTANEOUSLY WITH STITCHES

This is one of the exercises I developed and taught across the nation to overcome the block experienced by so many who say: "I am not creative; I cannot design." They want the security of a line drawn by someone else! All who try can create their own pieces and, often for the first time, experience the satisfaction of feeling free with stitches and enjoy the process. Remember that you are doing something to satisfy yourself, not striving for a masterpiece to be hung in a gallery, what I call the Smithsonian syndrome. I stitch for fun and enjoy the doing. I do not stitch to impress others.

For this exercise, nothing is to be predrawn, either on paper or on cloth. I set up limits on size and materials ahead of time because limitations spark creativity. Absence of limits brings uncertainty. The finished piece is to be 10 by 7 inches, which you should be able to finish in a day or so. The background cloth should be just that: unobtrusive, yet with a little texture for interest. Stretching the cloth over a frame is helpful. Select yarns of different values of a single color, some thick, some thin, a variety of textures. Having no limits on color would immediately bring the confusion of different choices.

Limited means give charm and strength to so-called Primitive Art. For example, pottery artist Lucy Lewis of Acoma, New Mexico, limits herself to using clay from the mesa, ink from the soil and plants, and a yucca leaf cut to a fine edge for a paintbrush. With these very limited means, I watched her create masterpieces treasured in Museums. Some of the great chefs of the world have concocted famous dishes because of specific restrictions imposed on them by circumstances. So it is with needle art: the very limitations stimulate the thinking process into finding solutions, and finding answers is what creativity is all about.

The theme of the exercise is to design from a force in nature, so that the piece unfolds in a logical way. You could choose the wind, creating patterns on the desert sand, or flames leaping up. For this particular exercise, try to imagine water flowing in a creek around two rocklike obstacles, a major one and a minor one, each diverting the flow of the water. The major one should draw the eye, as a piece of jewelry around your neck. The minor one should not be a replica of the major one but somewhat related to it; size is less important than emphasis in establishing the major-minor relationship. Think carefully about where you will place these obstacles: not exactly on the same horizontal or vertical line, nor along either diagonal. Mark these two places.

Picture the water flowing from outside your piece in more or less parallel lines, anticipating the first obstacle. Start by working on the major obstacle, trying to give it dimension with a stitch such as Raised Spider Web which could be worked over a bead or with heavy knots on top of each other. Leave a breathing space around the obstacles, a space with a pleasing shape. Later you may want to go back to it, adding more stitches, little beads, or groups of French Knots. Mark the place of your minor obstacle. You can work it now or later. It can be a block of overlapping stitches such as Bullion Knots or a group of small Spider Webs, Cross Stitch Flowers... try to invent something.

You can determine the flow of water using a yarn that is easy to manipulate and not too thin. Play with it on the cloth, feeling what the water would do. When you have established your line, not too close to your obstacle, pin it down and couch it with a variety of stitches. You can knot the yarn itself or hump it up in places like small inch worms, with anchoring stitches on each side. Let the yarn flow around your minor obstacle before it runs out of the picture, with lines flowing as they would in nature.

On either side of the obstacles, you might try stitches that lend themselves to changing widths—the Square Chain, Vandyke, Herringbone and Palestrina Stitches. The stitch itself might not evoke flowing water, but the general direction of the line is what is important. This is an exercise for putting to use the stitches you know. A four-ply yarn can be separated along the way, with each ply tacked down, simulating little rivulets. Groups of Raised Seed Stitches and little knots might suggest splashing water or pebbles lying in a quiet backwater where the viewer's eye can rest. If you are afraid of losing your free line, you can pin it or use chalk, but as much as possible compose as you go along. Let your flowing lines have their direction justified by the obstacles. Watch the spaces between the lines so that you produce pleasant, open shapes.

Be a good craftsman. Let your ideas grow and unfold; execute them as well as you can. In stitchery, much of the success of a piece lies in the beauty of the stitches. Freedom is a good thing, but it is not a license to be careless. If an idea is worth developing, it is worth doing well. In the end, you will find great satisfaction in knowing that you can be free with stitches.

WALL HANGINGS AND SPACE DIVIDERS

The severity of contemporary interiors has much to do with the vogue of wall stitcheries, just as the stark, cold walls of medieval castles brought forth the use of tapestries.

You might be inspired by a piece of cloth you have on hand and decide later what you will do with your completed stitchery. Or you might want to adorn a specific place in your home—perhaps a bare wall in a hallway.

When planning a wall hanging for a particular spot, I like to take a large sheet of paper, such as shelf paper, and pin up what I feel is a satisfactory size for the space to be covered. It is a good idea to leave the paper up for a few days until you are satisfied that it is the right size and shape for the spot.

Design your wall hanging either freehand or with a planned design. In selecting a material, it is stimulating to experiment with a variety of backgrounds, including unlikely materials with texture. Let the background speak and suggest designs and stitches.

Plan the general lines, and then follow them with needle and thread, improvising with stitches. If you have acquired freedom with the needle, ideas will come naturally as you proceed, because your eye will have gradually become trained to possibilites with stitches. Imaginative needlework will emerge from doodling with needle and threads. As you stitch along, invent new ways of working a stitch that you have previously practiced in its basic form. A striking wall hanging can be made while you are practicing, reviewing, and inventing stitches.

If you are working on a space divider, use stitches which look well on both sides of your stitchery. Merge the beginning and the ends of the threads into the stitching with two or three Running Stitches into the line.

With wall hangings, space dividers, and screens, people can explore new worlds of creativity right in their own homes at little expense.

Tapestry by Genaro de Carvalho, Bahia, Brazil. The artist uses swift stokes of the scissors to cut out his great stylized birds and his lush Brazilian jungle plants. He uses colored papers, which he assembles in large, vibrant collages. From these, the wall hangings are stitches by the women of Bahia. This tapestry is 4 feet 2 inches by 3 feet 4 inches. (Courtesy of Dr. and Mrs. Stanley M. Gartler, Seattle, Washington.)

MORE IDEAS FOR YOUR HOME

There is a limit to the number of "pictures" a woman can make for the walls of her home, but countless articles around the house can be adorned with stitches and stamped with her individuality. They include table mats, tray cloths, tablecloths, runners, bedspreads, head boards, cushions, chair seats, and so forth.

As I have suggested earlier, for the beginner, a practical way of using stitches right away is to plan a number of table mats to be used as gifts, each mat with a different border or design illustrating a stitch or a combination of stitches. The mats can be bought plain and hemmed or they can be made from yardage such as heavy linen, or cotton homespun, which is inexpensive and comes in many attractive colors. I like to make mine a generous size, about 13 by 19 inches after hemming. The first mat might be worked with blocks of runnings stitches, the next one with laced running stitches, and so on.

Six table mats designed and worked by the author. They are embroidered in white on red cotton homespun. The first four mats are worked in Running Stitch and Fly Stitch joined at the base, Chain and Running Stitch, Breton and Chain Stitch, and Renaissance Stitch. The mat with the elks (bull, cow, and calf) was made for a hunter. The last mat is made with Running Stitch, Fly Stitch joining hands, and Chain Stitch in the center.

If your dishes are all white, try colored mats blending with the color of the walls or repeating the dominant color of a picture, and embroider them with white threads of different weights.

Using a striped material is fun and a good way to develop freedom with a needle. The stripes can run vertically or horizontally and can be of even size or irregular. Some of the stitches can be light and airy, like the Chevron, the Herringbone, or the Breton; or they can be solid, like the Fishbone or the Closed Cretan.

You can also plan an original tray cloth for a present. Besides being original, it will be personal and useful. Designs and stitches can be placed on the place mats and tray cloths in a variety of ways (Figures 515-520).

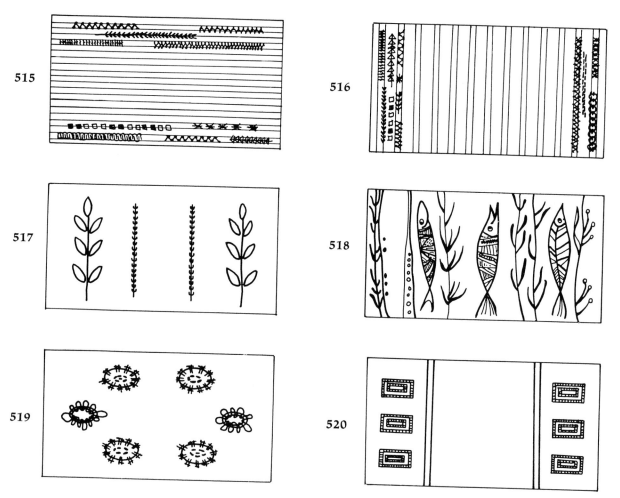

For tablecloths and runners, choose a material that is easy to launder and iron. Modern linens are easy to iron. Use a ready-made plain cloth, or buy yardage. Measure your table and add about 10 inches all around to hang over the edge. Cloths can be made to hang over the lengthwise ends and not the sides. Narrow bands of material can be used to make a single cloth by embroidering the edges together.

One good plan is to have a basic, plain tablecloth, with different table runners placed over the center. Before designing a tablecloth or runners, you may find it useful to set the table with plates, silverware, and glasses to see what part you want to embroider.

Keep in mind that you can use white thread on colored tablecloths; a red cloth is attractive for Christmas and Valentine's Day. A variety of designs for tablecloths and runners are shown in Figures 521-529. (For other tablecloth designs, see pages 79, 99, 104, and 150.

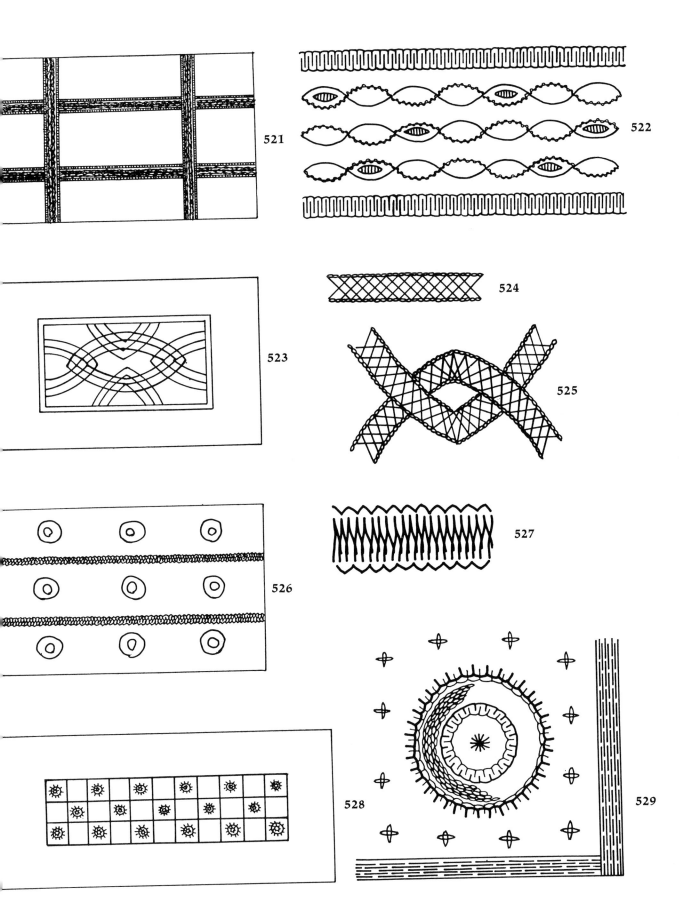

521

522

524

523

525

526

527

528

529

Blue Danish tablecloth embroidered in Buttonhole, Chain, Whipped Chain, and Outline Stitches in several shades of blue. (Courtesy of Dr. and Mrs. Stanley M. Gartler.)

English coffee table top designed and worked by Mrs. L. Devereux. Abstract shapes in blues and greens appear through the transparent organdy. The motifs are embroidered in turquoise, lime, and black. (Courtesy of *Embroidery*, The Embroiderers' Guild, London, England.)

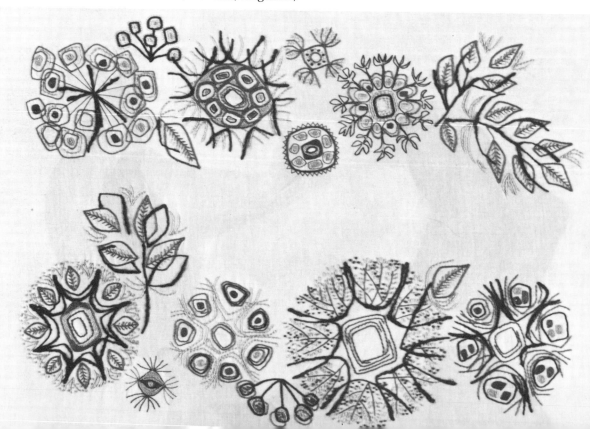

A decorated bedspread can add a great deal to a plain room. If you are searching for ideas, try cutting shapes that appeal to you with paper and scissors. Either place these shapes on the bedspread in regular sequences or let them fall freely. Move them around until the design satisfies you. When it does, pin the shapes on the cloth, trace around them, and embroider your design. Repeated bold motifs look well on bedspreads. You can also treat the bedspread as an oversize sampler, working several areas in rows of stitches in groups, vertically, horizontally, or in curved lines, using a variety of coarse threads. You can use the same idea for a headboard (Figures 530-532) or for cushions.

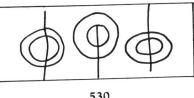

530

531

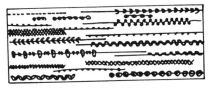

532

Cushions are full of possibilities. Use them to practice stitches or to try out design ideas. They make welcome gifts (see cushions shown on pages 127 and 191.

Why not use a stitchery for a chair seat or a stool? The Japanese cover seats with beautiful Kogin embroidery (Pattern Darning). Their neat, timeless linear designs go well with contemporary furnishings.

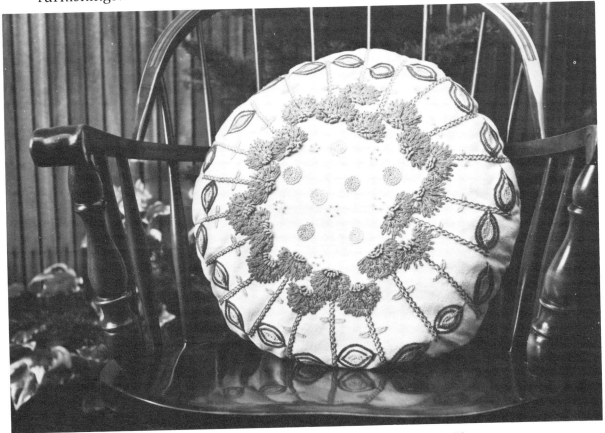

Cushion by Joan Carbary. While three of her children were working on "Summer Meadow," Joan was inspired to design and stitch this cushion. (Photograph by the author.)

CLOTHES

Clothes offer great scope for original stitchery. They become a walking source of joy. More people will see and appreciate the piece of clothing you originated than will see a stitchery hung in an exhibit. It is one of the easiest, most satisfying ways of obtaining a one-of-a-kind distinctive garment for yourself, for a member of your family or for a friend; and you can do this even if you are a beginner. You can start using the stitches you have learned by practicing them horizontally or vertically on the yoke of a blouse or dress, or around a skirt. Some materials have woven lines or stripes that make the task easier, or you can draw guidelines lightly with an erasable pencil. Try contrasting knubby stitches such as the Palestrina Knot with a flat open stitch like the Herringbone.

The color and texture of the background cloth is a matter of personal choice. I enjoy off-white, clear navy, light blue, and burgundy red—it really all depends on the way I feel! You do need to choose a suitable background for the yarns you intend to use.

If the garment is already made, you may want to unstitch a facing or an underarm seam or remove a pocket to embroider it. If you work on a garment that is already cut, reinforce the edges of the pieces to prevent stretching. It is easiest to stitch on the cloth before the garment is cut, with the sewing line drawn on. For sheer or stretch fabrics such as T-shirt material, I occasionally iron on to the back the sheerest weight of a one-sided fusible interfacing cut the size of the design and follow the manufacturer's instructions. One advantage is that the design can be drawn on the interfacing and reversed if it is not symmetrical; or else the lines can be basted through to show a stitching line on the front.

For placement ideas, keep a scrapbook or folder of illustrations of decorated clothing you like, from advertisements and magazines as well as rough sketches of placements you have seen or better still your own original ideas. The ethnic costumes of many countries and cultures provide an endless source of ideas. You can add excitement to blouses, dresses, and sweaters by working embroidery around the neck and down the front, in rows or freeform, around the sleeves, or lengthwise along the top of the sleeve, as in done in Central European ethnic blouses.

An embroidered pocket on a jacket, apron, or dress can transform it. Women in all parts of the world have embroidered bands around their skirts. You can also embroider belts and bags. A young girl turned her bikini into a sampler; it was delightful and very individualistic!

Whatever design and placement you select, the most effective results are obtained when the eye focuses on a definite area, a cluster, rather than on small scattered spots; these may be individual gems, but they are not exciting on clothing. An area of color holds the attention, and either a variety of colors or variations of one color add interest. For instance, the petals of a flower might have three different reds—from a pure red, to a purplish red, and an orange-red—or a green spray might have added blue-green and yellow-green. Adjacent colors of equal value give sparkle. The eye tends to blend them into one shimmering color.

Dress lengthened by Susan Ayrault for her daughter Lisa. Susan added a piece of material and embroidered over the seam line, incorporating the new material into the design—an imaginative way of lengthening a little girl's dress. The lighter shade is repeated in Twisted Satin Stitch over the darker added piece. The darker color is repeated over the light part of the dress.

Dress by Susan Ayrault. Susan made this dress for 5-year-old Lisa, using the collar as a review sampler. The many bright colors of the embroidery contrast with the olive green of the material.

I am partial to a moderate use of variegated threads for flower shapes; their changes in value have built-in sophistication. For instance, for foliage you can thread your needle in such a way that the light green comes out at the top, getting gradually darker as you go down. There is no substitute for placing colors you like next to each other and seeing how they react and perhaps introducing a third one to enliven or tone down the first two. Do you want the effect to be quiet, soft, and low key, or do you want it to sing and have varied textures? Central European countries often use a brilliant red on white. They give it zing by adding a small amount of black—an idea I used on a creamy white evening gown embroidered in red with three different weights of thread; when I added a little black, the whole gown sparkled. Use your favorite colors—those that make you happy.

I like to use pearl cottons in a variety of weights because they wash well and remain crisp. For a different texture, on some clothes I use fine 100 percent orlon yarns which come in a great variety of colors in small skeins. I embroidered a creamy white cotton dress with orlons in saturated colors (see page 10). It is a great success, has been many times in a washing machine, and remains as fresh as it ever was. A number of other synthetic fibers may also be suitable. If the clothes have to be washed, test for color fastness and shrinkage; if they do not have to be washed, crisp crewel wools work well.

I have taught clothing embellishment for many years, using different approaches. Besides rows of stitches, borders or medallions, one of my favorite approaches is to use flower shapes, stylized and clustered closely together. Flower shapes are not difficult to embroider and the results always meet with instant success. It is a help, though not essential, to have a plastic template of circles and ovals in different sizes. You can then match a center circle or oval with larger outer ones, matching horizontal and vertical marks for accuracy. You can also use coins, a thimble, a spool, or any other circular object. If you like to plan the whole design before you start, cut a variety of circular and oval shapes out of paper. Place them on the garment near each other and move them around until you have achieved a placement you like—some touching, others with slight spaces between them for foliage. Pin them in place.

At this point, you can make a tracing of your placement to keep as a reference. Using an erasable pencil (I use one the color of the thread), outline the shapes on the cloth or make paper templates for each one. I am always careful not to have lines that cannot be erased on the right side of my work, since I often change from my original plan as I proceed. I like both spontaneous and controlled designing. Have a general plan in mind for the effect you want but avoid planning too many details ahead of time. The fun comes from letting the shapes and colors clamor for the next step. As you go from one motif to another and change yarns, fasten the end behind the part you have just worked. This will make each unit independent of the next so that, if you change your mind and want to undo something, your yarns will not overlap each other.

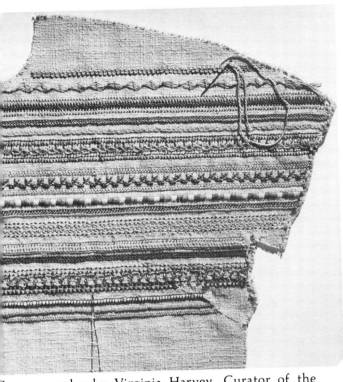

Blouse sampler by Virginia Harvey, Curator of the Costume and Textile Study Collection at the University of Washington. Mrs. Harvey decided she would make something useful while experimenting with stitches. (Photograph by William Eng.)

Detail of a white striped blouse used as a sampler, embroidered front and back in creamy white to create a yoke effect. The collar is turned up. (Worked and photographed by the author).

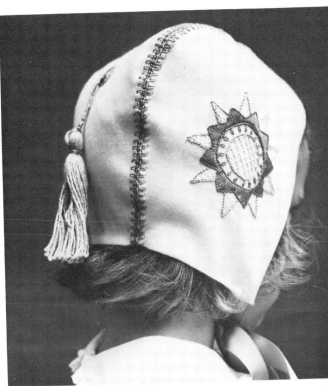

A Brittany bonnet embroidered by the author in three shades of blue on white wool, with the sun motif. (Photograph by the author.)

Detail of SPRING DYNAMICS, page 69, by Wilcke Smith, showing her imaginative use of the Raised Cross Stitch.

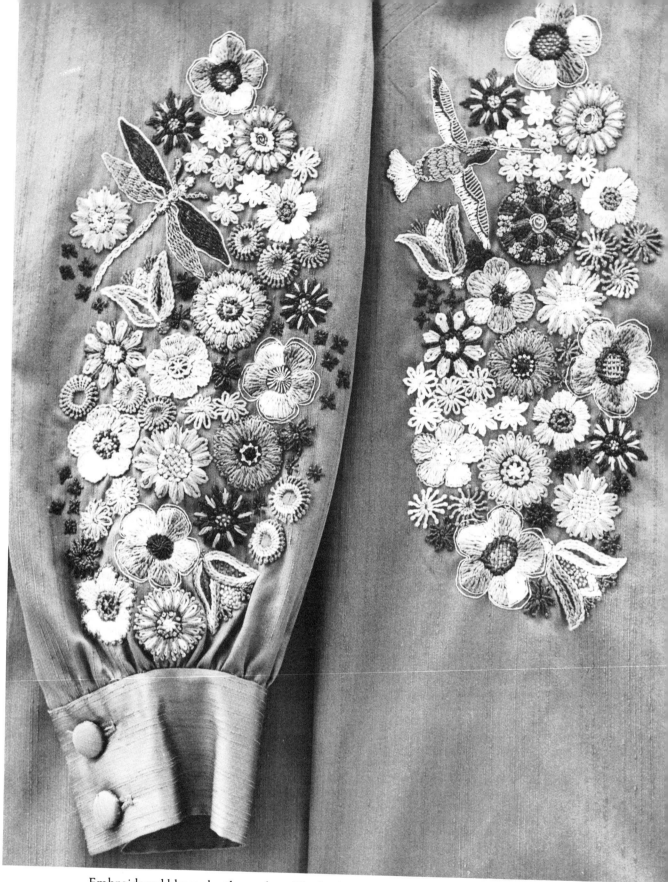

Embroidered blouse by the author. The background cloth is deep red, the embroidery is worked mostly with pearl cottons in warm shades of red and pink, with a few gold highlights. The design developed as the work progressed, with the shapes being chalked in lightly. One sleeve is embroidered from the shoulder to the elbow; the other from the elbow to the wrist. Most of the flower shapes are described in the text. (Photograph by the author.)

212

EMBROIDERING FLOWER SHAPES

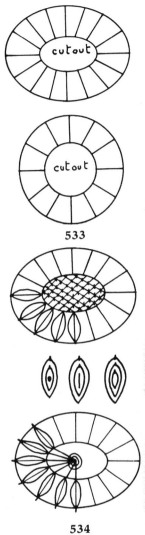

The description of a number of flower shapes will be followed by a review of centers which can be used with any of them. Suggestions for foliage, also decorative joinings of seams and of edges will follow. In this way you can create your own mix of alternatives in your own color scheme and have a piece you can truly call your own.

The adornments described need not be limited to clothing. They can be used on cushions, bags, wall hangings, framed pictures, blocks for a quilt, and many other things.

A successful method I developed for beginners and used for many years starts with cutting out a paper shape such as Figure 533, either a 1½ by 1 inch oval or a 1½ inch-diameter circle, cutting out the center and marking around it twelve or sixteen equally spaced lines. For twelve marks, think of a clock: two verticals and two horizontals, dividing the dial into four quarters and each quarter divided into three. For sixteen marks, divide each quarter in two and again in two. Baste the shape on the garment with sewing thread. This is the only time the needle will pierce the paper.

When you begin to embroider, avoid using starting knots which do not wear or iron well. I usually work a few very small Running Stitches at a place that will be covered up. Work Single Chains all around over the lines on the paper, the needle coming up and going down just outside the paper without sewing through it. The chains can be started on the inside, with the anchoring stitch on the outside, or they can be started on the outside with long anchoring stitches joining in or near the center (Figure 534). These could be used as the base for a Woven or Whipped Spider Web.

When the Chain Stitches have been worked, cut off the basting stitches from the back. Carefully snip the paper in two or three places; it will pull out easily. Work a second row of Single Chains inside the first possibly using a different color value. Then work a third Chain inside; if there is not sufficient room, or for the sake of variety, try using a Straight Stitch or a French knot.

There are many ways of varying the basic Single Chain idea. You can add different stitches such as Long-Stemmed French Knots, Fly Stitches or others illustrated on Figure 535. Two rows of Long-

533

534

535

Stemmed Chains can be worked in different values with a Straight Stitch in each center for a third value (Figure 536).

Try making flower shapes with Twisted Chains, turned up or down. These can be anchored with a long stem or one to three small stitches (Figure 537).

537

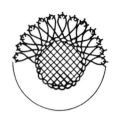

536

Threaded Chain

Children love to work with the easy Threaded Chain. Start with a Double Cross which serves as a base for chains (Figure 538). Come up at A, outside the cross, thread under the first edge, and return to A. Continue around. A second Threaded Chain can be worked around the first. The center can be woven, and Long-Stemmed French Knots can be added between.

I am very partial to a flower shape I made up with petals of Single Knotted Cable Chain, anchored with Bullion Stitches. I frequently use two values of the same color for alternate petals, such as a medium and light blue or a deep and light rose.

538

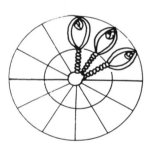

Draw a shape with an erasable pencil or chalk. Make the total width about 1½ inches and the height 1¼ inches, with twelve divisions (Figure 539). A milliner's needle, which is long and of even thickness, makes the work easier, as does a small hoop. Using pearl cotton size 5, start with a Single Knotted Cable Chain on the first division, a relaxed chain anchored halfway down (see Figure 433).

After working the stitch through points A, B, C, D and E, go down at F (see Figure 440) almost to the center of the flower. Come back up at E and push the needle almost but not quite through. Work a Bullion Knot with as many twists as are necessary to cover FE. Pull through, evening the twists, and go down at F. Repeat all around using a different value for alternate petals. For added beauty, I work a single French Knot in gold metallic thread in the center, another one inside the base of each chain, and clusters of three Long-Stemmed French Knots between petals.

539

Bullion Stitches can also be placed on the outside or toward the center of Single Chains or Fly Stitches (Figure 540). If you find Bullion Knots difficult, or if you just want a change, try using Long-Stemmed Knotted Cable Chain with Ribbed Spider Web over the stems. This can also be very effective (Figure 541).

540

541

Another variation is to make a Single Knotted Cable Chain with heavy yarn such as pearl cotton size 3, with the anchoring stitch EF just below C, encircling the small Twisted Chain (see Figure 434). The result is a textured three dimensional petal, with a long or short stem or with three anchoring stitches (Figure 542). You can also use pearl cotton size 5 for small petals. The combinations are endless.

542

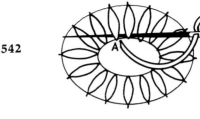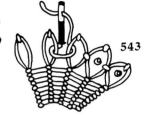

543

Ribbed Detached Chain

This stitch variation (Figure 543) was taught to me in Mexico by an embroideress who used variegated pearl cotton size 5 and sometimes size 8. Neither of us could speak the other's language, but we communicated beautifully and taught each other with joy. The shape was roughly 1½ inches horizontally by 1⅛ inches vertically. The center was ¾ inch horizontally by ⅜ inch vertically. She drew it in with a pen! For accuracy and peace of mind, I later basted a paper template with its center cut out and with sixteen divisions marked on it. All these measurements can and should be varied as you adapt the shape to your needs. For example, you could make it circular, with twelve or fourteen divisions.

Work a Single Detached Chain, a little loose, over each division, without piercing the paper, with the tying-down stitch on the outside. Then snip and slide out the template. Change to a tapestry needle with a long thread. Starting at A, work a Ribbed Spider Web, back over one chain, and forward under two all around; keep it snug pushing the needle down without pulling down the shape, and perhaps changing color values, until you have reached about two-thirds of the way up the chains.

The remaining ends of the chains are then tied together: Come up between two chain ends, about half way up. Without piercing the cloth, go under one side, then over it; next go over the other side, then under it. Go back down at the start, pulling the sides together. You might want to add a French Knot inside the stretched chains. There are countless center possibilities, if you feel the need of center stitches.

For a flower bud (Figure 544), make a triangular paper shape ¾ inch long, drawing five divisions on it. Baste it on the cloth and work Single Chains—first number one, then two on the opposite side, three in the middle, and so on, for balance. Take off the basting and the paper. Come up at A between chains two and four. Work Ribbed Spider Web from right to left, back over the number two chain, and forward under two and four. Continue. After going back over the number one chain, go down at B, and come up at C between chains one and five. Turn the work around and continue to DE, and so on, back and forth from right to left, until you reach F, pushing the stitches towards the base. Tie the rest of the chains as in the full flower. Add Long-Stemmed French Knots for stamens.

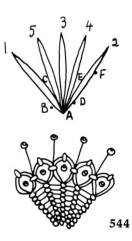

544

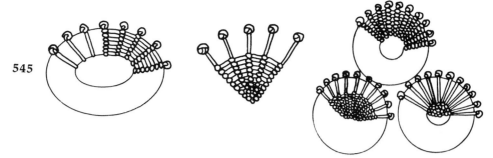

545

The same flower shapes and buds can also be worked over a base of Long-Stemmed French Knots (Figure 545), with the ribbing either all the way to the top or two-thirds of the way. I like to work clusters of three round shapes based on ¾ inch circles with twenty-four Long-Stemmed French Knots, using size 8 pearl cotton in different values of one color. Sometimes I work three or four rows of Ribbed Spider Web, leaving the rest of the Stemmed Knots free.

Threaded Straight Stitches

Threaded Straight Stitches can produce countless varieties of flower shapes and medallions of many sizes, from very small to large enough to use around a skirt. Playing with these will soon convince you that you can be creative and come up with ideas of your own.

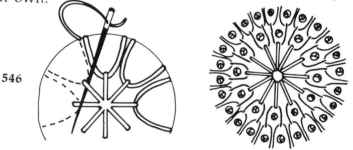

546

Work eight Straight Stitches, each under ¼ inch long, with pearl cotton size 5, or twelve stitches with pearl cotton size 8, almost to the center. Slide the needle under each Straight Stitch (Figure 546), without catching the cloth. Work as many rows as you like, changing color values; thread under the edges of the last out-stretched arms, and end the last row with the arms outstretched or joined together. Some threadings can overlap. Many stitches can be added effectively. The center can start with an Eye Stitch or with Fly Stitches (Figure 547). Spider Web Stitches can be worked around this base, or Straight Stitches around an open space which can be filled with French Knots or any stitch you choose.

Threaded Straight Stitches can also form designs, such as growing forms, overlapping each other (Figure 548).

547

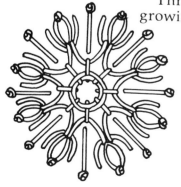

548

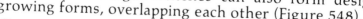

Woven Staight Stitches

Over a row of Straight Stitches (Figure 549), weave from right to left over and under as many rows as you need, reversing under and over at the end of each row. I like to use two yarns threaded in a needle as a Straight Stitch foundation (Figure 550), weaving over and under one side of each double stitch and alternating rows. Figure 551 shows Straight Stitches held in pairs with Back Stitches.

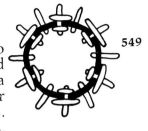

549

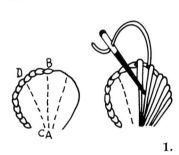

550

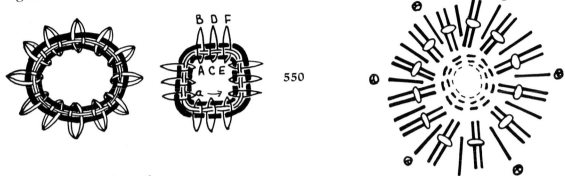

551

Ideas for more realistic flowers

Petals can be filled in a number of ways. It is interesting to see how various cultures work this out.

Satin Stitch is frequently used. One way to give a sharp edge to petals is to outline them with Split Stitch, working the Satin Stitches just over the outline. Work half of each petal at a time. You may want to draw directional lines to keep the correct slant, using a pencil the color of your thread (Figure 552-1). Start with the center stitch AB, then CD, bisecting the half petal. Continue filling. Small compensating stitches may be needed so that no cloth shows and there is no overlapping. I like to start those from the outside, nudging the point of the needle down between the adjoining stitches. If your edge is not smooth, work Outline, Chain, or Back Stitches on the outside.

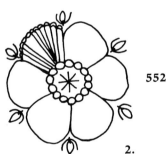

552

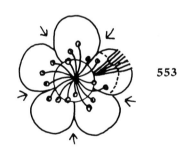

553

1.   2.

One of my favorite ways of working Satin Stitch petals is the Chain Outlined Satin Stitch used in Hungarian embroidery (see Figure 321). It slightly raises the edge and gives a crisp outline (Figure 552-2). One of many ways to fill petals is with Long-Stemmed Fly Stitches, arms together (Figure 553). Add interest by using threads with close values of one color, or variegated threads. This gives you built-in sophistication. Long Satin Stitches can be anchored with a Triple Palestrina Knot for added texture (Figure 554).

554

555   556   557

Here are more ideas: Try working Darning Stitches around circles, changing color values; or Straight Stitches outlined with a darker color; or Roumanian Stitches (Figures 555-557). Figures 558-564 will provide you with more stitch combinations: Straight Stitches and Satin Stitches; Outline Stitches and Seed Stitches; Long-Stemmed French Knots anchored with Chain Stitches; Long-Stemmed French Knots in clusters; groups of Threaded Detached Chains between large shapes; flowerets of white Single Chains with a yellow French Knot in the center (I worked this on a navy blue blouse; it provided cheerful accents amidst vibrant colors); Straight Stitches close together from the center, in different color values, worked from outside in. You can also use clusters of Raised Cross Stitches or Cross Stitch Flowers in three or four color values, either as individual small flowers sometimes overlapping or in groups where a space needs to be filled.

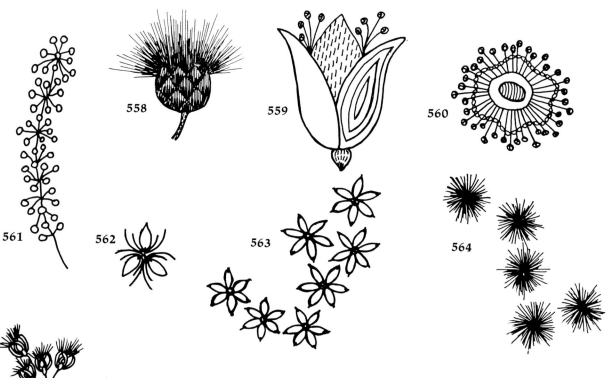

558   559   560   561   562   563   564   565

Effective sprays can be designed (Figure 565) with small Single Twisted Chains encircled by the same thread slipped through the anchoring stitch. These can be about ½ inch high in pearl cotton size 5 (I like a strong yellow), with added light yellow stamens made of two strands of floss just bursting out. Once you get started, you will find that the possibilities are endless, and you will know the joy of creating your own flower shapes.

DETACHED AND SEMIDETACHED PETALS

Flower shapes can be worked with petals detached and anchored only at the base; or they can be semidetached, anchored at the base and at the top. Detached petals can be made in several ways. One of the simplest starts with Running Stitches around the shape, using sewing thread, working as many stitches as you need petals (Figure 566). With a twisted yarn (floss will not work), come up at A, go over the Running Stitches, then under at D without piercing the cloth. Go down at B, pull through. Come up between AB at C. Split the AB yarn at D, without piercing the cloth. Weave over and under from the top of the petal down over the three yarns, pushing the weaving toward the top to make a compact petal. When you reach the base, go down at B and start the next petal. When all the petals are worked, clip the Running Stitches on the back of the cloth. The petals will be free. The sea anemone on the pant leg page 11 was worked in this way.

566

You can also work Running Stitches in groups of four, with loops through three Running Stitches and one stitch through the fourth, giving a base of seven threads for weaving (Figure 567). Starting at the top without piercing the cloth, weave over and under each of the successive two sides of the three loops and of the last stitch, working from top down, pushing up for compact texture. When the weaving is complete, clip the Running Stitches at the back.

567

Another method of working detached petals is one I use not only for flower shapes but for any detached petals, as for those on a jacket around the neck and on the pockets. I used pearl cotton size 5 in different colors. Stranded floss does not work well. Each petal is ¾ inch long, not quite ½ inch at the base. You can of course make them any size, depending on the weight of the thread. The needle goes through the cloth ONLY at the base. Mark where the base will be. Insert a T or corsage pin where the point of the petal will be, bringing it out lower than the base (in the center if it is a flower).

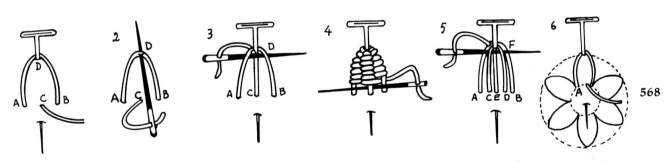

568

With the needle and thread, come up at A (Figure 568-1). Circle the relaxed thread around the pin, and go down at B. Come up again at C, pull through. With the point of the needle, split the thread at D (the top of the petal), without piercing the cloth. You will need to take off the pin while you split the thread (2). Return the pin to its place. Start weaving back and forth over the three threads, without pulling too much from side to side so that you keep a proper width for the petal (3). As you weave, use the needle to pack the woven threads up toward the tip for a compact texture until the base is reached (4). Take the needle and thread down to the back, remove the pin, and start the next petal. If heavier petals are needed, work two loops around the pin, AB, CD, E to F, splitting both loops without going through the cloth (5). Start weaving back and forth over five threads.

For a flower shape with detached petals, using pearl cotton size 5, a 1½ inch circle with a ½ inch center works well (6), or mark any size circle your threads warrant. If you don't want to mark the circles with chalk, you can make a template of the circle and run stitches around it which you can take off later. Another alternative is to trace the circles on tissue paper or sheer nonwoven interfacing; baste these down and tear them off when through. Mark five or six spokes for correct placement; then start at A, and so on.

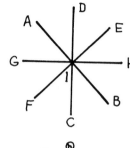

Semidetached petals

Semidetached petals are best worked with a hoop. With a sharp erasable colored pencil, mark the center of the flower and draw lightly a Double Cross Stitch 1½ inches across (Figure 569). With pearl cotton size 5, come up at A, ¾ inch from the center, and go down at B, 1½ inches from A. Continue around, laying 1½ inch spokes. Go down at H, and come up in the center at I, to the left of AB.

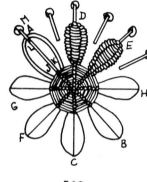

Change to a tapestry needle and work a Ribbed Spider Web snugly toward the center, backward over one, forward under two, pushing the stitches toward the center as you go around so that the center will rise up. Continue until the center is ⅜ inch in diameter. Go down and end the thread behind the web. Change to a darker value or to a gold thread, and work a Ribbed Spider Web snugly three times around. Go down at the end of the third row.

For the petals, using two close values of your chosen color for alternate petals, come up at J. Work a relaxed Detached Chain, and go down at K, anchoring it up at L, the same hole as A, with a ¼-inch Long-Stemmed French Knot. The anchoring knot can be made larger by twisting the needle twice over and under the thread. Come up again at L. Weave over and under the three threads without pulling so that the petals stay rounded. As you weave, push the needle toward L for a compact texture. Go down between J and K. Remember to change values for alternate petals. When all are filled, change to the lighter value or to gold and work Long-Stemmed French Knots between the petals.

569

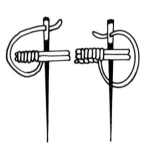

570

Semidetached petals or shapes

These are worked in a variety of ways: over Foundation Stitches or relaxed Straight Stitches, Buttonhole, Chain, Outline, and so on, each one creating a different effect. On one, two, or three Straight Stitches you can whip over and under or Buttonhole over without picking up any cloth (Figure 570). In Figure 571, each petal is made of two sets of relaxed Straight Stitches starting and ending in the same hole, with Detached Buttonholes worked toward the outside to help curve the stitches. For long semidetached lines, use a base of Outline Stitches. You can weave over two, three, or more Straight Stitches laid parallel to each other with or without a gap between (Figure 572). If two Straight Stitches start from the same hole, the

571

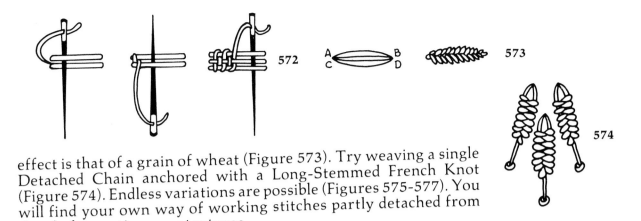

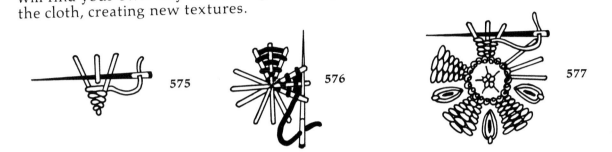

effect is that of a grain of wheat (Figure 573). Try weaving a single Detached Chain anchored with a Long-Stemmed French Knot (Figure 574). Endless variations are possible (Figures 575-577). You will find your own way of working stitches partly detached from the cloth, creating new textures.

Centers

Centers of flower shapes can be filled in many ways, depending partly on the size of the shape and on how large the center is. Here are a few suggestions which have been illustrated in preceding flower shapes; French Knots in a circle—either spaced, close together, or filling the whole area—using one color or several mixed (these can be worked on top of each other for a raised center); Long-Stemmed French Knots in different lengths, like stamens (these can go over the petals); Raised Cross Stitches; Palestrina Knots, single or double; Spider Webs, ribbed or woven, worked sometimes only partway, with fine or heavy threads; Couched Filling with two or three values of a color; and Woven Filling.

Foliage and leaves

A small amount of gracefully curved foliage between flower shapes adds interest and balances the spaces. In the right proportion, green is what sparks your other colors. I enjoy using variegated green, planning so that the tips are light and the lower parts dark. Try light sprays with Single Chains along a stem, Fern Stitches, light Blanket Stitches back to back, Coral Knots (spaced or close), Long-Stemmed French Knots. The Chinese use their Knot in effective sprays, in which each group of three curves is worked in light, medium, and dark green silk, with the lower stem couched. (Figure 578).

Leaf illustrations are shown throughout the book made with stitches that include Running, Stem, Flat, Fishbone, Leaf, Herringbone, Buttonhole, Feather, Cretan, Fly, Chain, Knots, Roumanian and others.

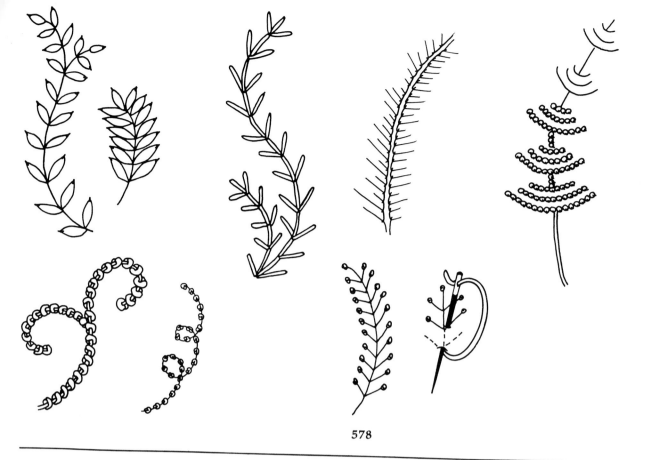

578

579

Crazy quilts provide imaginative stitchers with endless opportunities to embellish already stitched seams creatively. This is a record of some of the stitch combinations used on the Bicentennial crazy quilt for the Governor's Mansion in Olympia, Washington. It was embellished by the members of the South Sound Creative Stitchery Guild. (Stitch drawings by Judith Weston.)

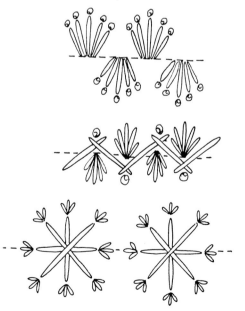

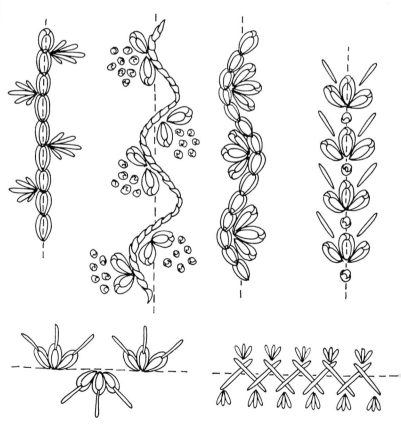

JOININGS

A garment can be greatly enhanced by decorative joinings stressing its structure. Embellishments can also be added to an already stitched seam (Figure 579). Ethnic clothing especially older examples will provide you with a wealth of techniques. I enjoy making samplers of joinings from different cultures.

From the earliest times, joinings had to be used to make wearable garments. Different cultures wove cloth in a variety of widths, many of them quite narrow. This in turn influenced the structure of the garments, using very little cutting; pieces were joined from selvedge to selvedge in a lasting way. From their utilitarian origins, the joinings became ornamental, and it may be that embroidery saw its beginning as an elaboration of joinings. Edges were frequently worked right against each other; others had spaces of varying widths between them depending on the stitch used.

If cut edges rather than selvedges are to be joined, work a small ¼ inch hem on each side or fold back the width of the stitch used to cover it. Press or baste in place. I like to baste my joinings on a piece of paper following a line I have drawn on it so that the two sides stay exactly opposite each other. If the edges are spaced, I use graph paper with inch divisions, the number of squares to the inch depending on the size of the stitches. Graph paper provides a straight basting line and definite stitching points. Pliable vinyl-type material can also be used instead of paper. The French use thin oil cloth.

People in the Balkans use a great variety of joinings on their blouses. I keep coming across new ones. I found one of my favorites on a white Roumanian blouse, worked in red cotton of about pearl 8 weight, with the edges close together (Figure 580). It must be worked with precision to be effective. The stitches are ¼ inch in height and width. Hem both edges with the smallest possible hem, and baste on paper with the two edges just touching. With an erasable pencil, mark dots on both sides of the cloth, ¼ inch apart and ⅛ inch from the edge. Work from right to left, slipping the needle between cloth and paper. Follow the diagrams; note that G is halfway between E and C and that H is halfway between D and F.

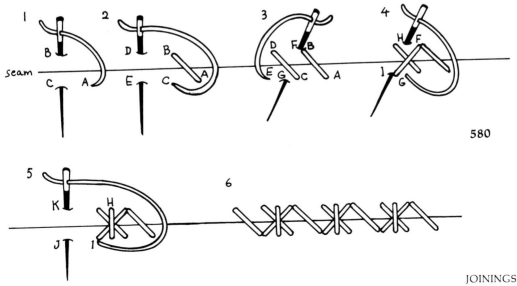

580

In old Russia, an effective small embroidered band was used either to join two edges or to cover already joined sleeve seams, in which case it was called a "masking" stitch. The joining stitch is worked vertically, drawing the edges together. It consists of a Cross Stitch with a Long-Armed Cross Stitch followed by a Cross Stitch with a Long-Legged Cross Stitch, repeating the succession while working from right to left. For the "masking" stitch, the needle is worked horizontally; it was taught to me by a Russian emigrée as she worked on my children's clothes. The crosses were very small, giving an elegant touch to the clothing. It can of course be made any size, and several rows can be worked close together for a border. It is easy to learn on a hardanger or aïda-type of cloth. For Russian joining, follow the diagram from A to Q; then repeat as from A (Figure 581).

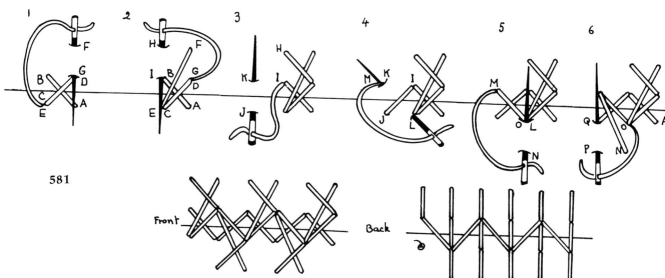

581

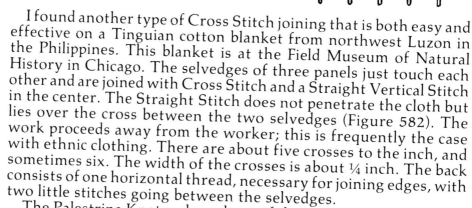

Front   Back

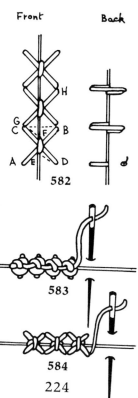

Front   Back

582

583

584

I found another type of Cross Stitch joining that is both easy and effective on a Tinguian cotton blanket from northwest Luzon in the Philippines. This blanket is at the Field Museum of Natural History in Chicago. The selvedges of three panels just touch each other and are joined with Cross Stitch and a Straight Vertical Stitch in the center. The Straight Stitch does not penetrate the cloth but lies over the cross between the two selvedges (Figure 582). The work proceeds away from the worker; this is frequently the case with ethnic clothing. There are about five crosses to the inch, and sometimes six. The width of the crosses is about ¼ inch. The back consists of one horizontal thread, necessary for joining edges, with two little stitches going between the selvedges.

The Palestrina Knot makes a beautiful joining that is much used in Italy (Figure 583) as is also the Palestrina Knot and Chain. The Squared Palestrina can be used in the same manner (Figure 584).

Triangular Joining is found in the earliest textiles of Asia, Europe, Africa, and South America (Figure 585). It is part of Moslem tradition and spread from the Near East around the Mediterranean to Spain, Portugal, and later to the colonies of these countries. It is also found in early Peruvian textiles. It looks best when worked with precision. Baste selvedges or small hems, or just turn back the cloth on a strip of paper on each side of a drawn line.

224

For clarity, in Figure 585, the diagrams show spaces between edges, but actually they should just meet. If you are using pearl cotton size 8 or 5, the points of the triangles should be ⅛ inch in from the edge, ¼ inch apart, the two sides staggered so as to create a zigzag effect. Some are worked in one color; others change colors every two inches or so, or whenever the thread runs out. I find it helpful to use a small ruler and mark every ¼ inch with a dot, ⅛ inch in from the edge, using a pencil the same color as the thread and remembering to stagger the opposite side.

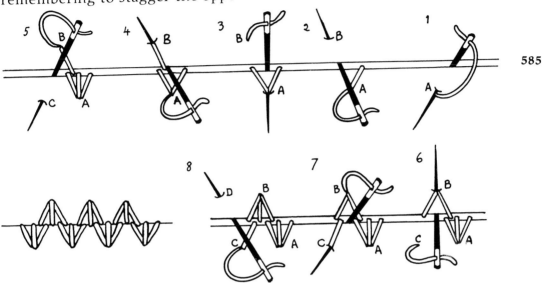

585

Work from right to left. Come up at A, ⅛ inch from the edge (Figure 585-1), and pull through. Slide the needle, slanting downward, under the lower edge between paper and cloth and come up again at A. Pull through. (2) Slide the needle upward under the upper edge. Come up at B, ⅛ inch to the left of A, so as to start the staggered triangles. Pull through. (3) Holding the thread up to the right, slide the needle downward under the lower edge, *TO THE RIGHT OF AB.* Come up at A, pull through. (4) With the thread circling counterclockwise, slide the needle upward under the upper edge, *TO THE RIGHT OF AB,* coming up at B. It is important that the needle always be pulled to the right, going into the point of the triangle, to make the triangle stitches even. (5) With the thread up and circled clockwise, slide the needle under the lower edge, coming up at C, ¼ inch from A. Pull through. (6) Circling the thread to the right, slide the needle upward under the upper edge, to the right of BC, coming up at B. (7) Slide the needle downward to the *RIGHT* of BC, coming up at C. Pull through. (8) Repeat the steps, beginning with step 2.

A variation worked with fine wool on a Peruvian pancho has an added Straight Stitch at each point of the triangles. It makes the joining wider and more decorative.

The Yugoslav Border Stitch described on page 92. (Zigzag Double Running) is also used as a joining, with points ¼ inch apart. The Roumanian Stitch (see Figure 453) can be worked spaced, close together, or in patterns. Try Feather Stitch or Herringbone, plain or laced. Raised Chain Band (see Figure 393) is another attractive joining. There are many Mexican and Guatemalan joinings based mostly on the Flat Stitch, the Roumanian Stitch, and the Cretan.

A delightful joining found in the University of Washington Textile Collection, Seattle, was on Greek pant legs with Feather Stitches worked over Cretan. For the overstitching, change to a round-pointed needle; work the Feather Stitch without going through the cloth, and fill the space (Figure 586). The original was worked with fine white threads. Try it with pearl cotton size 3. I use the Greek idea frequently when I want the joining space to be filled solidly.

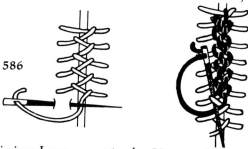

586

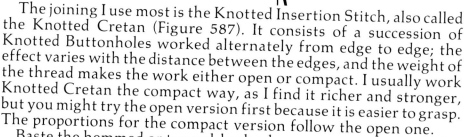

The joining I use most is the Knotted Insertion Stitch, also called the Knotted Cretan (Figure 587). It consists of a succession of Knotted Buttonholes worked alternately from edge to edge; the effect varies with the distance between the edges, and the weight of the thread makes the work either open or compact. I usually work Knotted Cretan the compact way, as I find it richer and stronger, but you might try the open version first because it is easier to grasp. The proportions for the compact version follow the open one.

Baste the hemmed or turned-back edges on a paper backing. For pearl cotton size 5, try using a strip of graph paper 10 squares to the inch, basting the edges 2/10 inch apart. The graph paper provides precise stitching intervals. It can be worked horizontally or vertically. I find the latter easier.

Come up on the left edge at A from inside the fold (Figure 587-1). Go down at B on the opposite side through both thicknesses, 1/10 inch lower. Pull through, over the thread from A. (2) Hold the thread down, counterclockwise. Slide the needle downward under both threads. Snug the working thread under the point of the needle. Pull through, making a knot close to the edge. (3) With the needle on the A side pointing to the B side, go down at C, 2/10 inch lower than A. Pull through, going over the thread from B. (4) Slide the needle downward under the two threads, circling the thread from C clockwise and pulling it snugly under the point of the needle. Pull through, making a knot close to the edge. (5) Continue back and forth. To end, slide the needle into the fold of the opposite side. Fasten after the basting is removed by cutting the threads behind the paper.

For the compact version, using the same cotton and graph paper, baste the sides 1/10 inch apart and make the distance between stitches 1/10 inch. Experiment with different weights and textures. If you are joining the seams of a wool jacket for instance, try using one strand of crewel wool for a narrow joining or a tapestry wool for a wider one, with colors either blending or contrasting. These joinings and many others you may discover add character to garments, whether the stitching actually joins the edges or is used over a stitched seam.

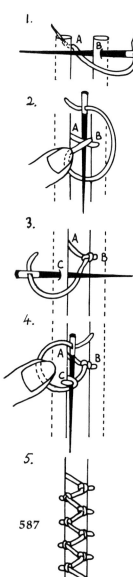

1.

2.

3.

4.

5.

587

EDGINGS

Edges of garments can be enhanced by rows of stitches worked close together, either repeating the same stitch, such as Chain Stitch, or using a successive variety of stitches. These are borders. Compact rows are usually most effective.

A true edging is worked over the edge which can be a selvedge, a hem, or the cloth turned back. The stitches can be spaced or close together; the possibilities are endless. Below are descriptions of a few I find particularly useful and decorative.

The Eskimo Laced Edge described on page 48 is an example of a decorative edging that is somewhat spaced. On the collar of a child's dress made of fine organdy, I made a hem ⅛ inch deep with six red Running Stitches to the inch using three strands of six-stranded cotton, lacing over the edge in blue. On a table mat, the hem was 3/16 inch, four Running Stitches to the inch, using pearl cotton size 5 and lacing with pearl 3.

Many cultures use a zigzag overcast stitch, worked over a folded hem, either a single row over the edge from left to right (Figure 588) or a double row, returning from right to left, filling the spaces (Figure 589). It is often seen in Mexico and Central America, with the return journey worked in a different color.

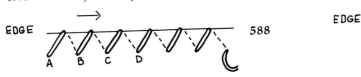

One variation adds an upright stitch on the first journey and fills in with a slanting stitch on the way back (Figure 590). Work an upright stitch at A over the edge and back at A, followed by a slanting stitch, coming up at B, then an upright stitch at B, and so on. From E go back over the edge, slanting and up at D, and so on.

Another attractive variation, used in old Russia adds groups of small stitches on the return journey. First work slanting stitches over the edge as in Figure 588. As you come up at E (Figure 591), work a small stitch to F, back to E, then to G, back to E. Finally to H, and back to E. Continue over the edge, come up at D, and so on.

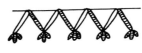

591

Another row can be added to the first, with little groups of three on the second row (Figure 592). I saw this done on yellow cloth with a fringed edge from Guatemala. The first row was worked in deep turquoise, the return journey in deep magenta. The two sides are identical, which makes it ideal for a scarf. It is both functional and decorative.

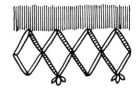

592

An edging Mexican women worked around the neck of white voile blouses with black thread is one I have not seen anywhere else, which is why I refer to it as the Mexican Edging. The size of the stitches and their distance apart vary with the weight of the thread. The hem on one example was a scant ¼ inch and the black thread used was about the weight of pearl cotton size 8.

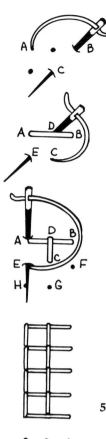

Working downward (Figure 593) come up at A from inside the basted hem, down at B, ¼ inch to the right, and up at C, ⅛ inch down between A and B. Pull through. Go down at D on the AB line, over the thread, and come up at E on the edge, ⅛ inch below A. Pull through. Work a Back Stitch from E to A in the same hole, then back to E, right on the edge. Pull through. Repeat E to F, down to G. Pull through. Go down at C in the same hole, up at H on the edge, down at E, and up at H in the same hole, and so on. It must be worked with precision to be attractive. I use a transparent ruler and mark dots ¼ inch from the edge, ⅛ inch apart, with a colored pencil that matches my yarn. It makes the stitching relaxed, precise and saves time. The stitch has many possibilities with added rows facing each other. French Knots could go in the squares, or Single Chains on the open side. The size and weight of thread can also be varied.

Buttonhole edges have many possible variations. Look at page 102 for ideas. A Buttonhole edging knotted in pairs is found in a number of cultures, especially in the Orient. I diagrammed one from a blouse made in Taiwan on an off-white cloth worked in indigo threads (Figure 594).

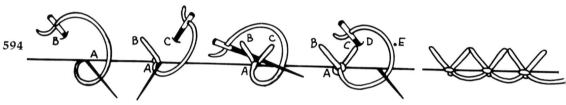

594

593

Baste a narrow hem turned to the right side of the cloth. Bring the needle and thread up at A from inside the hem. Holding the thread down with your left thumb, go down at B just outside the hem, to the left of A, and come up at the edge, over the thread coming from A. Pull through. Go down at C. Come up at the edge over the thread from A. Pull through. Slide the needle under the two slanting stitches from left to right. With the thread under the point of the needle, pull through forming a knot. Continue buttonholing and knotting in pairs, D to E and so on, forming even Vs and triangles. The back and the front are alike. For a firmer edge, a knotted top can be worked with knots close together. Knotted Buttonholes are used by embroiderers under a variety of names and by means of different techniques. One way is illustrated in Figure 246.

The Turkomans of western Turkestan work a Tailor's Buttonhole on the edges of some of their stunning coats, an idea we might well adapt for use on a jacket or a vest. The heavy cloth is not turned back, but lighter cloths would be. The stitch can be worked with the edge toward you, sideways, or away from you. Some cultures do it one way, others another, with the same results.

I personally favor Louisa Pesel's technique for Tailor's Buttonhole which she diagrammed at the Victoria and Albert Museum in London while studying Turkoman coats. She illustrated it in her Eastern Samplers series in 1913. It is the buttonhole technique I was taught as a young girl in France. It is worked with the knotted edge away from the worker, with the garment on one's lap. This gives good control over the knots. I studied Turkoman coats at the Los Angeles County Museum of Art and find the result especially beautiful when Stem and Outline Stitches are added to cover the base of the Tailor's Buttonhole.

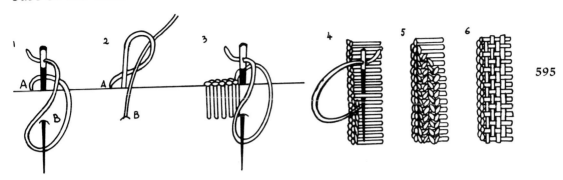

595

Work from left to right (Figure 595). Start with two or three small Running Stitches in the opposite direction, going back to A. These will be covered up. With the thread from A up, slide the needle behind the cloth and come up in front at B. Do not pull through. With the thread from A snugly behind the needle, pass the thread from the eye of the needle left to right over and under the point of the needle. Pull the needle through, lifting the thread up to the edge and tightening the knot. Repeat. The knots should be close together, with the Straight Stitches not quite touching each other. A firm twisted thread works well. The Turkomans used a twisted silk with a Z twist, upper right to lower left. Since our eyes are accustomed to an S twist, upper left to lower right, the Z twist gives the Turkoman stitches a different look.

Using a tapestry needle, work Outline Stitches close to the knots over each of the Straight Stitches, without piercing the cloth (thread held up). Follow this with a row of Stem Stitches (thread held down). These two rows together look like a Chain. If there is room, you can repeat these until the Buttonhole base is covered. I have worked it on dark blue wool flannel using red three-ply wool. It makes an interesting, beautiful braidlike edge. It can also be worked with Running Stitches over and under the base stitches, in alternating rows, using different color values.

You have, I hope, learned many stitches; this should give you freedom of choice in embellishing clothing. It is important to choose the right stitch and the right thread for the effect you want. Use each stitch often enough so that you may become relaxed and free with your needle. Use what you have learned to create original work. If you try, YOU CAN BE CREATIVE. It will bring much joy into your life and into the lives of those around you.

INDIANS AND BUFFALOS by the author. A stitchery with a theme, this mural for a boy's room is worked on handwoven linen. It is embroidered in colored cottons in shades of green, blue, blue-green, brown, and gold, with small touches of red. The design was first worked out with scissors and paper. Outlines were lightly drawn on the linen. The stitches were chosen as the work progressed to express texture, motion, and depth.

230

Conclusion

The four young women whose samplers are reproduced in color on page 7 all started out with the fixed notion that they could neither stitch nor design. If you felt this way when you started to read this book, I hope that by now you have changed your mind as they did.

Working with their samplers was a new experience for them. They enjoyed choosing and mixing colors. New ways with stitches became a never-ending source of delight.

The tempo of Susan's creativity amazes me; she is always busy producing beautiful things for her home, adding original designs to her little girl's clothes or to her own, making unique presents for her family and friends.

It was Elizabeth, active and persuasive, who talked me into teaching the four friends. She is now teaching and inspiring others, and is especially successful with small children, who are fascinated with the magic of stitches.

Besides helping children with their individual pieces, Elizabeth guides groups of them into stitching delightful murals, full of life and enthusiasm, like "Summer Meadow" shown on page 6.

Isobel and Lois took a little longer to strike out on their own. Before starting on her sampler, Isobel insisted that she would never be able to create spontaneously with a needle. Yet, after she had finished her sampler, in two exhilarating afternoons, she produced the lively sparkling beetle shown below. I shall never forget the light in her eyes when she brought me her delightful creation. I had made several unsuccessful attempts to inspire her. I had spoken of stylized sunflowers or wild grasses for the pocket of a garden apron, but these were my ideas, not Isobel's. She found her inspiration on the cover of a garden magazine, an ugly little brown beetle, about 1½ inches long, a most unlikely subject. But it proved to be the needed catalyst. She suddenly visualized it quite large, in sparkling greens and blues and gold; the stitches flowed from her needle. Like everyone else, her small son fell in love with it, and he now has it framed in his room.

BEETLE by Isobel Johnson. The sparkling beetle, 6 inches long and 6½ inches wide, is worked in gold, green, and blue, with small touches of red.

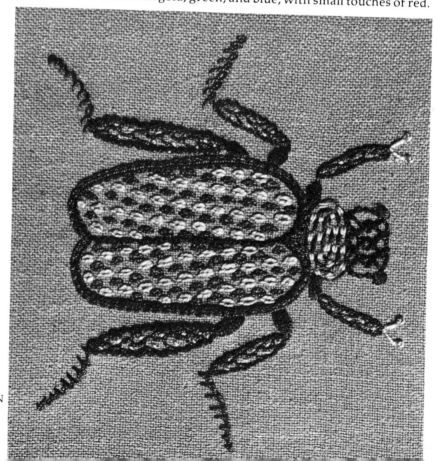

Lois was the one who found it hardest to accept the idea that she could design and create in a way that would truly express her personality. The delightful "Lion" stitchery shown on the title page is the first thing she produced completely alone. She found her inspiration in the Mexican Indian painting shown below. Her "Lion" is a joy to all who see it. It was fun for her, and rewarding. Many people today are making the same discovery about embroidering.

Gradually, more and more schools are successfully exploring stitches as a means of artistic expression. Mariska Karasz, Mary Ann Spawn, Wilcke Smith, and many other talented artists are giving new vitality to the medium; works by these artists are reproduced in color on pages 15, 6, 11. Every country in which the art of embroidery has been practiced has developed its own style. It is my fondest hope that this book will foster the growth of the American style that is now in the process of emerging.

Racing Hydroplanes. Stitchery, 20 by 19 inches, on burlap by David Carbary, 11 years old.

A black and white reproduction of this painting by a folk artist of Tonala, Mexico, inspired the "Lion" stitchery by Lois Packer shown on the title page.

Index of Stitches

-A-

Afghanistan Reversible Stitches, 47
Algerian Eye Stitch, 63
    Filling, 63
Alternating Stem Stitch, 72
Arrowhead Stitch, 92
    Interlaced Yugoslav Border, 93
    Yugoslav Border, 92

-B-

Back Stitch, 52
    Double (Closed Herringbone), 81
    Threaded, Double, 55
    Threaded, Single, 55
    Triple, Closed, 55
    Triple (Hungarian), 55
    Whipped, 55
Back and Running, 53
Back Stitched Chain, 122
Basket Filling Stitch, 61
Basket Stitch, 97
    Closed, 98
    Open, 97
Basque Knot, 158
Basque Stitch, 131
Bayeux Stitch, 168
Blanket Stitch, 101
Bokhara Stitch, 174
Bosnia Stitch, 94
    Triangle, 97
Braid Stitch, 147
Breton Stitch, 90
    Variation, Point de Veuve, 91
Briar Stitch, 108
Broad Chain, 144
Bullion Knot, 151
    Chained, 152
    Long-Stemmed, 152
    with single knotted chain, 163
Buttonhole Stitch, 102
    Blanket, 101
    Closed, 102
    Crossed, 102
    Double, 104
    Filling, 105
    Knotted, 160
    Outline, 103
    Raised Edge, 105
    Single Feather, 103
    Spaced, 101
    Spiral, 103

Tailor's, Turkoman, 228
Up and Down, 106
Up and Down, Double, 107
Up and Down, Filling, 107
Whipped, 105

-C-

Cable Chain, 140
    Double, 140
    Knotted, 160
    Knotted with Bullion, 214
    Slipped, 140
Cable Zigzag Chain, 141
Catch Cretan Stitch, 110
Centipede Stitch (Loop), 118
Chain and Buttonhole Band, 124
Chain and Fly Stitch, 129
Chain Outlined Satin Stitch, 125
Chain over Chain, 122
Chain Stitch, 121
    Back Stitched, 122
    Broad, 144
    Cable, 140
    Cable, Double, 140
    Cable, Slipped, 140
    Chain and Buttonhole Band, 124
    Chain and Fly, 129
    Chained Cross, 136
    Checkered (Magic), 132
    Closed Double, 136
    Closed Square, 135
    Closed Threaded Square, 135
    Crested, 146
    Cross, 136
    Detached, 126
    Detached Filling, 127
    Detached Filling, Slipped, 128
    Detached, Long-Armed, 128
    Detached, Slipped, 127
    Detached Twisted Chain, 137
    Double, 136
    Edging Stitch, 227
    Flowers, Detached, 129
    Heavy, 144
    Hungarian Braided, 145
    Interlaced, 124
    Knotted Cable, 160
    Knotted Zigzag, 163
    Length Variations, 122
    Outlined Satin, 125
    Raised Band, 145
    Ribbed Detached, 215

Rosette, 139
Russian, 128
Single Knotted Cable, 161
Spine, 144
Spine, Laced, 144
Spine, Whipped, 144
Square (Open), 132
Square (Closed), 135
Square Closed Threaded, 135
Threaded, 124-214
Threaded, Detached, Double, 128
Threaded, Detached, Single, 128
Threaded Square, 133
Twisted, 137
Twisted, Detached, 137
Whipped, 122
Zigzag, 126
Zigzag, Cable, 141
Zigzag, Long-Stemmed, 130
Zigzag, Twisted (Spanish), 138
Chained Bullion, 152
Checkerboard Running Stitch, 33
Checkered Chain (Magic), 132
Chevron Stitch, 91
Chinese Knot, 157
Closed Basket Stitch, 98
Closed Buttonhole Stitch, 102
Closed Cretan, 109
Closed Feather Stitch, 107
Closed Herringbone (Double Back
    Stitch), 81
Closed Square Chain, 135
Closed Threaded Square Chain, 135
Coral Knot, 153
    Snail Trail, 153
Coral Zigzag Knot, 154
Couched Filling, 167
Couching, 166
    Variations, 167
Crested Chain, 146
Cretan Stitch, 109
    Catch, 110
    Closed, 109
    Filling, 110
    Laced (Interlaced Band, Double
        Pekinese), 110
    Open, 110
    Slanted, 110
Crewel Stitch (Outline, Stem), 71
Crisscross Herringbone, 83
Cross Stitch, 64
    Double, 65
    Flower, 70
    Oblong, 66
    Raised, 70
    Slav (Long-Armed), 68
    Upright, 65
Cross Stitch, Chained, 136
Crossed Buttonhole Stitch, 102

-D-

Darning, 49
    Kogin, 51

Pattern Darning, 51
Surface Darning, 49
Detached Chain, 126
    Ribbed, 215
Detached Chain Filling, 127
Detached Chain Flowers, 129
Detached Split Stitch, 143
Detached Twisted Chain, 137
Dot Stitch (Seed Stitch), 56
Double Back Stitch (Closed Herring-
    bone), 81
Double Buttonhole Stitch, 104
Double Cable Chain, 140
Double Chain, 136
    Closed, 136
Double Cross Stitch, 65
Double Flat Stitch, 76
Double Herringbone, 84
    Interlaced, 88
    Variation, 87
Double Knot (Palestrina), 154
Double Laced Band, Tuareg, 39
Double Pekinese Stitch (Laced
    Cretan), 110
Double Running Stitch (Holbein),
    45
Double Slanted Feather Stitch, 108
Double Threaded Running Stitch,
    37
Double Up and Down Buttonhole
    Stitch, 106

-E-

Edgings, 227
Eskimo Laced Edge, 48
Eye Stitch, 62
    Algerian, 63

-F-

Feather Stitch, 107
    Closed, 107
    Long-Armed (Spine), 109
    Rosemary, 108
    Slanted, 108
    Slanted, Double, 108
    Slanted, Triple, 108
    Slanted, Variations, 108
    Straight, 107
    Straight, Double, 108
    Straight, Triple, 108
Fern Stitch, 78
Figure of Eight Stitch, 173
Fillings,
    Algerian Eye, 63
    Basket, 61
    Buttonhole, 105
    Couched, 167
    Cretan, 110
    Detached Chain, 127
    Fly, 114
    Four-sided, 64
    French, 73
    Satin, 60

Seed, 56
Slipped Detached Chain, 127
Star, 63
Tête-de-Boeuf, 129
Up and Down Buttonhole, 107
Wave, 93
Fishbone Stitch, 76
Open, 77
Raised, 77
Flat Stitch, 75
Double, 76
Flower, Cross Stitch, 70
Fly Stitch, 113
Chain and Fly, 129
Filling, 114
Fly and Two Ties, 114
Interlaced, 113
Whipped, 113
Zigzag, 115
Four-Sided Stitch, 63
Filling, 64
French Filling (Stem Stitch), 73
French Knot, 149
French Knot Border Stitch, 150
French Zigzag Band, 96

-G-

Guilloche Stitch, 61

-H-

Heavy Chain, 144
Herringbone Stitch, 81
Closed (Double Back), 81
Crisscross, 83
Double, 84
Double Interlaced, 88
Threaded, 84
Tied, 84
Triple, 84
Variation, 87
Holbein Stitch (Double Running), 45
Huichol Zigzag, 94
Hungarian Braided Chain, 145
Hungarian Stitch (Triple back), 55

-I-

Insertion Wave Stitch, 93
Interlaced Band Stitch (Laced Cretan), 110
Interlaced Chain, 124
Interlaced Fly Stitch, 113
Interlaced Yugoslav Border Stitch, 93
Interwoven Cross Stitches, 70
Italian Hemstitch, 63
Italian Sheaf Stitch, 99

-J-

Joining Stitches, 223

-K-

Knotted Buttonhole Stitch, 160
Knotted Cable Chain, 160
with Bullion, 214
Knotted Pearl, 157
Knotted Zigzag, 163
Kogin, 51

-L-

Laced Cretan (Interlaced Band, Double Pekinese), 110
Laced Spine Chain, 144
Laced Woven Band Quadruple, 42
Laced Wheat-Ear Stitch, 144
Ladder Stitch, 118
Leaf Stitch, 78
Length Variations, Chain Stitch, 122
Line Shading (Stem Stitch), 74
Long and Short, 61
Long-Armed Cross Stitch (Slav), 68
Long-Armed Detached Chain, 128
Long-Armed Feather Sttich (Spine), 109
Long-Legged Cross Stitch, 68
Long Stem Stitch, 72
Long-Stemmed Bullion Knot, 152
Long-Stemmed French Knot, 150
Long-Stemmed Zigzag Chain, 130
Loop Stitch (Centipede), 118

-M-

Magic Chain (Checkered Chain), 132
Mirror Work, Shisha, 178

-N-

New England Laid Stitch, 173

-O-

Oblong Cross Stitch, 66
Open Basket Stitch, 97
Open Chain (Square), 132
Open Cretan Stitch, 110
Open Fishbone Stitch, 77
Outline Buttonhole Stitch, 103
Outline Stitch (Crewel, Stem), 71

-P-

Palestrina (Double Knot), 154
Knot and Chain, 157
Random, 157
Reverse, 157
Small, 158
Squared, 155
Triple, 155
Pattern Darning, 51
Pekinese Stitch, 56

Double (Laced Cretan), 110
Spaced, 57
Petal Stitch, 130
Petals Detached, 219
Semi Detached, 220
Plait Stitch, 69
Point de Veuve, 91
Portuguese Stem Stitch, 74
Pueblo Stitch, 142

-Q-

Quadruple Laced Woven Band, 42

-R-

Raised Bullion Knot, 151
Raised Chain Band, 145
Raised Cross Stitch, 70
Raised Edge Buttonhole Stitch, 105
Raised Fishbone Stitch, 77
Random Palestrina, 157
Renaissance Stitch, 172
Reverse Palestrina Knot, 157
Ribbed Detached Chain, 215
Rosemary Stitch, 108
Rosette Chain, 139
Roumanian Joining, 223
Roumanian Stitch, 172
Running Stitch, 31
Checkerboard, 33
Connecting Variations, 43
Double (Holbein), 45
Threaded, Double, 37
Theaded, Single, 37
Whipped, 33
Russian Chain, 128
Russian Joining, 224

-S-

Sashiko, 52
Satin Stitch, 60
Chain Outlined, 125
Filling, 60
Twisted, 60
Scroll Stitch, 119
Seed Stitch (Dot), 56
Filling, 56
Threaded, Double, 56
Threaded, Single, 56
Whipped, 56
Semi-Detached Petals, 220
Sheaf Stitch, 98
Italian, 99
Guatemala, 98
Shisha, Mirror Work, 178
Single Feather Stitch, 103
Single Knotted Cable Chain, 161
Slanted Cretan, 110
Slanted Feather Stitch, 108
Slanted Feather Stitch Variations, 108
Slav Cross Stitch (Long-Armed), 68
(Long-Legged), 68

Slipped Cable Chain, 140
Slipped Detached Chain, 127
Slipped Detached Chain Filling, 128
Small Palestrina Knot, 158
Snail Trail, 153
Sorbello Stitch, 158
Spaced Buttonhole, 101
Spaced Pekinese Stitch, 57
Spanish Stitch (Twisted Zigzag Chain, 138
Spider Web Stitch, 175
Lozenge, 177
Raised, 177
Ribbed, 177
Ringed, 178
Woven, 176
Spine Chain, 144
Laced, 144
Whipped, 144
Spine Stitch (Long-Armed Feather), 109
Spiral Stitch, 103
Split Stitch, 141
Detached, 143
Split Laid Work, 142
Square Chain (Open), 132
Closed, 135
Threaded, 135
Squared Palestrina, 155
Star Filling, 63
Star Stitch, 67
Stem Stitch (Crewel, Outline), 71
Alternating, 72
French Filling, 73
Line Shading, 74
Long, 72
Portuguese, 74
Whipped, 74
Straight Double Feather Stitch, 108
Straight Feather Stitch, 107
Straight Stitch, 62
Threaded, 216
Woven, 217
Straight Triple Feather Stitch, 108
Surface Darning, 49

-T-

Tête-de-Boeuf Stitch, 129
Filling, 129
Thorn Stitch, 79
Threaded Back Stitch, Double, 55
Threaded Back Stitch, Single, 55
Threaded Chain, 124, 214
Threaded Detached Chain, Double, 128
Threaded Detached Chain, Single, 128
Threaded Herringbone, 84
Threaded Running Stitch, Double, 37
Threaded Running Stitch, Single, 37
Threaded Seed Stitch, Double, 56
Threaded Seed Stitch, Single, 56

Threaded Square Chain, 133
    Closed, 135
Threaded Straight Stitch, 116
Tied Herringbone, 84
Triangle Stitch, 97
Triangular Joining, 225
Triple Back Stitch, Closed, 55
Triple Back Stitch (Hungarian), 55
Triple Herringbone, 84
Triple Slanted Feather Stitch, 108
Triple Palestrina, 155
Tuareg Double Laced Band, 39
Turkoman Edging, 228
Twisted Chain, 137
   Detached, 137
Twisted Fly and Two Ties, 115
Twisted Satin Stitch, 60
Twisted Zigzag Chain (Spanish),
   138

-U-

Up and Down Buttonhole Stitch,
   106
Upright Cross Stitch, 65

-V-

Vandyke Stitch, 119

-W-

Wave Stitch Filling, 93
Wheat-Ear Stitch, 143
   Laced, 144
   Whipped, 144
Whipped Back Stitch, 55
Whipped Buttonhole, 105
Whipped Chain, 122
Whipped Fly Stitch, 113
Whipped Running Stitch, 33
   Variations, 34
Whipped Seed Stitch, 56
Whipped Spine Chain, 144
Whipped Stem, 74
Whipped Wheat-Ear Stitch, 144
Woven Straight Stitches, 217

-Y-

Yemenite Embroidery, 188
Yugoslav Border Stitch, 92

-Z-

Zigzag Chain, 126
   Cable, 141
   Coral, 154
   Double Running, 92
   Fly, 115
   French Band, 96
   Huichol, 94
   Knotted Chain, 163
   Long-Stemmed, 130
   Twisted (Spanish), 138